JUDAISM

JUDAISM

A Sociology

STEPHEN SHAROT

DAVID & CHARLES

NEWTON ABBOT · LONDON

VANCOUVER

To my parents

MS: Judaism -- History -- Modern
Period, 1750 -

0 7153 6752 8

© Stephen Sharot 1976

Set in 10pt on 13pt Times, printed in
Great Britain by Redwood Burn Ltd
Trowbridge & Esher
for David & Charles (Publishers) Limited
Brunel House   Newton Abbot   Devon

Published in Canada by Douglas David & Charles Limited
1875 Welch Street   North Vancouver BC

Contents

Acknowledgements

I am indebted to the Harkness Foundation, the Commonwealth Fund of New York, which provided me with the opportunity to do research in the United States under very favourable conditions.

I would like especially to thank Dr Bryan R. Wilson whose expert supervision of my doctoral thesis provided me with much encouragement and intellectual stimulation and whose comments on the manuscript were most valuable.

I must also thank Professor Ilya Neustadt and Pele and Hannah Gut for providing congenial working conditions, respectively in the University of Leicester and in Israel. I am grateful to Audrey Craig who typed the manuscript. Finally, my thanks to my wife, Tami, who helped me with translations from Hebrew but who otherwise was a welcome distraction.

A large part of Chapter 1 first appeared in a modified form in *Comparative Studies in Society and History*, Vol 16, No 3 (June 1974).

Introduction

Modern Judaism, in a historical and comparative framework, has gone largely uninvestigated in sociology. A number of recent studies of contemporary Jewish communities, mainly in the United States and using quantitative methods, have provided valuable statistical data on the relationship between religious identity and practices and social variables; but sociologists of religion have paid scant attention to the enormous changes that have occurred, especially since the eighteenth century, in the practice and ritual forms of post-biblical Judaism. Where sociologists have studied change in modern Judaism, they have generally limited their analyses to one society, and research has been almost exclusively focused on Judaism in the United States.[1]

There are a number of intellectual histories of modern Judaism[2] but these have rarely touched on problems which are of interest to the sociologist. The historians have traced the development of religious ideas among an intellectual élite; the sociologist of religion is interested more in the religious beliefs and practices of the majority, and in showing the interrelationships between religion and other cultural and social dimensions of society. This analysis will be concerned more with changes in religious ritual than with changes in religious belief. In the context of the modern Western world, Judaism may be classed as a comparatively ritualistic religion. Unlike Christianity, which sets forth general principles of action and, especially in Protestantism, leaves decisions in particular cases to the conscience of the believer, Judaism prescribes highly detailed patterns of religious behaviour. Most Jews measure religiosity by the number of rituals that are kept, and by the

1

frequency of their performance, and the major differences between individual Jewish religious groups are seen largely as dissimilarities in the form and content of their respective religious services.

Whilst this book is devoted primarily to the sociology of a religion, the fact that Judaism is associated with a particular people, the majority of whom live in a diaspora, means that it must at the same time be a study in the sociology of minorities. In recent years a few sociologists have moved towards a comparative analysis of minorities in a wide range of societies. What has rarely been attempted, however, is a comparative analysis of a *single* religiously distinctive ethnic group in a number of societies. The Jews are an obvious candidate for this kind of study since they have inhabited many widely different socio-cultural environments, and it is only possible to explain the variant developments in modern Judaism by comparing the Jewish communities within the wider societal contexts.

A crucial problem for the comparative analysis of Jewish communities is posed by the question: why are some Jewish communities more like their gentile neighbours than others? The concepts *acculturation* and *deacculturation* are of use here in comparing Jewish communities in terms of their distinctiveness from the gentile environment: *acculturation* is defined as the change of the minority's culture to that of the 'host' or 'core' society, and *deacculturation* is defined as the change of the minority's culture away from that of the 'host' or 'core' society. The major cultural difference between the Jew and his non-Jewish neighbour has historically been a religious one, but Jewish communities may be compared along a continuum, ranging from those which retain or reinforce the distinctiveness of their religion to those which adopt, or take as models, the religious beliefs, practices, and organisational forms of the non-Jewish environment. An analysis of acculturation does not involve measuring deviation from some ideal-type Judaism, Talmudic or otherwise, which may never have existed. Rather, it is a matter of noting, over a delimited time period, the loss of beliefs and practices which the Jews did not share with non-Jews

2

and the adoption of beliefs and practices from non-Jews.

Although the major concern here is to account for variations in acculturation, it is not possible to ignore assimilation – the extent to which members of the minority come to interact socially with the majority.[3] Minority groups may be seen as ranging from those who have no social contact with the majority to those who are disappearing through intermarriage. Although many Jewish groups have disappeared through assimilation, the majority of Jewish communities are placed between the two extremes. The greatest number fall between communities whose contacts with majority members were few and generally restricted to highly formal secondary relationships, such as the buyer-seller relationship, to communities whose contacts with majority members were many and included relationships at a primary group level.

It is obvious that acculturation and assimilation are generally interrelated; either may be studied as a dependent or independent variable of the other, but neither can be reduced or explained wholly in terms of the other. Empirically, the degree of interrelationship between acculturation and assimilation varies enormously, but certain limited generalisations may be made. One is that while substantial or even total acculturation of a subordinate ethnic group need not necessarily involve substantial assimilation, substantial assimilation will nearly always involve substantial acculturation. An ethnic group may retain its cohesiveness and social boundaries despite its adoption of cultural patterns of the majority or core group, but an ethnic culture is almost bound to disappear if the ethnic population is absorbed by the majority. Thus, any attempt to explain a minority's acculturation must take into consideration factors affecting its social differentiation from the majority.

It can forcibly be argued that a comparative analysis of social units which share important characteristics is likely to be more fruitful than an analysis of social units which differ in almost every respect. Within a narrow range of comparison, the investigator can 'control' common factors, treating them as parameters, and then proceed to examine the influence of the factor or factors which are not held in common. If the sociologist attempts to compare social units which differ widely, his inability to 'control' any of the variables makes it very difficult to show the relative importance of the many indepedent variables. However, the small number of certain kinds of social units may mean that there is a choice of a wide-range comparison or no comparison at all.

Comparison of Jewish communities in the present volume is in the first instance made by considering communities which differ very widely with respect to their non-Jewish socio-cultural environments, and then of communities which inhabit socio-cultural environments which are similar in a number of significant respects. As the range of comparisons become more restricted, certain factors relevant to the comparisons of the wide range can be treated as parameters. In Chapter 1 the religious changes in the Jewish communities of 'pre-modern' China, India, the Middle East, and medieval Europe are compared. The most striking contrast here is between the Eastern communities, who adopted much of the local religion and culture, and the European communities, who retained and even strengthened their religious distinctiveness. In successive chapters the comparative range is narrowed to Western societies, and particular attention is given to the Jewish communities in eastern Europe, Germany, France, Britain, and the United States from the eighteenth century to the present day. These communities came to differ in their cultural and religious distinctiveness, in the strength and cultural expressions (religious and secular) of their Jewish identity, and in the changes they made in the form and content of their religious services. The religious and cultural differences are analysed in relation to the socio-economic composition of the Jewish communities, to the dominant non-Jewish religious and cultural environments, and to the wider social structures, especially as they affected the relationships between gentiles and Jews.

1 Judaism in 'Pre-Modern' Societies

Dispersal and isolation

After the Temple of Solomon was destroyed and Judea captured by the Babylonians in 586 BCE (before the Common era), the major part of the Jewish population was exiled from its homeland to Babylonia, while some fled to Egypt. From that period only a minority of the Jewish people continued to live in what had been the kingdoms of Israel and Judah, and in the following centuries the Jews gradually settled throughout the Near Eastern and Mediterranean empires. On the destruction of the Second Temple in CE 70 and the crushing of the Jewish revolt against the Romans the Jews became a truly exiled people. Their further dispersion followed the political expansion and long-range trading routes of first the Roman and then the Arabic empires. From the area of the first diaspora, the Middle Eastern and Mediterranean territories, the Jews dispersed farther north and west into Europe and a smaller number settled farther south in the Sahara and farther east in the Caucasus, Turkistan, Afghanistan, India, and China.

With the decline of the empires and the contraction of world trade, the connections between many Jewish communities were severed. The Chinese Jewish communities, which were predominantly composed of Jewish traders who had settled in China from about the ninth century CE, were effectively isolated from other Jewish communities from about the twelfth century. The Jewish community in Kaifeng, which began in the eleventh or twelfth century and was the only community to survive until the nineteenth, had by 1605 lost contact not only with Jews from the West but also with other Chinese Jews. [1]

Jewish communities in India also had little or no contact with

5

other Jewish communities for a long period. The Cochin Jews, whose existence on the Malabar coast of India from the end of the tenth century is firmly established, became effectively isolated from other Jews from the thirteenth century. Jews from Spain and Portugal migrated to the Malabar coast and intermarried with the Cochin Jews from the early sixteenth century, but the isolation of the Cochin Jews was effectively broken only with Dutch rule in the second half of the seventeenth century. The origins and date of settlement of the Indian Jewish community, the Bene Israel, who resided in the villages of Konkan, are obscure, but their isolation from other Jewish communities lasted longer than that of the Cochin Jews. The Bene Israel probably lost contact with other Jewish communities, including other Indian Jewish communities, early in the second millennium, and sustained contact with other Jews began again only in the nineteenth century. However, there is evidence that the Bene Israel were known to Western Jews in the twelfth century and that contacts with Cochin Jews were frequent in the eighteenth century. [2]

There was also little contact between the majority of Jewish communities under Christendom and Islam up to the nineteenth century. In the fourteenth and fifteenth centuries Jews from Spain and Italy migrated to North Africa where they culturally absorbed a number of North African Jewish communities, although in some cases the European Jews were culturally absorbed by the Oriental Jews. Other Jewish communities under Islam, such as those in the Grand Atlas of southern Morocco, the Algerian desert, Ethiopia, Yemen, Kurdistan, the Caucasus, and Afghanistan, were isolated not only from the Jews under Christendom, of which some were not even aware, but also from other communities under Islam. Both during the centuries before Islam, and in the first centuries of the Arabic political unification, communication between communities was precarious. From the tenth to the thirteenth centuries mobility and connections between the communities were comparatively high, but these declined again with the break-up of the Arabic empire. [3] In the Middle and Far East the isolation of many

6

Jewish communities resulted in the development of religious practices which were not shared with other Jewish communities. In contrast, the European Jewish communities formed a vast network with many ties, and, although numerous local variations developed, there remained a basic unity in religious beliefs and practices.

The connections between the majority of Jewish communities considered here were broken only after the post-exilic characteristics of Judaism had evolved into stable and distinctive forms. The Babylonian Talmud had been codified about CE 500 and was accepted by most Jewish communities as authoritative over the Jerusalem Talmud. Babylonia had been the most important cultural centre of Jewry from at least the third century and it was clearly the centre of the study of the Torah from the seventh to the eleventh centuries. During this period Babylonian-Persian Jewry was highly centralised: the communities were already scattered, but they all recognised the *geonim,* the chief judicial leaders, of the Talmudic academies in Sura and Pumbedita as the legitimate religious authorities.[4] The Jews who migrated from Persia to areas as far east as India and China in the last centuries of the first millennium came, therefore, from the centre of Talmudic Judaism. From Persia the authority of the Babylonian Talmud came to be accepted by most Jews under Islam and, in the last centuries of the first millennium, by the growing Jewish communities in Europe. Thus, at the time of the settlement of Jewish communities over many parts of the world and before their connections were broken, Judaism had become clearly identified with an ethnic group, the Talmud was widely diffused, and other religions in the monotheistic tradition (Christianity and Islam) were clearly distinguishable from Judaism.

It is clear that Jews were not initially disposed to acculturate to the environmental non-Jewish religio-cultures. Although, like all the major world religions, Judaism had been syncretistic in its formative stages, it had become a comparatively distinctive religion with clearly defined boundaries setting it off from other religions. Jews had come to put a great emphasis on the

7

maintenance of their strict monotheistic beliefs, to protect them from the 'idolatrous' beliefs and practices of non-Jews. This insular, as opposed to syncretic attitude predisposed them further to construct social barriers between themselves and non-Jews. Adherence to Judaism involved, therefore, both the construction of religio-cultural barriers against other religions, and voluntary segregation from non-Jewish groups. Hence, an explanation of variations in levels of Jewish acculturation requires an analysis of those aspects of the religio-cultures and social structures of the 'host' societies which would either strengthen or reduce the Jews' religious doctrinism and voluntary segregation.

Levels of acculturation

An obvious place to begin a comparison of levels of acculturation among Jewish communities is the Middle East; in contrast with Europe and the Far East, the Jews had not transplanted their culture to an alien environment, but were, from the outset, very much a part of the indigenous culture. The expansion of the Arabic empire facilitated the widespread dispersion of Jews over the Middle East, but in many areas Jews were established long before the advent of Islam. In its formative stages Islam incorporated many religious, legal, and moral conceptions from the Jews, and even after the boundaries between Islam and Judaism were clearly drawn, Jews and Muslims continued to share many beliefs and practices.

Levels of Jewish assimilation and acculturation to Islamic societies have varied greatly over different areas and periods. Although, following the Islamic conquests, significant numbers of Jews were totally assimilated, often by conversion, into the 'host' population, the rate of assimilation was rarely high enough to reduce the overall numbers. In contrast to the Christians and Zoroastrians, who were unable to adjust to their newly acquired minority status, the number of Jews increased in the centuries after the Islamic conquests.[5] The Jews remained a distinct socio-cultural group under Islam, but they shared far more of the culture of their non-Jewish neighbours than the Jews in

8

Europe. The influence of Judaism on early Islam had been considerable, but after its crystallisation Islam in turn had an influence on Middle Eastern Judaism. As in most cases, the subordinate minority were acculturating to the dominant majority, rather than the other way round.

In general, there was little that outwardly distinguished Jew and Muslim: they spoke the same language and wore the same clothes, despite occasional regulations seeking to differentiate Muslim and Jewish dress. It has often been said that the Middle Eastern Jews were 'Arab in all but religion', but this oversimplifies and distorts the true situation. Religion pervaded Middle Eastern culture and a distinction betwen 'religious' and 'secular' areas of culture is often difficult to make. For example, adoption of the dominant language was bound to have implications for the minority's religion. By about CE 1000 the majority of Middle Eastern Jews had, like the rest of the population, adopted Arabic,[6] and this involved the adoption of Arabic ways of thinking and Arabic religious concepts. The Jews used Arabic for translating and teaching the Bible as well as discussing Jewish law and ritual. Although the Muslim's emphasis on the study of the Arabic language also influenced the Jews to study Hebrew, the use of Arabic for both secular and religious purposes contrasts with the development of language barriers between Jews and Christians in Europe. [7]

Furthermore, if we take the term 'religion' to mean not just the 'orthodox' doctrines of Judaism and Islam but all the supernatural beliefs and practices found among the Middle Eastern population, then there was considerable overlap between the religion of Muslim and Jew. Much of the 'popular' religion shared by Muslim and Jew was pre-Islamic. One central cult, especially important in North Africa, which had many pre-Islamic elements but which was brought into the framework of both Islam and Judaism in the Middle East, was that of pilgrimage to the tombs of saints. Both Muslims and Jews sought the intercession and protection of the saints, offering them candles and oil lamps and performing rituals by their tombs. Family pilgrimages were made when important family

9

events occurred and collective pilgrimages were made on the anniversary of the death of the saint. In addition to certain saints worshipped by both Muslims and Jews, the two religious groups shared many magical practices and beliefs associated with witchcraft, sorcery, divination, ecstatic prophecy, demons, the evil eye, the magical significance of numbers, and the protective power of amulets. [8] In many cases the 'popular' cults appear to have attained a greater place in the total religious system of Middle Eastern Jews than the distinctive beliefs and practices of Judaism. The trend from local religious diversity to Talmudic uniformity, which had occurred under the Roman and Persian empires and which was at first strengthened under Islam, was reversed in the later Middle Ages when local religious customs again assumed importance. A European Jew who made a number of visits to North African Jewish communities between 1906 and 1916 found widespread ignorance of Judaism but a great variety of 'popular' cults and magical practices. In the interior of Morocco he found that the religious beliefs of the Jews had a polytheistic character which approached fetishism. [9]

In addition to sharing much of the 'popular' religion of their neighbours, Jews were also influenced by more 'orthodox' Islamic practices. The short, intense features of Muslim prayer impressed the Jews, whose services displayed far more decorum than European Jewish services. Like the Muslims, the Jews practised polygamy, and the religious position of Jewish women deteriorated in Islamic environments. In the highlands of Yemen, where Islamic women did not attend the mosque, Jewish women did not attend the synagogue and were completely cut off from the religious life of the men. [10]

Although most Middle Eastern Jewish communities shared much of their culture with their Muslim neighbours, their distinctiveness as religious minorities varied greatly, even among those who had little or no contact with other Jewish communities. For example, the Yemenite Jews had no contact with Jewish communities outside Yemen but their religio-culture remained very distinct from that of their non-Jewish neighbours; they had evolved certain unique religious practices, but, like the

Jews of Europe, prayer in the synagogue and study of the Talmud were central. [11] They provide a sharp contrast with other isolated communities which were highly acculturated, such as the Mountain Jews of the Caucasus (Tats), the Jews in Kurdistan, and many communities in the interior of North Africa.

There are few studies by trained observers of Middle Eastern Jewish communities before their disintegration in the last few decades, but two studies, one of Jews in north-east Iraq and the other of Jews in the north-west Sahara of Algeria, provide interesting sources for comparison, especially since both communities had no significant contact with other Jewish communities. [12] In the former case the Jews were highly acculturated to the environmental Kurdish culture: in addition to sharing values with respect to such areas as marriage, family, and honour, they also held common magical beliefs and worshipped at the same holy graves. The Jews observed the Sabbath, dietary regulations, and the purity laws, but they had virtually no knowledge of the Talmud, and religious learning was not important. In contrast, the Jewish community in Ghardaia in the north-west Sahara shared few religious practices with the neighbouring Muslims. They adhered rigidly to traditional Jewish values and practices; they prayed in the synagogue three times a day, and religious learning was highly valued in the community. Integrated with 'orthodox' Jewish practices were local magico-religious practices whose historical origins were often lost, but only a few of them were held in common with Muslims. The customs peculiar to the Ghardaia Jews sometimes functioned to uphold traditional values; for example, at the age of five years every boy had to undergo an elaborate ceremonial initiation which served to dramatise the importance of religious learning for Jewish males.

The Jewish communities under Islam varied greatly in their levels of acculturation to the culture of the majority, but on a continuum of religious acculturation most of the Middle Eastern communities may be placed mid-way between the highly acculturated Jewish communities of the Far East (India and

11

China) and the very strong sub-cultural distinctiveness of the pre-nineteenth century European Jewish communities. In the early Middle Ages Jews migrated from the Middle Eastern centres and transplanted their religio-culture to 'alien' environments: the majority migrated to Europe and a much smaller number migrated farther east. The contrast between the development of Judaism in East and West is striking: in the West the Jews not only retained but reinforced their religio-cultural distinctiveness, while in the East the Jews adopted much of the local culture and religion into their own system.

The Jews of China provide one of the few documented Jewish communities which were entirely absorbed, culturally and socially, by a 'host' society. There were probably a number of small Jewish communities in both inland and coastal Chinese towns by CE 1200, and a number of communities, some quite large, are known to have existed in coastal towns between the fourteenth and seventeenth centuries, but the community in Kaifeng was the only one to survive into the nineteenth century. By the end of the nineteenth century, the Jews of Kaifeng too had almost entirely disappeared through assimilation, but there is historical evidence of their substantial acculturation long before this.

There is no doubt that the first Jewish settlers in Kaifeng were Talmudic Jews; in 1850 they still had all the prayerbooks and scrolls required for daily and Sabbath services and for all the festivals and fasts. It appears, however, that Chinese influences entered the Jews' beliefs and practices at an early stage, and Western visitors in the seventeenth and eighteenth centuries found a highly acculturated community whose religion combined certain distinctively Jewish beliefs and practices with beliefs and practices from the environmental Confucian, Buddhist, and Taoist religions. The Jewish temple was still flourishing and the Jews still practised a number of traditional Jewish commandments such as abstinence from pork, but the attenuation of their Judaism was observed in their poor Hebrew and ignorance of many Jewish rites and festivals. The influence of the non-Jewish religious environment was clearly visible in the architecture of their temple, the use of non-Jewish ritual objects, the observance of Chinese seasonal festivals, ancestor worship, the absorption of Chinese rituals into the rites of passage, and the use of inscriptions written on stone tablets for the transmission of religious beliefs. The inscriptions on both the stone tablets and temple archways were written in Chinese, used Chinese terms for God, contained quotations from Confucian writing, and proclaimed that the principles of Confucianism and the religion of the Chinese Jews were the same. [13]

Unlike the Chinese Jews, the Jews in India increased in number, but during their period of comparative isolation from other Jewish communities their Judaism lost much of its distinctiveness, they adopted many Hindu customs, and they were assimilated into the caste system. In the sixteenth and seventeenth centuries, European Jews migrated to India and established an orthodox form of Judaism among the Cochin Jews. The Jews from Europe probably intermarried with the wealthiest families of the established Jewish community, but they came to form a White Jewish caste and completely distinguished themselves from the indigenous Black Jews. A third caste, composed of the slave and servant converts of the White Jews, also emerged.

Little is known of the religion of the Cochin Jews before their contacts with Western Jews, but it is evident from the thirteenth century tombstones that even then they had an imperfect knowledge of Hebrew and the Bible. There is more information of the pre-Westernised Judaism of the Bene Israel who, unlike the Cochin Jews, did not come into sustained contact with early European Jewish immigrants to India. A more distinctive Judaism was introduced to the Bene Israel in the nineteenth century by Cochin Jews, Jewish immigrants from the Middle East, and, somewhat paradoxically, by Christian missionaries who translated the Bible into Marathi and taught Hebrew. But before the recent period of contact with non-Bene Israel Jews, the Judaism of the Bene Israel took highly acculturated forms. The Bene Israel observed the Sabbath, some of the holy days, some dietary regulations, and circumcision, but knowledge of Hebrew had been lost and they had adopted a number of religious beliefs and practices from their Hindu neighbours, especially from the higher castes – they objected to the remarriage of widows and they believed that the eating of beef was prohibited by the Jewish religion.

The Bene Israel held a comparatively low-caste position; in the villages of Konkan their traditional caste occupation was oil pressing, and in Bombay, where they concentrated in the nineteenth century, they became a caste of clerks. In addition, the Bene Israel were divided into two sub-castes: the *Gora* or 'White' Bene Israel, who claimed they were pure descendants of the first Jewish settlers in India, and the lower caste *Kala* or 'Black' Bene Israel. [14]

Although most Jewish communities under Islam retained a greater religio-cultural distinctiveness than the Jews of China and India, it is the Ashkenazi Jewish communities of medieval and early modern Europe which provide the strongest contrast with the Jewish communities of the East. The Ashkenazi came to put an enormous emphasis on the strict interpretation of religious law and the observance of religious ritual; a 'wall' was built around the Torah to lessen the possibility of ritualistic mistakes. In the twelfth and thirteenth centuries, the *Haside Ashkenaz* ('pious men of Germany') established more rigid precepts against contact with Christian symbols and imposed upon themselves an even stricter ritualism than that required by the Talmud. [15] The cultural distinctiveness of the Jews was not limited to religious beliefs and practices but came to encompass such spheres as everyday language and clothes. Yiddish developed as the distinctive everyday language of the Jews, and in eastern Europe, from the seventeenth to the early twentieth centuries, Jewish appearance and clothes visibly set them apart from non-Jews: the men grew long beards and sidelocks and wore long black caftans and large hats. That special clothes came to signify the orthodox Jew illustrates the encompassing importance of Judaism to Jewish society in Europe. The religious law of the Talmud and its commentaries, codified in the

Shulhan Arukh in the sixteenth century, regulated life in the traditional Jewish community, prescribing ritualistic observances and regulating social, business, and filial relationships as well as dress, diet, and hygiene.

Jewish society in the medieval and early modern period was a traditional one in the sense that change was only accepted if it could be legitimised by values and practices handed down from the past. Legitimacy had to be found in the codes of religious law, and this gave enormous significance to religious scholarship. Men were regarded as superior to women since they were the main 'carriers' of the religion, bearing the major part of the 'yoke of the Law'. Women had only to learn enough to read their prayers and perform their special ritual activities, but it was the duty of every man to study, and a large proportion did devote part of the day or a certain day of the week to the study of the law. It was common for the wife of a scholar to manage both the home and a business while her husband devoted his time to study of the sacred texts.

At the *chedarim* (schools) boys first learnt to read and write Hebrew and Yiddish. This was followed by the study of the Pentateuch when the boy began to understand, translate, comment, and interpret; and finally he progressed to the study of the Talmud. The aim of the *cheder* was to turn the more capable pupils into scholars who would study at the community-maintained *yeshiva* (advanced educational institution) from the age of twelve or thirteen. Only a minority studied at a *yeshiva,* but the teaching of the basic aspects of Judaism to the majority was a secondary function of the *cheder* compared with the primary function: the rearing of scholars. Since the hope of most fathers was to see their sons become *yeshiva* students, they regularly tested their sons and asked learned men to give an opinion on their sons' talents for study. Demands by the child for logical justification of religious rules and norms were welcomed by adults as an indication of the child's intellectual precocity. At the *yeshivot,* boys analysed the Talmud and its commentaries, compared the different interpretations, and attempted to reconcile apparent

15

contradictions in the sacred writings. Students did not achieve rabbinical status at the *yeshivot;* they had to study for a minimum of six years after marriage before they could receive the scholarly title which entitled them to rule on religious questions. These titles, which accorded the holders special privileges within the community, were awarded by the rabbis officiating in the community, and the status of the title depended on the scholarly status of the rabbi who awarded it.

The three major status attributes in the traditional Jewish community were learning, wealth, and lineage (the scholarship and wealth of ancestors and relatives). Since wealth was not always sufficient to achieve status in the community, many prominent merchants and bankers sought to obtain rabbinic standing. If a man could not achieve high scholarly status, the next best thing was to support his son-in-law while he studied. Marriages and dowries were arranged according to the bridegroom's religious scholarship.

There were no estates within the Jewish community and many gradations of wealth and learning. Wealth had a precarious basis because of the insecure conditions of Jewish life; and high status based on a scholarly lineage had to be validated by the individual's own scholarship. Educational opportunities were formally open to all males, but environmental factors made the opportunities more accessible to some. In eastern Europe, for example, a child born into a scholarly and wealthy family residing in a centre for rabbinical scholarship in Lithuania had an environment far more conducive to study than a child born into a non-scholarly poor family residing in a small village without a rabbi in the Ukraine. Thus, long rabbinical lineages developed. If a rabbi had no son, he generally obtained a scholarly son-in-law to carry on the rabbinical tradition in his family.

The status system was given expression and sanction in the synagogue. During public prayer the women were segregated in a special section or room above the synagogue hall from which, through special windows, they could hear and see the men at prayer. Scholars and wealthy men sat at the Eastern Wall towards which all faces were turned when prayers were said. Those seated farthest from the Eastern Wall had the lowest status. It was an honour to be called to the reading of the Torah, but certain passages were more honorific than others and these were given to the scholars. The rich displayed their wealth and reinforced their status by pledging large sums for charity when 'called to the Torah' and by donating scrolls, curtains for the Ark and other ritual objects in the synagogue. [16]

Jews and Christians held many magical beliefs in common, but even in this sphere there were important differences between them. The invocation of demons and the distinction between white and black magic were of minor significance for the Jews compared with their importance in the Christian religio-culture. Another difference was that magic did not have an anti-establishment function among the Jews; the more scholarly Jews emphasised the need for both adherence to the legalistic rabbinical classification of magic and knowledge of the mystical cabbalistic writings. Talmudical scholars were often the greatest miracle workers. [17] Thus, although there was some cultural overlap in magic between Christians and Jews, this was of limited significance, and in general the religio-cultural distinctiveness of the Ashkenazi Jews remained very marked in most parts of Europe up to the end of the eighteenth century.

In comparison with the Ashkenazi, the Sephardi Jews of the Iberian peninsula adopted a greater part of the dominant culture. Judaism was less encompassing in the socio-cultural system of the Sephardim, and from the thirteenth century onwards references to non-observance of the religious law by the Jews in Spain are common. The Ashkenazi observed a greater number of rituals, interpreted the religious law in a stricter fashion, and took greater heed of their rabbis. [18]

Environmental culture and social structure

Any explanation of the different levels of acculturation among Jewish communities must take into consideration demographic distribution. The Jewish population in each single community was not, however, a significant independent variable: urban concentration did not guarantee, and rural distribution did not necessarily weaken, continuing socio-cultural distinctiveness. A few of the Chinese urban communities were fairly large at one time, but they disappeared, while Jewish communities in rural areas in India, the Middle East, and Europe increased in number. The largest urban communities were found in the Near Eastern and Mediterranean areas where many Jewish communities occupied entire quarters of the towns. In Europe most communities were not large; the number of Jewish families in a few commercial centres reached the hundreds but European Jewry was widely distributed in many towns and villages, especially in eastern Europe.

Far more significant than the number in each community was contact with other communities, and here the greater density and communication of Jews within Europe must be considered. In the High Middle Ages western and central Europe contained most of the European Jews, but there was a movement east in the latter part of the medieval period, and, in the early modern period, the vast majority of European Jews lived in eastern Europe. In the pre-modern societies mobility between communities was low, but the Jews were more mobile than most, and, although often infrequent and irregular, the network of contacts and ties between the European communities supported the knowledge of, and identification with, a 'people' which stretched far beyond the immediate community. This was not the case for the Jews of the East and some parts of the Middle East, many of whom knew little or nothing of a Jewish people outside their own immediate community.

Although the most acculturated communities are to be found among those isolated for long periods from the centres of Jewish settlement, there are also examples of isolated communities which retained a very high level of religio-cultural distinctiveness, and the history of Western Jewry since the eighteenth century has shown that large numbers, extensive communication, and a sense of identity with a far-ranging 'people' do not prevent substantial acculturation. It is clear that small numbers and lack of contact with other communities only made a community particularly susceptible to an absorbent environment. An explanation of variations in the level of Jewish religious acculturation requires, therefore, an analysis of those aspects of the religio-culture and social structure of the 'host' societies which would affect the cultural and social barriers between minority and majority.

In the cultural environments of the 'pre-modern' societies under discussion, religion was central and played a very important part in the dominant groups' orientations to religious minorities. The major religions in China were both syncretistic and culturally pluralistic; they combined and reconciled diverse beliefs and practices, and little or no attempt was made to demand the exclusive allegiance of worshippers. In accommodating non-Jewish practices into their religion, the Chinese Jews were following the general Chinese practice of observing sacraments from a number of religious traditions — Buddhist, Taoist, etc — side by side.

Confucianism, the official Chinese state doctrine, was neither a state religion nor a church in the Western sense; the literati espoused a doctrinal orthodoxy and emphasised the necessity of performing certain rites, but there was little or no attempt to coerce others. The Chinese political elite permitted and encouraged religious syncretism if it was politically efficacious and it tolerated diverse religions as long as they were not hostile to the state. Max Weber wrote, 'the most important and absolute limit to practical tolerance for the Confucian state consisted in the fundamental importance of the ancestor cult and this-worldly piety for the docility of the patrimonial subject'. [19] There was little or no formal constraint on Chinese Jews to conform to non-Jewish beliefs and practices as long as they recognised the ancestral cult and religious status of the Chinese emperor. In addition, neither religious nor nationalist notions predisposed the dominant group to separate the Jews from other Chinese. The concept of nationalism or of a nation did not arise in China since the empire was regarded as the universe, composed of concentric circles, becoming increasingly barbarous the farther they lay from the Chinese core. [20] Like the

Muslims, with whom they were sometimes categorised, the Chinese Jews lived within the universe and were not, therefore, subject to any differential legal, political, economic or social treatment.

The important elements of the Chinese social structure, the extended family, clan, and political rule by a centralised bureaucracy, did not dispose the Jews to enter a peculiar structural niche in the society. The original Jewish settlers in Kaifeng were probably specialists in manufacture, dyeing, or pattern printing of cotton fabrics, but economic diversity among native Kaifeng Jews is illustrated by a 1512 inscription which mentions degree-holders, civil and military officials, farmers, artisans, traders, and shopkeepers. In the fifteenth, sixteenth, and seventeenth centuries, a number of Jews attained high political and military posts and others were successful as physicians and scholars. [21]

The majority of Kaifeng Jews were members of the small Chinese merchant-artisan class which occupied a social position between the mass peasant base and the literati, but from the beginning of the fourteenth century Kaifeng Jews entered the scholar-official class in increasing numbers and some held important positions. In contrast to the free towns in Europe, Chinese towns were seats of the mandarinate, and the ambition of most merchant families in the towns was to break into the scholar-official class. [22] The literati was not a completely closed class, and in the large, wealthy, imperial city of Kaifeng, Jews as much as others could take advantage of the limited opportunities for mobility. Song Nai Rhee has argued that the civil service system transformed Jewish intellectuals into Confucian literati, a transformation which affected their total philosophical and religious perspective. Some members of the Jewish community, who were more conscious of their religious distinctiveness, disapproved of the Confucianisation of the Jewish intellectuals, but as members of the Chinese elite the Jewish scholar-officials were bound to have an important influence on the whole community. In addition, participation in the civil service contributed towards intermarriage and assimilation; the Jewish

20

literati had to leave Kaifeng since, like all other civil servants, they were prohibited from holding official positions in the place of their birth.[23] It may be hypothesised, therefore, that the substantial acculturation and assimilation of the Chinese Jews was related both to the Chinese cultural orientations (religious syncretism and pluralism) and to the Chinese social structure which permitted the socio-economic integration of the Jews in Chinese society.

Like the Chinese religions, the general dispositions of Indian Hinduism towards minority religions were syncretistic and culturally pluralistic. The dominant Hindus tolerated other religions which did not threaten the caste system and the supremacy of the Brahmins, but although they were pluralistic in the sense that they did not actively attempt to enforce a Hindu monopoly, the assimilative character of the caste system and the syncretism of the Hindu religion resulted in a virtual monopoly of Hinduism over much of India.[24] Although the Bene Israel had only acquired the status of a low caste, it had presumably been to their advantage to accept voluntarily certain Hindu rituals and the caste system; it was difficult for an alien and therefore impure group, which was not economically self-sufficient, to exist outside the Hindu community. Once the Jews had adopted the caste system and some principal practices of Hinduism, their own distinctive beliefs and rituals were tolerated within the Hindu community itself.

Although the general orientations of Hinduism strongly disposed the Jews to substantial acculturation, the Indian social structure did not strongly dispose them to substantial assimilation. Srinivas has described Indian society as subject to two opposed types of solidarity: the solidarity of village and the solidarity of caste.[25] Indian villages were largely autonomous units; there were no large-scale inter-regional religious institutions in India, and the authority of the secular rulers rarely extended to the internal affairs of the village. For many centuries the Bene Israel resided in the villages of Konkan, and it is clear that their close association with non-Bene Israel occasionally resulted in intermarriage. However, the solidarity of caste

21

reinforced the social boundaries of the Bene Israel and enabled them to increase in number. As in China, the Indian Jews were not singled out for differential treatment as Jews, but unlike in China, the very integration of the Jews into the Hindu religio-social system contributed to their social preservation.

In contrast to the syncretistic religions of the East, Islam developed out of a monotheistic tradition and inherited from it strong dispositions to doctrinism. Islam was flexible in incorporating folk beliefs and practices of the nominal Muslim population, but its syncretism was slight in comparison with the inclusive tendencies of the Eastern religions, and the dominant Islamic groups were consistent in their rejection of distinctive Judaic beliefs and practices. Again, in contrast with Eastern religions, which were generally content to coexist peacefully with other religions, Islam has often been markedly monopolistic; it has sought, often with success, to establish itself as the only religion in a particular area by converting or eliminating non-Islamic religious groups. Islamic monopolism was, however, mainly directed towards pagans or non-monotheists and the Islamic disposition toward the Jews was, in general, more pluralistic than monopolistic. Mohammed established the general principle that adherents of non-Islamic monotheistic faiths should be allowed to live under Muslim rule, and although in its early warrior phase this principle was not consistently upheld, Arab religious pluralism became firmly established once the Arabs had conquered vast territories containing large non-Islamic populatinns.

The broad pluralist disposition of the dominant Arabs towards other monotheists was formulated in a number of treaties which provided for the protection of the persons, property, and religious observances of minorities in return for payment to the Islamic rulers. During the High Middle Ages this pluralism was interrupted by two outbreaks of monopolism, limited in time and scope: one in Egypt from 1012 to 1019 under al-Hakim and the other under the Almohad conquerors of North Africa and Spain in the 1140s. In both cases, Christians as well as Jews were given the choice of conversion to Islam or death. Such occurrences were, however, very rare in the Arab world. The general condition of non-Muslims declined under the rule of foreign 'barbarian' military castes in the fourteenth and fifteenth centuries, revived under the Ottomon Turks in the sixteenth and seventeenth centuries, and then deteriorated again, but over long periods and up to recent times, the Jews under Islam enjoyed a comparatively secure existence, free from persecution.

Within the framework of general religious pluralism, the Jews were subject to a certain amount of differential treatment, although, again, this varied considerably between periods and provinces. Some, but by no means all, of this differential treatment was motivated by a desire to secure the monopoly of Islam over its nominal adherents and to protect Islam from 'deviant' religions. In order to demonstrate the superiority of Islam over other religions, numerous restrictions on non-Muslims were introduced concerning such matters as modes of dress, size of buildings, and interfaith contacts. These restrictions, which applied to Jews as well as other religious minorities, were seldom enforced, and in fact discrimination was very intermittent.[26] Non-tolerant and segregationist policies were more likely to be found where the Muslim population adhered to a sectarian form of Islam. In the Yemen, under the rule of the Sh'ites, conditions were particularly oppressive; Jews were regarded as ritually unclean, they were subject to many restrictions, and in the seventeenth century they were forced out of the towns to live in special areas on the outskirts. As the only non-Muslim religious minority in the Yemen, the Jews were without rights, and they were forced to seek Muslim patrons who would provide them with protection in exchange for payment.

Many Jewish communities under Islam were subject to heavy fiscal discrimination, but with a few exceptions, such as the Yemen, other forms of discrimination were slight or non-existent. The Jews had undergone a transformation from an agricultural people to one of merchants and artisans in the seventh and eighth centuries, but since there were few restrictions in the economic sphere they undertook a great variety of occupations and did not become economically differentiated from urban Muslims. The Middle Eastern Jews shared both in the prosperous mercantile period from the ninth to the thirteenth centuries and in the economic decline in the later Middle Ages and following centuries. [27]

In most cases, the residential separation of the Jews was voluntary: there were no legally segregated quarters, but predominantly homogeneous religious quarters were customary in Muslim towns and there was no degradation associated with living in one. The Jews also had their own semi-autonomous community organisation to which the Islamic rulers delegated substantial political authority and which was entrusted with the task of collecting taxes. But despite fairly distinct living quarters and community organisation, close and intimate association with Muslims was not uncommon. [28]

A comparison of the highly acculturated Kurdish Jews of Iraq and the more culturally distinctive Ghardaia Jews of the north-west Sahara shows a considerable difference in the level of social interaction with Muslims. The majority of Kurdish Jews were manual labourers, living in the villages and small towns of Islamic Kurds. In the small towns they lived by choice in a separate quarter adjacent to the Muslim quarter, but many Muslims lived in the Jewish quarter, and some even lived in Jewish households as lodgers or workers. Jews and Muslims visited each other and ate in each others' houses. In contrast, the Ghardaia Jews were highly segregated both from the neighbouring Arabs, who belonged to the Malekite sect, and the neighbouring Berbers, who belonged to the puritanical Ibadite sect. The Ghardaia Jews lived in a ghetto-like quarter, performed specialist economic functions for the Muslims, and interacted with Muslims only in impersonal relationships. [29] In general, however, the social boundaries enclosing the Jews under Islam were limited and took mainly voluntary forms.

Like Islam, Christianity was an insular religion with only limited dispositions to syncretism; the Christian church was flexible in incorporating pagan folk beliefs and practices which

24

did not present articulate religious alternatives or challenges, but it was consistent in establishing clear boundaries with alternative religious systems, such as Judaism. The Christian Church differed from Islam, however, in so far as it was far less disposed to take a pluralistic stance towards other monotheistic faiths.

The fact that the Jews were the only deviant religious group whose existence was tolerated by the central organs of the Church is important to an understanding of the situation of the Jews in medieval Europe. Muslims were not tolerated except on a temporary basis in Spanish and Italian areas, and Christian heretics were bloodily suppressed. The Jews were the sole recognised representatives of religious dissent, the only group to fall outside the otherwise complete religious monopoly of the Church. The ecclesiastical doctrine, formulated by the Church fathers and the early popes, stated that the Jews should be tolerated in a submissive state until the end of days, at which time their conversion would herald the second coming of Christ. The Church taught that the exile and submissive state of the Jews was a God-inflicted penalty for the Jewish repudiation of Christ and could thus be regarded as evidence for the truth of Christianity. This doctrine did not mean that the Church should not attempt to convert Jews, but conversion by force was in general officially prohibited.

The policy of limited pluralism with regard to the Jews was held relatively consistently by the Papacy and the higher ranks of the Church throughout the medieval period; with a few exceptions, the central offices of the Church counselled tolerance and restraint during intolerant periods, and they passed decrees whose purpose was to protect Jews and safeguard their property. The Church had little executive power outside the pontifical states and feudal lordships of individual bishops, but the principles of the Church toward the Jews were very influential in determining the policies of secular rulers who generally found that the existence of a Jewish community was congruent with their economic and fiscal interests. The official Church policy of limited tolerance was, however, little appreciated or known by the Christian masses and the lower levels of the Church hierarchy; local and regional clerics, particularly parish priests and wandering monks, were often supporters or leaders of anti-Jewish outbreaks. During periods of unrest, such as the times of the crusades and the Black Death, neither the Church nor most secular authorities were able or willing to prevent massacres of whole Jewish communities. Thus, although European Jews were often protected by sovereign powers, outbreaks of persecution were far more frequent under Christianity than under Islam.

The Church was rarely directly responsible for the persecutions and massacres, but it provided encouragement and legitimation for such activities by its teaching on the Jewish deicide of Christ as well as its emphasis on Jewish social inferiority and unworthiness. Populist outbreaks against Jews occurred only after the Church had established an effective monopoly in Europe. The first major pogroms in Europe occurred at the end of the eleventh century when the lower stratum of the crusaders extended the principle of revenge on the infidel to native Jews. In the thirteenth century the accusation that the Jews murdered Christian children for their Passover rituals replaced the crusading ideologies as a pretext for massacre, and in the fourteenth century the popular image of the Jew became an integral part of the growing demonology: the Jews were accused of being Satan's associates on earth and widespread large-scale pogroms followed the accusation that the Jews had caused the Black Death by polluting the wells. [30]

It should be emphasised that the massacre of Jews was not an expression of racial or nationalistic antipathy. In the medieval period national self-consciousness was weak, especially in Germany; the Germans thought of themselves as members of a tribe (Saxons, Franks, Bavarians, etc) or as citizens of the Holy Roman Empire. The Jews were distinguished, both in law and in popular beliefs, not in terms of race or nation, but in terms of religion; they were seen as 'deliberate unbelievers' whose rejection of Christianity could only be explained by their association with Satan. The popular beliefs that conceived of Jews as 'monsters' with demonic features provided clear justification for their destruction without remorse or guilt. [31]

The tragic side of European Jewish history should not obscure the fact that there were long periods when a limited tolerance, sanctioned by the Church, did prevail. But in order to safeguard its virtual religious monopoly, the Church found it necessary to segregate that group over which its religious authority did not extend. The segregation of the Jews by the Church began in the early centuries after Christ when the Church was having little success in converting the Jews and when Judaism was regarded as a dangerous proselytising competitor, but the Church continued its policy of segregation long after Judaism had ceased to be a threat. The Church regulations providing for the segregation of the Jews were extended and elaborated in minutest detail in the later Middle Ages.

Although the voluntary ghetto was common throughout the medieval period, it did not become an enforced legal institution until the fifteenth century. The Jews did not oppose the legal institution of separate quarters, but many did object to the Jewish badge which was first instituted, under the auspices of the Church, in the thirteenth century and then took one and a half centuries to become firmly established. The increased emphasis of the Church on the segregation of the Jews in the latter part of the medieval age reflected the fears of churchmen that the Jews encouraged, directly or indirectly, the development of Christian heterodoxies and sectarian deviations. [32]

The majority of European states came to follow the Church's segregationist and discriminatory programme, but religious orientations of the dominant group cannot alone account for the clear legal, economic, and social separation of the Jews in medieval society. It is also appropriate to consider the Jews' position and functions in the social and economic structures of European feudal societies.

In the early Middle Ages the Jews were welcomed by many European rulers as a class of merchants who could provide valuable services in international and wholesale trade. In the Carolingian period the terms 'Jew' and 'merchant' were used almost interchangeably. The Jewish occupational structure was at first diversified in trade, crafts, and credit facilities, and despite the antagonism of the Church many Jewish communities achieved social prestige and political influence by their association with the secular rulers. From the period of the Crusades a class of gentile wholesale merchants grew, and the Jews were increasingly restricted to money lending, which was forbidden to gentiles by the canonical prohibition of the Church. The Jews lost the high status they held prior to the first Crusade and came to be despised more and more as a people identified with usury. Jewish participation in agriculture constantly declined: many Jewish land-holdings were expropriated, but in any case their insecure situation put a premium on owning property that could be moved. The prohibition on joining guilds and other discriminatory legislation and practices prevented Jewish participation in a number of crafts and occupations. In consequence, the European Jews developed from a people with a wide variety of occupations to a predominantly mercantile people with a strong emphasis on the money trade. [33]

In addition to their economic specialisation, the Jews were further separated by the corporate structure of medieval society. Within the feudal system of estates, the Jews formed a distinct corporation with their own relatively autonomous jurisdiction. The legal status of the Jewish 'estate' came to be denoted by the term 'serfdom', but the question of who had jurisdiction over the Jewish 'serfs' was much disputed. The powerful popes of the twelfth and thirteenth centuries proclaimed the perpetual serfdom of the Jews to the Church, and they issued decrees concerning the Jews which they declared were binding on the whole of the Christian world. This theological doctrine of Jewish 'serfdom' was disputed by the emperor in Germany and the monarchs of Western Europe. The royal theory of Jewish serfdom became an actuality in Western Europe by the end of the thirteenth century, and in Germany jurisdiction over the Jews shifted from the imperial crown to the German princes and cities by the fifteenth century.

Jewish 'serfdom' should not be equated with villeinage; the

Jews were, in many respects, the 'chattels' of the sovereign power, but in a feudal context they were comparatively free, since they lived under the sovereign's protection and enjoyed a considerable measure of corporative autonomy and independence.

The necessary alliance the Jews had to make with the monarchs was in turn a contributing factor to their economic differentiation in medieval Europe. In return for substantial fiscal contributions and economic services, the monarchs protected the Jews and their property, facilitated their economic enterprises, and sometimes authorised certain economic functions, such as money lending, to be performed exclusively by Jews. Some monarchs exploited other estates via the mediation of Jewish money lenders; the monarchs extorted large contributions from the Jews who in turn charged high interest rates for their loans. The alliance of the Jews with the monarchs antagonised both the nobles, who were often in debt to the Jews, and the burghers, who resented Jewish economic competition. The combination and interpenetration of economic antagonism and religious hatred had tragic consequences for the Jews.

With the decline of feudalism, the growth of the Christian merchant classes, and the greater emphasis on national and cultural identities among the Western European nations, the economic functions of the Jews were found to be increasingly dispensable. The massacres and expulsions from the Western nations in the thirteenth, fourteenth, and fifteenth centuries led to a Jewish migration to Poland and Lithuania where the continuation of feudal structures, the absence of a native merchant class, and the greater ethnic heterogeneity of the general population provided a more congenial environment. [34] In eastern Europe, the Jews entered a comparatively wide variety of occupations, but, in general, they remained a trading and artisan group, mediating between the nobility and the peasant masses. Eastern Europe had few cities, and the majority of Jews lived in small towns and villages, nearer to non Jews than did the ghetto Jews of western Europe. Despite this proximity, intimate association between Jews and gentiles was rare. [35]

In the feudal and early modern European states the Jews had considerable self-government and judicial autonomy; in return for taxes paid to the rulers, the Jews were permitted to elect their own leaders who employed salaried functionaries to administer communal institutions, represented the community in external relations, supervised the collection of taxes, and had certain sanctioning powers to enforce social and religious conformity. The most severe and effective formal sanction within the Jewish community was the *cherem* (excommunication) which ranged from threatened, and temporary, to permanent excommunication. The excommunicant was excluded from all religious facilities and might also be exluded from economic and social relationships. Since this meant exclusion from all society, the excommunicant was forced into a terribly isolated situation. It was not, of course, possible for a Jew to be unaffiliated with the community and yet remain a Jew; Jewish identity was a corporate identity.

The corporation or *kehilla* employed a number of salaried functionaries to administer community functions and staff the many organisations which the community maintained. The community employees combined secular and religious roles in varying degrees; the more secular functionaries included the *shtallanim* (interceders for the community) and tax collectors, and the more religious functionaries included the rabbis, cantors, beadles, slaughterers, and scribes. Although the *kehilla* employed professional rabbis, the rabbinate was largely independent and autonomous. The performance of rabbinical roles (scholar, teacher, judge, and ritualistic adviser) was not dependent on an appointment or office, and the professional salaried rabbis often accepted the judgement of the private rabbis who supported themselves by fees. A formal rabbinical hierarchy did not exist; the local autonomy of the rabbinate meant that the only hierarchy was an informal one based on number of followers and recognition of outstanding religious scholarship.[36]

As noted, the Sephardi Jews were less culturally distinctive than the Ashkenazi, and this difference may be related to the more tolerant conditions in Spain and Portugal up to the end of the fourteenth century.

The Iberian Jews were persecuted by the Christianised Visigoths in the seventh century, but the Arab conquest of Spain in the eighth century brought a long period of pluralistic tolerance which was only interrupted for a short period in the twelfth century by the fundamentalist Almohads. The Church in Christian Spain made many attempts to curtail the rights of Jews, but a combination of circumstances, which included the presence of a large Muslim population, made for a comparatively secure and settled Jewish existence. This came to an end in the late fourteenth and fifteenth centuries when renewed Christian monopolism took the form of massacres, forced conversions, and expulsion.

During the long period of pluralism, the Sephardim were not greatly separated from non-Jews in social or economic spheres, and they played a significant part in the cultural and economic life of Spain. Unlike the Ashkenazim, they were active in most occupations and a few rose to eminence and influence in the Spanish courts. [37]

Where the Sephardi rabbis were more strict than the Ashkenazi in their religious rulings, they were responding to the greater non-Jewish tolerance towards, and social interaction with, the Jews. They made a number of rulings which were intended to counteract the close contact with the Arab population and the concomitant adoption of Arab customs, but it is doubtful whether the Sephardi rabbis, whose authority was not as great as the Ashkenazi rabbis, were very successful in this. Where the Sephardim did observe certain religious practices to a greater extent than the Ashkenazim, these were often observances, such as lustrations, which were also practised by the Arabs.

Where the Ashkenazi rabbis were more lenient in their religious rulings, this reflected the greater persecution and separation of the Jews in central and north-west Europe. The occupational specialisation of the Ashkenazi Jews meant that they had to depend on non-Jews for many goods and services

31

which did not always conform to the religious requirements of Jewish law. For example Jews often depended on non-Jews for bread and wine, and the Ashkenazi rabbis had to modify the law to legitimise the deviance from certain talmudic injunctions which this involved. The Ashkenazi rabbis also modified religious laws to avoid persecution. For example, they ruled that it was permissible to put out a fire on the Sabbath since it was common in Germany for a Jew to be thrown into the flames if his house caught fire.

Since revenge against the Christian persecutors was not possible and exhortations for a supernatural revenge appeared to have little effect, the Ashkenazi Jews tended to accept persecution as a just retribution by God for past Jewish sins and failure to observe the religious·law. They atoned for these unknown sins by abstinence and self-affliction; the number of religious fasts increased and a number of new rituals, such as flagellation on the eve of the Day of Atonement, were introduced. Many laws and customs developed in connection with the martyrs of pogroms, and a new type of religious poetry dealt with persecution and sacrifice. [38]

Early modern Europe

The important changes in post-medieval Europe – the Renaissance, Reformation, and Counter-Reformation – had comparatively little impact on the cultural distinctiveness and social position of the majority of European Jewish communities. Forced conversions and expulsions became less frequent after the fifteenth century, but most rulers maintained or even reinforced Jewish segregation. With one exception, Jewish communities were largely untouched by the development of secularism and individualism among the non-Jewish upper stratum during the Rennaissance period. The exception was Italy where the rich Jewish loan-bankers were socially accepted by the Renaissance Christian élite who were themselves bourgeois and involved in commercial operations. Italian Jewry, and particularly its upper class, made significant contributions to the Renaissance and adopted the Italian language, fashion, and modes of behaviour. In many respects Italian Jewry was a Renaissance society in miniature; the Jewish patricians who were the nucleus of this society lived in luxurious houses, commissioned artists, and employed scholars who were versed in both religious and secular knowledge. [39]

In the second half of the sixteenth century the Counter-Reformation put an end to the tolerance of the Italian Renaissance. Jews were expelled from certain areas but in most Italian states there was a return to the segregation of the medieval period: Jews were forced to wear distinctive garb and live in ghettos. The segregation imposed by the religio-political authorities was not reinforced by any vehement anti-Jewish feeling of the Italian people; violent outbreaks were rare and continued friendly association is demonstrated by the number of occasions during the seventeenth and eighteenth centuries when the Church found it necessary to prohibit Christians from joining Jews in social recreations such as dancing. For this reason, and because their segregation was a totally involuntary one, Italian Jews continued to adopt Italian fashion and culture. Those who could not endure the forced segregation and attendant pauperisation either emigrated to northern Europe or converted. [40]

In northern Europe the immediate effects of the Reformation and the increased independence of the German states from the imperial powers were further anti-Jewish measures and expulsions, especially from the Lutheran states. The expulsion of Jews from German cities in the fifteenth and early sixteenth centuries resulted in a greater dispersal of the Jews over rural districts, but the trend was reversed in the early seventeenth century when the Protestant rulers readmitted the Jews with improved privileges in order to use Jewish commercial and financial skills in the development of their states. The Counter-Reformation introduced measures to segregate Jews, but as the Church continued to uphold the principle that the Jews should be tolerated until the end of days there were few expulsions from Catholic lands, and in the Habsburg possessions there was even some improvement in Jewish status. [41]

33

Comparisons

It is now possible to make a number of statements accounting for the gross differences in levels of Jewish acculturation in the societies discussed. It should be emphasised, however, that with regard to a number of the 'isolated' communities, our conclusions will have to be very tentative. The historical data is often sparse and, in some cases, almost non-existent. It is not possible to trace the religio-cultural developments of the Chinese, Indian, and many Middle Eastern communities over the centuries since much of our information derives from Europeans who visited and described the communities after they were 'discovered'. In many cases we can only compare a number of static pictures of communities at the end of their periods of isolation and from these attempt to reconstruct their histories. However, what independent historical evidence we do have suggests that where the distinctiveness of Judaism became highly attenuated, the process occurred over a long period and cannot be explained in terms of the characteristics and orientations of the first generation of Jewish settlers. If the original Jewish settlers had been predisposed to cultural and social absorption by the 'host' society, the community would not have survived centuries of isolation from other Jewish communities, even in a highly attenuated form.

The size of the Jewish community and the distance from the major centres of Jewish settlement are important variables but should not be overemphasised. Comparatively small numbers, and lack of contact with other Jewish communities, could only make a community particularly malleable to its cultural and social environments. One important cultural dimension was the strength of the boundaries of the dominant religion of the majority. Jewish acculturation was much greater in those societies where the dominant religion was syncretic than in those societies where the dominant religion was insular. Although the differences between Judaism and the environmental religious systems were initially much greater in China and India than in the Middle East and Europe, the syncretism of the Eastern religions contributed to the much greater loss of Jewish religio-cultural distinctiveness in the East.

Another important dimension was the strength of the dominant group's disposition to demand allegiance to its religion within its defined territory. As might be expected, syncretic religions were more disposed to pluralism and insular religions were more disposed to monopolism. The greater the tendency of the dominant group to coerce the Jews into accepting he majority religion, the more the Jews emphasised their religio-cultural distinctiveness. The greater the tendency of the dominant group to accept the existence of Judaism, the more likely the Jews would acculturate to the majority or core culture.

Both religio-cultural and social structural dimensions influenced the extent to which the Jews were separated socially from non-Jews. Where Jews were separated, they were less likely to adopt the non-Jewish religio-culture. Where Jews were not so separated and social contracts with non-Jews were more frequent and intimate, acculturation was far more likely. The extent to which the Jews were separated within a society was often related to the dominant group's disposition to monopolism or pluralism. A total monopolistic policy, if successful, would have resulted in the disappearance of the Jews, but successful monopolism was very rare. Even when Jews were forced to convert to Christianity, they often remained unassimilated, and this drove the dominant group to segregate them still further.

Although attempts at a total monopolism by means of massacres, forced conversions, and expulsions were not uncommon in Christian Europe, periods of pluralism were generally longer. Variations in social separation have, therefore, to be considered within the framework of pluralism, although it is obvious that Jews were more likely to be separated from non-Jews in those societies whose pluralist stance was of a comparatively limited form. In some cases segregation of the Jews was motivated by the dominant group's desire to impose or retain its religious monopoly over the non-Jewish population. In medieval Europe, however, the Jews were segregated by more encompassing barriers long after Judaism had ceased to be a threat to Christian monopolism.

35

Some spheres of separation of Jews from non-Jews were little related, at least in any direct way, to the religious motives and orientations of the dominant group. Differences in the social structures of 'host' societies were also relevant. The feudal structure of European societies made for the separation of Jews in the economic, social, and political spheres. Jews were less segregated in Middle Eastern societies, but the convergence of religion and state under Islam involved the political separation of religious minorities. In China and India Jews were not politically separated and corporate Jewish polities did not develop. The Indian caste system did make for some social separation of Jews but, in contrast to the Middle East and Europe, the Jews were separated within the dominant religious system and not outside it. The social separation of Jews as a caste in India implied a substantial Jewish acculturation, while in the Middle East and Europe, the greater the social separation of Jews from non-Jews, the greater the tendency of Jews to retain or reinforce their religio-cultural distinctiveness.

2 The Eighteenth Century

Migration and dispersion

From 1500 to 1640 Polish Jewry enjoyed a period of relative security. This came to an end when the Greek Orthodox Ukranian peasants and Cossacks rebelled against the Roman Catholic nobles and massacred large numbers of Jews. Further massacres occurred during the Muscovite-Swedish invasion of Poland and these events mark the beginnings of a westward movement of European Jews. Pogroms were not, however, the major cause of emigration from Poland in the seventeenth and eighteenth centuries. More important was the deteriorating political situation and economic decline of Poland and the politically more secure and economically more favourable situation in central and western Europe. The vicinity of the foreign border was an important factor; the majority emigrated from Lithuania and the western regions of Poland and settled in Germany, especially Prussia. A few migrated to western Europe, especially Amsterdam and London, but the westward movement was small compared with the mass emigration after 1880, and eastern Europe continued to have the largest concentration of European Jews. [1]

In contrast with the migration of Ashkenazim from eastern Europe, which was related to the political disintegration of the Polish commonwealth, the expulsion of the Sephardim from Spain (1492) and Portugal (1498) was part of the Spanish ruler's policy to eliminate religious minorities in order to achieve a strong national state around the throne and Church. Jews were given the choice of expulsion or conversion, but many of the converted Jews *(marranos)* continued to practise Judaism in secret and they became a special object of the Spanish Inquisition's investigations and persecutions. The majority chose to remain Jews and leave Spain, but a substantial minority remained in Spain and joined the class of *marranos* which had grown throughout the fifteenth century. Many *marranos* later fled the Spanish Inquisition and reverted openly to Judaism in their adopted countries. [2]

Over half of the Iberian Jews migrated to the Ottoman empire, others settled in Italy, Morocco, southern France, and South America, and in the seventeenth century Sephardi Jews started new Jewish communities in England, Holland, and North America. In Europe the Sephardim settled in the developing commercial centres, and, in general, they remained more prosperous, secular, and acculturated to non-Jewish society than the Ashkenazim. In the new western communities, however, Ashkenazi immigrants from central and eastern Europe soon outnumbered the Sephardim. The Amsterdam community grew from 200 Sephardim in 1609 to 2,400 Sephardim and 21,000 Ashkenazim in 1795. [3] An English census in 1695 found a total of 548 Sephardim and 203 Ashkenazim in London, but by 1720 the number of Ashkenazim exceeded the number of Sephardim, and in 1800 only about 2,000 of the total British Jewish population of 20,000 were Sephardim. [4] In North America, the number of Ashkenazim exceeded the Sephardim from about 1735, but the total North American Jewish population was only about 2,000 in 1800. The distribution of European Jews at the time of the partitions of Poland (1772–95) was as follows: [5]

Poland-Lithuania (mostly annexed by Russia)	800,000
Habsburg empire:	
Hungary	75,000–100,000
Bohemia-Moravia	70,000
Galicia (annexed from Poland)	200,000
Germanies (including Posen annexed from	
Poland by Prussia)	175,000–200,000
Italy	30,000
France	40,000
Holland	50,000
England	20,000

Polish Jewry was spread over a large area. Jews often represented half the population in the larger Polish towns, but most Jews lived in small rural towns *(shtetls)* and villages. The 1764 Polish census reported that there were only twelve Jewish communities with a population of over 2,000, and that 26.9 per cent of the Jewish population lived in villages with an average of twenty-five Jewish families. [6]

Widespread distribution over rural areas was also a feature of the Jewish population in the Habsburg empire, the German states, France, and North America. In Europe most states limited Jewish rights of domicile and only allowed small numbers of 'tolerated' or 'privileged' Jews to live in the cities. The only large Jewish community under the Habsburgs was Prague with a Jewish population of 8,000 in 1791; in the Germanies, the large communities were found in Hamburg, which, together with nearby Altona, had 9,000 Jews; Berlin, and Frankfurt, each with over 3,000; and a few other towns with over 1,000. The vast majority of central European Jews were widely scattered in medium and small communities. [7]

Prior to the French Revolution, the bulk of the 40,000 Ashkenazim in France lived in the eastern border territories which had been annexed from Germany in the sixteenth- and seventeenth-century wars. In 1789 the Jewish population in the city of Metz numbered 2,000, but most Jews in Alsace lived in villages and small towns. The majority of the 3,000–4,000 Sephardim in south-west France lived in two cities: Bordeaux and Bayonne. In Paris in 1789 there were about 150 Sephardim and 350 Ashkenazim. [8] The North American Jewish population included few frontiersmen but it was highly dispersed and geographically mobile; there were only five organised Jewish communities prior to the American Revolution. [9] Two-thirds of the 30,000 Italian Jews were concentrated in ten urban communities, but only the Dutch and British communities were concentrated in the capitals: half of the Dutch Jews were concentrated in Amsterdam and three-quarters of the British Jews were concentrated in the City of London with only one-quarter elsewhere. [10]

Levels of acculturation in the eighteenth century

From around the turn of the seventeenth century the religio-cultural homogeneity of European Jews began to break up; the communities began to differ in the extent of their acculturation to non-Jewish society. Since religion was pervasive in all spheres of life in the traditional Jewish community, acculturation to non-Jewish society necessarily involved some deviation from the traditional religio-culture. In other words, acculturation necessarily involved secularisation in the sense of an increased compartmentalisation of the 'religious' and the 'secular'.

The religio-culture of the eastern European Jews remained quite distinct from the religio-culture of the non-Jewish majority. In the second half of the eighteenth century, eastern European Jewry was divided in two religious camps, the hassidim and *mitnagdim* (the opponents of the hassidim), but this was a division within the context of a distinctively Jewish religio-culture. In both groups all aspects of society – familial, economic, political, educational, and the stratification system – were regulated by the Jewish religion.

The hassidic movement, which gained support from large numbers of east European Jews in the second half of the eighteenth century, deviated from some aspects of 'Orthodoxy': it emphasised pantheism rather than dualism, ecstaticism rather than asceticism, and communion with God through prayer rather than the systematic study of the Talmud and its commentaries. The movement was not, however, a 'contra-culture'; it brought into prominence, and extended, certain aspects of the religious heritage. 'Orthodox' doctrine declared that God had created the universe out of nothing, but it postulated a radically transcendental God and a world devoid of sacred qualities where man attempted to carry out God's law. God's transcendentalism meant that the individual was not directly moved by God on earth to carry out His wishes, so the individual had to discern the appropriate religious behaviour by reference to the sacred writings. Hassidism presented a more monistic cosmology: God was omnipresent and his sparks of holiness permeated the world. The spiritual and the material world were ideally one, and, by perfecting himself through love and worship of God, man could help purge God's sparks of holiness of their defilement, contribute to the attainment of perfection in the higher realms, and thereby deliver the divine presence and the people of Israel from their captivity, achieving complete unity of the two worlds.

Hassidism may be said to have re-enchanted the world by emphasising God's omnipresence and bringing his angels and spirits down to earth, but the world of the Jewish masses was, in any case, far from disenchanted; the majority believed in saints, angels, demons, spirits, and such notions as the Evil Eye and the protective power of amulets. Moreover, hassidic mystical doctrines rested on cabbalism, especially the cabbalistic school of Luria (1534–76), which was an important aspect of Jewish tradition. Hassidism popularised the cabbalistic teachings; it replaced the esotericism and asceticism of the elitist mystic groups by a practical mysticism which emphasised joy rather than suffering and sadness. In contrast to the extreme forms of self-mortification practised by many Jewish mystics and 'scholar-saints', the hassidim demonstrated and stimulated the primary virtue of joy in their *shtiblech* (prayer houses) by shouting, clapping, dancing, drinking, whirling, and turning somersaults.

Direct communion with God was at first enjoined on all hassidim, but it gradually became the special task of the leaders, the *zaddikim,* the saintly intermediaries between God and the hassidic communities. The doctrine of the *zaddik* was present in the teachings of the first leader, Rabbi Israel Baal-Shem-Tov (the Besht for short), but the doctrine assumed greater importance among the third-generation hassidim. When the Besht died in 1760, the leadership was taken by Rabbi Dov-Ber of Meseritz and it was his disciples who dispersed to found the dynastic centres of the *zaddikim.* Thereafter the charisma of the *zaddik* was inherited by his sons, but if he did not have a son his charisma could sometimes be transferred to a son-in-law or a disciple. Each dynasty had its devoted followers who gathered on festivals and other occasions to celebrate at the *zaddik's* court, which varied in lavishness according to the size and wealth of the adherents. Life in the court focused on a fanatical devotion to the *zaddik* who would descend from the spiritual heights and direct his activities for the good of his followers, healing the afflicted and performing miracles.

The authority of the *zaddikim* clearly had a different basis from that of the religious leaders of the non-hassidic Orthodox, and it was the most eminent 'scholar-saint' of the eighteenth century, the Gaon Rabbi Elijah Vilna (1720–97), who persuaded the heads of the official communities to persecute the hassidim. The Gaon did not hold an official position in the community, but he held charismatic authority derived from his ascetic saintliness and scholarly reputation. The source of the more traditional type of charisma, as exemplified by the Gaon, differed from that of the *zaddik,* the divinely elected intermediary with thaumaturgic powers. The qualities of the *zaddik* did not, however, represent a complete break with the past; the veneration of, and pilgrimages to, saints were part of an ancient Jewish tradition.

The opposition of community and rabbinical leaders to hassidism was intense, especially in Lithuania, but the hassidim did not allow themselves to be forced into the position of a seceding sect. Although some hassidic leaders were critical of the communal and rabbinical establishment, they did not distinguish themselves as a 'band of saints' opposing a 'kingdom of evil'. A few hassidim criticised the scholars, especially for their elitism and their contempt for the non-scholarly masses, but the anti-intellectualism among the early hassidim subsided as the movement spread from the Ukraine to the more scholarly centres of northern Poland. The hassidim respected the sacred texts and, although they deviated in a few ritualistic matters, they conformed to the complex system of Jewish rituals as codified in the *Shulhan Arukh.* In this they differed from the heretical movements of Sabbatai Zevi and Joseph Frank in the seventeenth and eighteenth centuries. The Sabbatians and Frankists believed that the observance of the ritual was unnecessary because the Messianic age had begun or was about to begin. In comparison, although many of the individual hassidim may have expected an imminent deliverance, doctrines of imminent Messianism were not part of their leaders' teachings. The Besht had written that, during a mystical experience, when his soul rose to heaven, the Messiah had told him that he would only come when the hassidic teachings had spread fully among the people. In general, the hassidim emphasised their adherence to tradition and, after a period of mutual accommodation, the conflict between the hassidim and *mitnagdim* declined. Many *zaddikim,* especially those in Lithuania and White Russia, became eminent talmudical scholars. By the beginning of the nineteenth century the hassidim and *mitnagdim* had joined together to combat the dangers to traditionalism of the secular Enlightenment. It is somewhat paradoxical that the hassidim, who were at first violently opposed by the religious establishment, were in the nineteenth and twentieth centuries to become the major 'carrier' of religious traditionalism. [11]

Hassidism remained largely confined to those parts of the Polish commonwealth which were annexed by Russia (the Ukraine, White Russia, Lithuania), and it spread only to the eastern provinces of the Habsburg empire (Galicia, Bukovina, Transylvania, Slovakia). The majority of Jews in central Europe continued to adhere to a largely unmodified traditionalism, but in the first half of the eighteenth century there were clear signs of acculturation to gentile society and of deviation from traditional religious observances among the rich stratum of German Jewry. Many adopted gentile clothes and abandoned the traditional Jewish clothes, there was a greater emphasis on material possessions, a new interest in science and philosophy, and an increased participation in worldly activities – music, dancing, hunting, playing cards, drinking, secular literature and art, attendance at the theatre, and ball games. Religious learning declined, the status of the rabbinate fell, men shaved their beards, rules of family purity and interpersonal morality were disregarded, and men broke the Sabbath by going to the post office and stock exchange. Secular patterns of behaviour were first noted in Hamburg among the Sephardim, who mixed with non-Jews in the stock markets and coffee houses, but they became prevalent among the rich Ashkenazim and touched ever greater numbers during the second half of the century. [12] Nevertheless, only a minority displayed extensive secularisation and acculturation prior to the 'emancipation' decrees around the turn of the century.

Among the first German Jews to acculturate to non-Jewish behaviour patterns were the Court Jews of the seventeenth and eighteenth centuries. As companions of the Court aristocracy, it was impossible for the Court Jews to observe the ritual minutiae, but they always married within the Jewish group, and their acculturation to non-Jewish society demonstrated a strict compartmentalisation between 'secular' and 'religious' culture. The Court Jews adopted the formal ceremonial, rich dress, courtly manners, titles, and marks of rank of the aristocracy, but they conformed to the major Jewish values such as religious scholarship and piety, they founded *yeshivot,* financed synagogues, read the cabbalah, and took an interest in Jewish magic, prophecy, and revelation. Many received rabbinical titles in which they took even greater pride than in their court titles. [13]

The compartmentalised acculturation of the Court Jews contrasts with the more extensive acculturation and secularisation of the small 'privileged' Jewish upper class in the northern German cities in the second half of the eighteenth century. These wealthy urban Jews mixed socially with upper-middle-class Christian businessmen, officials, and nobles, and they adopted in large measure the values and behaviour patterns of their Christian friends and acquaintances. It was from among this small Jewish upper-class stratum, living in Berlin, Hamburg, Konigsberg, and Breslau, that the exponents of the *Haskalah,* the Jewish Enlightenment, appeared. [14]

Interest in branches of knowledge of non-Jewish origin had grown in the first half of the eighteenth century, but prior to about 1760 there was no attempt to re-interpret traditional values from a secular perspective. In contrast, the most famous of the early 'enlightened' Jews, Moses Mendelssohn (1729–86), used rationalist philosophy to defend Judaism; but while he urged Jews to adapt themselves 'to the customs and constitution of the land in which you live', he also emphasised that they should 'adhere firmly to the religion of your ancestors'. [15] He argued that Jewish ritual should be retained in total since it was this and not Jewish doctrine which distinguished Judaism from other religions. A more radical *Haskalah,* expounding deism, rationalism, and humanism, and discarding much of the traditional ritual, developed in the last years of the eighteenth century. Mendelssohn's theory was then reversed: it was argued that Jewish doctrine was unique to Judaism and that ritual was a secondary embellishment. This change in ideology was a response to the decline in observance and the growing number of conversions in the last two decades of the century. In 1792 Saul Ascher argued that the only way to stop conversions was to replace ritual prescriptions by a set of dogmas. [16]

The values of the Enlightenment dominated the intellectual culture of the famous Berlin salons of Jewish hostesses around the turn of the century. The salon Jews rejected the particularistic elements in Judaism, accepted the negative aesthetic evaluation of the Jewish religion, and adopted the view that Jewish culture represented a lower state of civilisation. In 1799, David Friedlander, a rich businessman, petitioned the Berlin Lutheran Councillor Teller 'in the name of many Jewish heads of families' with a proposal that they would accept Christianity and even baptism if they were not required to believe in the divinity of Jesus. The proposal was refused, but many rich urban German Jews were baptised in the early years of the nineteenth century. In 1806 nearly 10 per cent of the Berlin Jewish community were converted. [17]

In France, Holland and England the most secularised, acculturated Jews were found among the Sephardim, especially the upper stratum, who mixed in Christian circles, adopted the life style of the *haute bourgeoisie,* and relaxed their observance of the religious law. [18] The Ashkenazim in the eastern provinces of France and the Ashkenazi immigrants in Amsterdam and

London were generally poorer and more visibly foreign than the Sephardim; they spoke Yiddish and wore distinctive clothes, long hair, and beards. But evidence that acculturation was not confined to the Sephardim is found in the sermons of Ashkenazi rabbis in Metz, Amsterdam, and London. The rabbis criticised their congregations for shaving their beards, dressing in new fashions, and attending the theatre and opera, and for their lax observance of daily prayers, the Sabbath, and some festivals. [19] In all three countries these secular tendencies were largely confined to a small number of rich Ashkenazim, but secular behaviour appears to have made the greatest inroads among the Ashkenazim in London. Rabbi Hart Lyon, the Rabbi of the Great Synagogue in London, who had formerly been a rabbi in Breslau, compared the London Jews unfavourably with the German congregations and lamented the lax observance of the dietary laws, the observance of Christian feasts, the immorality of the young, the disregard of the laws of purity, the number of mixed marriages, and the endeavours 'to associate with Gentiles and to be like them'. Religious scholarship remained important for most French and Dutch Ashkenazim, but Rabbi Lyon said that the London Jews wasted their time in coffee houses and clubs playing cards, instead of devoting some hours, when free from business, to the study of the Torah. He complained bitterly that Jews neglected to teach the Torah to children and young people. R. Tevele Schiff, who succeeded Lyon as rabbi in 1765, also complained of having no pupils to teach and no friends with whom he could study the Torah. In the English community, religious knowledge was no longer the primary criterion of status. Unlike the east European Jews, whose segregation made possible a distinctive status system based on religious values, the acculturated English Jews' status system was based almost exclusively on one of the criteria important in the 'host' population's status system: wealth. The immigrant rabbis suffered from loss of prestige and loss of functions. The more limited role accorded to religion, and the lower estimation of it, in the English communities meant that the rabbis' status was not as high as in the countries from which they had come. In

England the rabbi was no longer the leader of the community, but a religious functionary, employed by a religious organisation, which limited even his religious powers. The chief role of the rabbi was to study the law, but in England this was not legitimised by a general value consensus which made study the duty of every man. Conflict was almost inevitable between acculturated Jewish laymen and the rabbis. Rabbi Lyon objected to the restriction on his authority, and in 1764 he left London to become rabbi in Halberstadt. Rabbi Schiff was also dissatisfied with the congregation. He tried to change his position and return to Germany on two occasions, but he died in England in 1791. [20]

Acculturation and secularisation were even more extensive in the eighteenth-century North American communities. The Ashkenazi immigrants were accepted into the Sephardi congregations and the first permanent Ashkenazi congregation was formed only in 1802. The integration of Sephardim and Ashkenazim was possible because of the comparatively secular nature of the Jewish immigrants, the small number distributed over large areas, and the absence of large differences in class and status. The amorphous nature of Jewish life in America meant that only the less traditionally religious Jews migrated there, and they were not too concerned about ritual differences. Since early Jewish migration to America was a migration of individuals rather than large families or communities, the dispersed immigrants often found themselves in an isolated situation, and they sought out other Jews without concern for ritual and ethnic differences. The synagogues, which had no rabbis to direct their activities, were social and community centres in which the Jewish immigrants from various lands integrated socially into an American-Jewish melting-pot. [21]In this society, the greatest deviation from the traditional religious community occurred. The minutes of the Shearith Israel Synagogue in New York provide evidence of trading on the Sabbath, non-observance of the dietary laws, and other deviations from the fundamentals of the religious law which had taken place. [22]

Environmental culture and social structure

In Poland-Lithuania both social structural and cultural factors contributed to the clear separation of the Jewish and non-Jewish populations. In many respects the kingdom of Poland was the most feudal European society; the divisions between the estates, each with its own legally defined duties and privileges, were strongly drawn. The country was ruled by a few large land-owning noble families who had deprived the Crown of any real power and severely restricted the independence of the small urban middle class. The Jews were an artisan and trading class occupying a social position between the nobility which, in addition to the large land-owners, included the 'middle gentry' and the poor 'barefoot' nobles, and the peasant masses, most of whom were serfs. [23]

As a separate estate the Jews had their own self-governing corporations, but their extensive autonomy was largely dependent on their economic functions. The nobles looked down upon trading occupations and despised the Jews, but they found the Jewish middlemen useful in resisting the economic and political demands of Christian merchants, many of whom were of German ethnic origin. Individual nobles owned whole towns and they effectively opposed the attempts of Christian merchants and artisans to introduce economic discrimination against the Jews. [24]

The occupational structure of the Polish Jews in the middle of the eighteenth century has been calculated as follows: 2–3 per cent rich merchants and financiers, nearly 40 per cent small traders including leaseholders and innkeepers, about 33 per cent artisans and other urban wage-earners, 10 per cent in community services, and 15 per cent unemployed and paupers. The urban Jewish population was stratified in a similar way to the gentiles: a top stratum of rich merchants and entrepreneurs, a middle stratum of small craftsmen and merchants who formed the majority, and a bottom stratum of wage-earners and paupers. The Jewish stratification differed from the gentiles in so far as status from religious scholarship was superimposed on status from wealth and inheritance. The urban Jewish communities were by no means harmonious; the artisans resented the arbitrary rule of the governing oligarchy, who were elected by a limited assembly of rich men and scholars, and there were occasions when artisans accused the leaders of arbitrary taxation and attacked the offices of the *kehilla*. These conflicts were kept within the confines of the Jewish community; there was never any question that the middle and lower strata would seek help from parallel classes outside the Jewish community. However divided the classes within the Jewish community, the ethnic-religious boundary was far more encompassing. The Christian merchants and artisans resented and feared the competition of the Jews who fell outside the jurisdiction of the guilds. [25]

In the villages and small towns, the majority of Jews, who were sub-lessees and employees, were nearly as poor as the serfs; only a few, who leased directly from the estate owners, were comparatively well off. The serfs, however, made little differentiation between them and resented all Jews as the agents of the land-owners and as the most visible source of their misery. Although most rural and small-town Jews lived in close proximity to the peasants, their interactions were almost exclusively confined to the economic sphere. There was an enormous cultural gulf between the Jews and the peasants, and the religious stereotype of the Jew, depicting him as a 'Christ-killer' and 'ally of anti-Christ', prevailed. The clergy, including some high church prelates, incited anti-Jewish feeling, and there were a number of ritual murder accusations and trials.

The rapid spread of hassidism in the last decades of the eighteenth century was related to Poland's economic decline and political disintegration. The Jews had to bear both their own economic losses and the hostility of the peasants, merchants, artisans, and lower nobility, who held the Jews responsible for their misery. Many petty lessees were deprived of their leaseholds, and expulsions from the villages and towns increased the number of destitute wanderers and robbers.

The social base of early hassidism was the lower-middle class in the rural areas — the middle and small lessees, innkeepers, small shopkeepers, peddlers, hawkers, and unemployed – whose economic situation was unstable and deteriorating. [26] A number of reasons may be given for the success of hassidism: its emphasis on communion with God through ecstatic prayer meant that non-scholarly Jews need not feel deprived of religious status; its emphasis on mysticism and joy provided some respite from the real world of increasing misery; its charismatic leaders stressed their responsibility to their followers at a time when the traditional scholarly élite had become remote from the Jewish masses; and lastly, its moderation and adherence to tradition enabled it to gain support from all strata in the community. Historians have noted the predominance of the lower stratum of religious functionaries (preachers, ritual slaughterers, *cantors,* and teachers) among the early hassidic leaders, but many of the chief opponents were also from this stratum, and rabbis were not entirely absent from the early leadership. Although the early hassidim were chiefly drawn from the non-scholarly, the followers and opponents cannot be clearly divided according to the economic and status divisions in the Jewish community. [27] The diffusion of hassidism throughout the different strata became even more prevalent as hassidism spread from south-west Poland to the less backward and more scholarly areas of northern Poland. By the beginning of the nineteenth century, hassidism had strengthened the Jewish community and reinforced the traditional religio-culture.

The partitions of Poland had little immediate impact on the social structure of eastern Europe and the position of the Jews within it; the Jews of Posen under Prussia, Galicia under Austria, and White Russia, Ukraine, and Lithuania under Russia continued to perform the function of a middleman commercial class. The 'absolutist' monarchs were not willing to countenance Jewish autonomy to the extent that had developed in the more loosely structured Poland; Russia reduced the autonomy of the *kehillot* in 1778 and Austria formally abolished them in 1785–9. But these measures did not significantly reduce the self-government of the Jewish communities; the monarchs could do little to prevent Jewish adherence to their religious law and the jurisdiction of the rabbis. [28]

In central Europe the great majority of Jews also remained clearly separate, legally, economically and socially, from the non-Jewish population. Although the central European states differed from Poland with respect to the political strength of their monarchs, they shared a number of similar social structural and cultural characteristics which resulted in the separation of the Jews. These included the estate form of stratification, the existence of semi-autonomous corporations, powerful land-owning nobilities, a small, politically weak bourgeoisie, a large peasantry, and a religious culture which included Jews in its demonology. Hungary's social structure most closely approximated to Poland: a powerful upper nobility secured the middleman position of the Jews in their estates and private towns. Hungary's Crown towns were mostly populated by Germans and, in contrast to Poland, the towns enjoyed a wide measure of autonomy. This meant that Jews had to struggle for domicile and trade rights in these towns. [29]

The position of the Jews within the social structure of Bohemia-Moravia was somewhat transitional between eastern and central Europe: the Jewish occupational structure resembled that of Polish Jewry, but the effective discrimination of Christian merchants and craft guilds resulted in fewer artisans and a concentration of Jewish tradesmen in wholesale and peddling. Joseph II's attempts to centralise, unify, and 'modernise' his empire included measures which were intended to assimilate Jews, both culturally and socially. He reduced the autonomy of the estates and corporations, released some occupations from guild control, removed certain trade restrictions, supported schemes to establish Jewish farming communities, and passed decrees intended to make the Jews adopt German names, dress, language, and culture. However, the universalistic principles set out in the Emperor's Edict of Toleration in 1781–2 were not implemented in a consistent fashion; most Jews remained subject to discriminatory measures, and only a small number of rich Jews benefited from the limited reform measures, supported the *Haskalah,* and adopted the German language and culture. [30]

As in Austria, the 'absolutist' rulers of the German states

51

reduced the autonomy of the corporations, including the Jewish *kehillot,* especially with respect to the law courts. The leaders of the *kehillot* were often appointed directly by the state governments and their affairs were subject to greater regulation. Nevertheless, the Jewish community was still a highly autonomous one: the *kehillot* apportioned taxes, supervised economic affairs and the distribution of charity, and regulated the many *kehillot* organisations: synagogues, cemeteries, schools, ritual baths, and so on.

State, guild, and local authority restrictions in Jewish domicile and occupations created a narrow Jewish occupational structure with very few artisans and a large number in petty trade and peddling. Economic specialisation reinforced the social barrier between Jews and Christians, both in the rural areas, where Jewish occupations were most clearly distinctive from the gentile rural population, and in the towns, where Jews were separated in ghettos. However, new opportunities in commerce in Germany resulted in a greater social differentiation within the Jewish community and enabled the small Jewish upper class to move out of the ghettos.[31] The development of mercantilism and political absolutism produced the Court Jews who provided credit for the German princes, supplied them with precious metals, moved supplies over long distances, and acted as intermediaries in diplomatic activities and negotiations.

The Court Jews were marginal men since they participated in, and oriented their behaviour towards, two widely dissimilar socio-cultural groups: the Court aristocracy and the Jewish community. The two sets of roles were performed in different contexts and at different times, and this insulation allowed them to constantly move between the Jewish religio-culture and the baroque style of life at the Court. Nevertheless, the Court Jews did have occasion to make choices between two sets of values and behaviour patterns. Their participation in the Court necessitated a comparatively secular behaviour pattern but, in general, the Jewish community appears to have been the more important cultural reference; they adopted the formal role signs of the aristocracy, but it was necessary for them to conform to the major Jewish religious values to gain some legitimacy among Jews for their leadership of the *kehillot*.

The heyday of the Court Jews ended about 1740, but, as part of their policy to expand commerce and industry, the 'absolutist' rulers continued to allow a small but increasing number of 'privileged' Jews to reside outside the ghettos and in the cities where Jewish domicile was formally forbidden. From the 1760s a number of these 'privileged' Jews gained access to Christian bourgeois circles, especially the learned societies where Christians and Jews focused on a common interest in 'secular' knowledge. Secular trends, especially evident in the intellectual sub-society, enabled Jews to enter what Jacob Katz has termed a 'semi-neutral society'; that is, a society which accepted Jews only incompletely and provisionally. The Germans who accepted Jews socially did not necessarily disagree with the views of those who justified their social rejection of Jews by emphasising the Christian character of European society and the belief that the Jewish religion kept Jews apart and made it impossible for them to fulfil the obligations of citizenship. 'Enlightened' Germans rejected certain Christian dogmas, but they recognised that they were products of a Christian society which they believed represented a higher level of civilisation than Jewish society. They expected that 'enlightened' Jews would finally accept Christianity or at least reject the particularistic elements in Judaism. Individual Jews were socially accepted as 'exceptions' who were not expected to behave like the mass of 'ordinary' Jews. [32]

The French victory over Prussia in 1806 caused many Germans to turn from universalism, rationalism, and humanism to nationalism, romanticism, and religion. [33] A decree in 1808 gave civic rights to all Jews and thus removed the legal foundations of 'privileged' Jewish status. Berlin society left the Jewish salons which were supplanted by the houses of the titled aristocracy and German upper-middle classes. [34] In place of the choice between the Jewish particularistic religio-culture and the universalistic culture of the Enlightenment, the 'privileged' Jews now faced a choice between the Jewish particularistic religio-culture and the German particularistic religio-culture. The two worlds were socially and culturally exclusive, and, since they could not contemplate identifying with the unacculturated Jewish masses, many chose apostasy. In the words of Heinrich Heine, who was baptised in 1825, baptism was a 'ticket of admission to European culture'. [35]

The political, economic, and social situation of the Jews in the French eastern provinces was similar to central Europe. The *kehillot* retained wide powers of autonomy, but there were signs of weakness in the late eighteenth century; the *parnassim* encountered difficulties in collecting communal taxes, opposition from both gentile officials and Jewish dissidents to their juridical claims, and tension with the rabbis over their respective powers. The Jewish leadership was drawn from a small rich stratum of army provisioners and bankers, but the Jewish majority were poor and worked in the traditional Jewish occupations — peddling, small shopkeeping, and money lending. Attempts to remove economic restrictions and enter the guilds were unsuccessful, and there was only a small number of Jewish artisans who worked exclusively for their fellow Jews. Anti-Jewish sentiment was common, especially among the smaller businessmen, who competed with the Jews, and the peasants, who borrowed heavily from them.

The Sephardim in south-west France included a higher proportion of rich merchants, and they were less politically and economically distinctive than the Ashkenazim. Most French Sephardim had arrived as *marranos* towards the end of the seventeenth century, and since they were admitted without formal recognition, they did not acquire an independent civil jurisdiction. They organised themselves along the lines of a merchants' guild, and, in the middle of the eighteenth century, they received official approval of their organisation which gave them authority to collect taxes for the civil and royal authorities as well as for their own communal needs. This type of semi-autonomous community organisation could not enforce religious conformity as effectively as the *kehilla*. In Paris, where there was minimal community organisation and control, deviancy from the religious law was possible without fear of any sanctions.

In 1776 the Sephardim obtained formal recognition of their commercial freedom, and in Bordeaux, the chief port of the French empire, they engaged in almost all aspects of trade. Government officials appreciated the commercial usefulness of the Sephardim, and, more generally, the Sephardim benefited from the change in the French economy, from one of fixed economic statuses and self-sufficient units to a more open growing economy with an emphasis on trade, especially international trade. Economic leadership was shifting from the guilds to the rich commercial capitalists who exchanged special privileges for the legal protection of the business contract. The emphasis on free economic competition rather than special privileges meant that the commercial capitalists were more likely to accept Jewish economic competition and to accept Jews socially. Although religious hatred of the Jews continued, social acceptance of Jews was reinforced by some diffusion of the new humanitarian views of religious tolerance. [36]

The comparatively universalistic values of commercial capitalism and a relatively high level of religious tolerance were prominent in both Amsterdam and London, the two most advanced commercial centres in the world. In Holland, despite alien status, restriction in domicile and occupations, and anti-Jewish sentiment, the Jewish situation was comparatively good: Jews were not subject to special tax levies, they were not forced to live in ghettos, and the rich Jewish merchants enjoyed a wide range of economic privileges. Most Jews in Amsterdam were petty traders, but there were also numerous craftsmen, diamond cutters and polishers, and professionals in medicine, law, and pharmacology. The rich stratum of Dutch Jews attained a comparatively high level of social acceptance, but the Jewish community was sharply delineated by the *kehilla* which exercised considerable control over the religious and social behaviour of its members. [37] In this, Holland, like other European countries, differed from England and America, being Jews organised in voluntary associations not autonomous communities.

55

In the seventeenth century a formal petition for the readmission of Jews into England was unsuccessful, but Jews were allowed to enter informally and no special laws were passed to regulate their status. British Jews could live in any part of the country, and although the immigrants remained aliens their children were British by birth. Restrictions on Jews, such as non-admittance to Parliament and the universities, were shared with non-Anglican Christians. The British Jews' refusal to take an oath on the New Testament excluded them from many professions, but in the courts they were admitted as competent witnesses and allowed to take a non-Christian oath. [38]

Since the British Jews had no distinctive legal status, a *kehilla* on the continental model did not develop, and without a legal ghetto the degree of segregation found on the continent could not be maintained. The first, mainly Sephardic, settlers established a voluntary semi-ghetto in the City of London, but from an early date small numbers of wealthy Jews migrated to more fashionable districts. In the 1695 London census, Jews were found in 48 of the 110 parishes, 681 of the 853 Jewish names extracted from the census were found in six parishes, and nearly half the names were concentrated in the two largest parishes. At the end of the eighteenth century the majority of Jews were still concentrated in the City and East End, but a limited dispersal of the richer Jews to Westminster and the countryside around London had gone on throughout the century. In addition, small numbers of itinerant merchants settled outside London in the market towns and sea ports. [39] Conditions in America were, of course, even less conducive to local concentration.

The British and American Jews were concentrated in trade and commerce, but in no area did they outnumber the non-Jewish bourgeoisie who were sufficiently secure to accept Jewish competition. In England many of the Sephardim and a few Ashkenazim were rich merchants and brokers, but the majority of the Ashkenazim were small shopkeepers, peddlers, itinerant fruit vendors, fishmongers, domestic servants, and charity recipients. [40] The division between rich and poor Jews was less evident in America where the majority were middle-class merchants with a few engaged in medicine and industry. American Jewry included a small upper-middle class, but there was no Jewish upper class, lower-middle, or pauper class.[41]

The long absence of Jews from England had not eradicated the medieval religious stereotype, but there was also a tradition of philo-semitism in England centred on the Puritan identification with the 'Hebrew' people. Attitudes towards the Jewish community appear to have varied with its size and social composition; between 1700 and 1765, when the community was small and comparatively wealthy, an increasingly favourable opinion can be traced in the newspapers and journals. With the more extensive immigration of poor Ashkenazim after 1765, public opinion became increasingly unfavourable, but more favourable views appear to have returned around the turn of the century.[42] The comparatively high level of religious pluralism in England, the philo-semitic tradition, and possibly the religious indifference of eighteenth-century English society, were conducive to the acceptance of at least the rich Jews by non-Jews.

Religious hatred of Jews appears to have been almost absent in colonial America and this, together with the comparatively secular nature of the Jewish immigrants, their small number, distribution over wide areas, and their middle-class composition, made for a greater social acceptance than in Europe.[43]

The comparatively high levels of social acceptance in England and America and the organisation of the communities on the lines of voluntary association in synagogues removed the possibility of enforcing conformity within the community. The voluntarily organised synagogues were faced with the problem of the unsynagogued and religious nonconformity, and at first synagogue leaders tried to enforce participation in the synagogue and religious observance by threat and use of sanctions. Many of the early synagogues in London had a system of fines for non-attendance of synagogue and committee meetings, for refusing to act as an honorary officer, for refusing

57

to be called to the reading of the law, and for non-attendance at mourning rites.[44] However, if a member did not accept the sanctions, the leaders could do little except expel him, and this may have meant little to a member who may have been able to join another synagogue or lost little by remaining outside such an association. In the 1750s excommunication was threatened against members of the Shearith Israel congregation in New York for breaking the religious law, but the penalties for religious nonconformity were soon lowered, and by the end of the century there were no longer any disqualifications for lax religious observance.[45]

Comparisons

Jewish society, like non-Jewish society, was divided into small and closely knit groups, but no Jewish community was entirely cut off from others; business and cultural connections brought different communities into contact and reinforced an identification with the Jewish 'people'. The effects of community size varied in relation to cultural and social factors: the small number and wide distribution of American Jews made them particularly susceptible to acculturation and assimilation, but in central Europe the small rural communities remained the most culturally distinctive, and the most acculturated Jews were found in the large urban communities.

Attempts to coerce the Jews to accept the dominant religion were not a feature of the eighteenth century. The Habsburg monarch Joseph II legislated for Jewish assimilation, but his decrees were not supported by an efficient or forceful administration and they had little effect. Most eighteenth-century rulers accepted the presence of a distinctive Jewish minority, but it is important to note the different reasons for this acceptance. In the medieval period an important basis for pluralism was the official Church view that the Jews should be tolerated until the second coming of Christ. In the eighteenth century the political power of the Church outside the papal states was greatly weakened, and even in Catholic countries the Church doctrine relating to the Jews was no longer an important basis for pluralism. Most European rulers tolerated the Jews within their territories because it was in their interests to do so; the Jews were a source of tax revenue and they often fulfilled valuable economic functions. This instrumentally based pluralism rarely extended from the political powers to other strata, and the rulers did not always guarantee the Jews protection from the attacks of peasants, who regarded Jews as their economic oppressors, or merchants and artisans, who regarded Jews as their economic competitors. It is difficult to disentangle the reasons for anti-Jewish outbreaks but an important contributing factor was the anti-semitic teachings of the Church and the place of the Jews in Christian demonology. In eastern and central Europe Jews were tried and executed for ritual murders, and priests incited mobs against the traditional 'enemy of Christ'.

The diffusion of Enlightenment values among the upper strata in central Europe and France resulted in more tolerant behaviour towards the Jews, but a genuine religious pluralism, accepting the legitimate coexistence of different religious beliefs, emerged only in Holland, England, and North America. A comparison of the eighteenth-century Jewish communities reinforces a finding from the last chapter: where the non-Jewish majority was largely intolerant, as in eastern and central Europe, the Jews were less disposed to deviate from their religio-cultural distinctiveness; but where a genuine religious pluralism was present, the Jews were more disposed to accept the culture of the majority.

The variation in the bases and extensiveness of pluralism had clear implications for the level of societal separation of the Jews: where gentiles displayed a genuine religious pluralism they were less likely to segregate Jews from their society. Tolerance towards Jews and their incorporation into the societal community were features of those societies which had moved farthest from the culture and social structure of European feudalism. Most eighteenth-century European societies retained, in large measure, the cultural and social structural features which had resulted in the extensive societal separation of the

Jews in the medieval period. The international political importance of the Catholic Church was reduced, but religious institutions, in the form of either the Catholic Church or the territorial Protestant churches, provided a powerful bulwark and legitimation of the secular rulers. In most Catholic countries the segregationist policies of the Church continued to prevail, and Jews were no less segregated in those Protestant countries where citizenship and polity were bound to the state Church. Where religious pluralism developed *within* Protestantism, as in Holland, England, and North America, this was extended in some measure to the Jews. Social acceptance of Jews was greatest in England, which combined a Protestant establishment with a comparatively high level of denominational pluralism, and in America, where there emerged a conception of the Church as ideally a voluntary association.

In addition to the level of religious pluralism within the dominant society, the separation of the Jews was related to the extent to which the societies were organised into estates and corporations. In most European societies, the nobility, bourgeoisie, and peasantry had distinct legal statuses, each with a limited range of rights, duties, obligations, and permitted or appropriate occupations. Most estates were internally differentiated in terms of wealth and status, but each estate was largely endogamous and felt a strong sense of social distance from the others. Where the estate system was strong, as in eastern and central Europe, the legal rights and duties of the Jews were strictly delimited. In eastern Europe, where the lines between the estates were sharpened by ethnic differences, the Jews formed a distinct middleman class under the protection of the powerful nobles. In central Europe and eastern France the Jews represented only a small proportion of the commercial classes, but their economic distinctiveness rested on the fact that their range of occupations was narrowly circumscribed. In England, where the remains of the estate system were very weak, and in America, where it did not exist, the Jews were not legally differentiated, and although they concentrated in commercial occupations they were not a visibly distinct economic group.

The extent to which semi-autonomous corporations remained an important aspect of the economic and political divisions in European societies had implications, not only for the economic differentiation of the Jews, but also for the social and community barriers between Jews and gentiles. The merchant and craft guilds excluded Jews economically and socially; in eastern Europe the Jews were their hated economic competitors, and in parts of central Europe and eastern France the Jewish proponents of free trade were seen as a threat to the previously guarded trade and craft monopolies. Where corporations were less important or absent and were replaced by free contract and economic universalism, as in Hamburg, Bordeaux, Amsterdam, London, and North America, it was possible for the Jews to enter the social circles of the gentile bourgeoisie. Moreover, where the Jewish community was itself a separate corporation both formal and informal sanctions supported a high level of religious conformity, but where the Jews were organised in voluntary associations traditional customs could be more openly disregarded.

Although both central and eastern European Jews were sharply separated from non-Jewish society, they differed in a number of respects which account for the success of hassidism in eastern Europe compared with the continuation of the more legalistic Orthodoxy in central Europe. In eastern Europe hassidism appealed to the very large Jewish lower-middle class, especially the rural lessees, who were deprived of status in terms of the Orthodox criterion of religious scholarship and whose economic position and security deteriorated sharply as Poland distintegrated. In central Europe the Jewish population was much smaller and less concentrated, it did not include a large class of rural lessees, political conditions were more secure, and economic conditions were improving rather than deteriorating.

As in eastern Europe, the majority of central European Jews confined their primary group relationships and cultural orientations to the Jewish sub-society, but in order to promote commercial development central European rulers permitted a few privileged Jews to live outside the Jewish community and freely associate with non-Jews. The 'privileged' Jews of central Europe and the Jews in western Europe and North America were marginal men since they no longer confined their primary group relationships and cultural orientations to the Jewish sub-society. However, the type of marginality varied according to whether an individual or group was involved and the extent to which conflicting choices were presented in cultural behaviour or social relationships. In central Europe the Court Jews were individual marginals who were able to move between two sub-societies and distinct cultures, but the salon Jews, who moved out of the Jewish sub-society and confined their social relationships and cultural orientations to a predominantly gentile intellectual sub-society, finally had to choose between social rejection or conversion to Christianity. Western European and North American Jews were expected to adopt the host culture, but there was less pressure than in Germany to adopt Christianity. In these cases Jews adjusted culturally by adopting the secular patterns of behaviour of the host society and reducing their religious observance from the traditional norm. This enabled them to continue to practise Judaism as well as to participate in the dominant society.

3 From The French Revolution to The Mass Migration

Separation and marginality

A comparison of the eighteenth-century communities has shown that the separation of the Jews and the autonomous Jewish community began to weaken in those societies where modern capitalism and the modern nation state were most developed. In the nineteenth century the economic and political differences between eastern Europe on the one hand, and central and western Europe on the other, became more pronounced, and in consequence the Jewish communities drew even farther apart in their social positions and religio-cultural orientations.

In Russia the Jews remained a legally defined alien group, and the policies of the authorities toward them alternated between cultural monopolism and social segregation. The attempts to russify the Jews, and eventually to convert them, included the conscription of Jewish youth into the army for long periods, the appointment of Crown rabbis, and the establishment of Crown schools, though these policies made little impression. Most important was the fact that, although there was an increase in the number of children taught in the official Jewish and Russian schools, the overwhelming majority of Jewish children continued to be educated in the non-official Jewish schools.

The Russian government restricted Jewish residence to the western provinces in an area known as the 'pale of settlement'. During the early 'liberal' phase of Alexander II's reign, select categories of Jews, including rich merchants, university graduates, certified craftsmen, and medical staff, were granted the 'privilege' of residing in the cities of the interior; but the vast majority were confined to the pale where, in a predominantly rural society, they formed a distinct urban occupational group. [1]

The Russian authorities made some attempt to encourage Jewish agricultural settlements, but in the main they pursued a policy of forcing the Jews out of the villages by expulsions and prohibiting their employment in the traditional Jewish rural occupations. Jewish migration from village to town quickened after 1861 following the emancipation of the serfs and the diminishing economic functions of the Jews in the villages and small market towns: factory-produced goods began to replace the hand-made goods of Jewish artisans; the increased capitalist concentration in trade and the expansion of the railways reduced the business of the small-town Jewish shopkeepers; and modern banks and loan associations began to compete with the small-scale Jewish money-lenders. Nevertheless, although the Jews represented a high proportion of the urban population, large numbers remained in the small rural towns. The Jews living outside the pale were successful in trade and industry, but in the economically backward and overpopulated pale, the vast majority in both town and country remained extremely poor small artisans and traders. [2]

The Russian government attempted to limit the activities of the *kehillot* in 1786 and 1796, but these remained fiscal units, responsible to the government for the collection of taxes, and highly regulatory bodies which appointed supervisors to see that members conformed to the ritual minutiae as codified in the *Shulhan Arukh*. In 1844 the *kehillot* were abolished, but the Jewish community retained an official legal status, and although certain functions, such as tax collection, were taken over by the state, the ineffectiveness and corruption of the Russian bureaucracy enabled the Jews to retain a high level of self-rule. [3]

The continued legal, vicinal, and economic separation of the majority of east European Jews contrasts with the breakdown of Jewish separation in western and central Europe. Complete citizenship was given to all French Jews in 1791 and legal emancipation was subsequently extended to many other European communities by the French occupation. After Napoleon's defeat the central European states reintroduced legal restrictions on Jews, and only the French and Dutch Jews retained their legal equality, but few states reimposed the former level of segregation. Central Europe was less advanced than western Europe in economic development and nation building, and the anti-Jewish legislation after 1815 was supported by those who wished to retain the semi-feudal order. Exclusion of the Jews was legitimised in nationalist as well as the traditional religious terms, but the developing capitalist economies and the declining importance of estates and corporations made the special Jewish status increasingly anomalous. An increasing number of liberties were attained in most German states in the 1850s and 1860s, and in 1871 the principle of citizenship, which was included in the constitution of the North German Federation in 1869, was extended to the whole Reich. In the Austrian empire the Jews attained citizenship in 1866–7.

As already noted, from the beginnings of the resettlement in England the Jews were British citizens by birth and they suffered only the same political disqualifications as other non-Anglicans. In 1828, however, a new law enabled the Catholics to take the Oath of Allegiance on the Christian faith, and the Jews were henceforth the only group who could not enter public office. After 1832 the reformed House of Commons passed all the bills for Jewish political emancipation, but the House of Lords successfully prevented the bills from becoming law. From 1847, the struggle centred on Lionel Rothschild who was elected five times by the City of London but was prevented from taking a seat in the House of Commons since he refused to take the Christian oath. Public opinion was overwhelmingly for emancipation and the House of Lords finally conceded. Rothschild took his seat in 1856.

The attainment of full legal and political equality was a slow process in many European states, but the Jewish separation of the late medieval and early modern period was almost irreversibly demolished between 1791 and 1813. The central European Jews were subject to civil disqualifications and excluded from a number of occupations until late in the century, but they were no longer isolated in ghettos, excluded from the major towns, or limited to a few despised occupations. The abolition of restrictions on residence enabled an increasing number of Jews to migrate from the rural areas, where the traditional Jewish occupations were declining as a result of the urbanisation of industry and the extension of the market, to the growing towns and capital cities. (See Appendix 1, Table B.) In contrast to Russia, where there was a strong element of physical coercion in the movement of the Jews to the towns in the undeveloped pale of settlement, the expanding economies of central and western Europe provided new opportunities for Jewish skills, and the movement to urban areas was often followed by a high rate of economic mobility.

In 1800 most German Jews lived in a belt of small towns and villages along the rivers Rhine and Main and in a strip along the eastern frontier from East Prussia to Posen and Silesia; only the cities of Berlin, Breslau, Frankfurt, and Hamburg had more than 3,000 Jews. The movement to urban areas often occurred in two stages, first from the rural areas to the neighbouring towns, and then to the major German cities. In Prussia there was a movement from the province of Posen, which was formerly part of Poland, to Berlin; the Jewish population of Prussia increased from 123,823 in 1816 to 325,587 in 1871, while the Jewish population in rural Bavaria dropped slightly, from 53,208 in 1818 to 50,648 in 1871. The proportion of Jews in urban areas was far greater than the proportion of non-Jewish population, but in comparison with the towns of the Russian pale the Jews remained a small minority in the German cities; the proportion of the Jews to the total population in Berlin increased from 1.7 per cent in 1816 to 4.8 per cent in 1880. [4]

Economically, the German Jews were highly mobile. In the commercial sphere peddling and petty trading declined and the proportion of large-scale and medium traders increased. A few entered agricultural and craft occupations, but in the second half of the century the trend was towards industry and the professions. In 1881 the Jews in Berlin accounted for 7.9 per cent of the city's legal profession, 8.6 per cent of the writers and journalists, 11.7 per cent of the medical personnel, 21.3 per cent of the wholesale dealers, 25.1 per cent of shippers and small businesses, and 25.8 per cent of those in the money market. [5]

A similar picture of urbanisation and economic mobility can be drawn for France, the Netherlands, and Italy. Dutch Jewry included a high proportion of paupers in the first half of the century, but the development of the diamond trade in Amsterdam in the second half resulted in increased prosperity and a greater concentration in the city. [6] In Italy the old traditional Jewish trades were abandoned after 1870, and although a large number of poor Jews continued to exist in Rome and one or two other Italian cities, Italian Jews displayed a high level of mobility into the middle and upper-middle classes. [7] After the French Revolution, the Jews in Alsace moved from the countryside to the larger commercial centres such as Strasbourg, Metz, and Mulhouse, and after the Franco-German War most of the 5,000 Jews who left the annexed territory migrated to Paris. In Alsace the Jews were very poor, but in Paris they came to form a middle class of shopkeepers, small-scale manufacturers, civil servants, and professionals. [8]

In the lands under the Austrian monarchy industrialisation was slower and more localised than in western Europe and in Germany after 1870. In the economically backward eastern parts of the Austrian monarchy (Galicia, Slovakia, Subcarpathian Ruthenia) the vast majority of Jews remained poor, but in other areas there was considerable economic mobility in the second half of the century. In Bohemia-Moravia, following the removal of the worst restrictive legislation after 1848, many Jews moved from the Jewish quarters and achieved considerable economic advance. In Hungary, the reluctance of the gentile upper class and second-generation bourgeoisie to seek employment inconsistent with the status of a 'gentleman' enabled the Hungarian Jews to predominate in the merchant and professional middle class. [9] However, most Jews who migrated from the eastern provinces to the urban areas of Hungary, Bohemia, Moravia, and Lower Austria only marginally improved their economic situation, and there remained a sharper contrast than in Germany and France between the small wealthy stratum and the large poor one.

In the early decades of the nineteenth century the Jewish community in London, where about two-thirds of British Jews were concentrated, was composed of a small rich upper class, a small middle class of shopkeepers, and a larger lower class of peddlers, hawkers, and charity recipients; by 1880 the middle class had grown considerably and the number of peddlers and hawkers had greatly diminished. After 1830 economic mobility was paralleled by migration from the original nucleus of Jewish settlement in the City of London to the West End and the north and north-western suburbs. [10] In the United States the German Jewish immigrants and their descendants settled widely in most American cities and towns, and progressed from peddling to owning their own shops which some expanded into large shops or chains. [11]

In addition to legal emancipation and vicinal and economic mobility, Jewish separation was further reduced by the limitation and, in some cases, abolition of the autonomy and functions of the organised Jewish community. In the first half of the nineteenth century most European states replaced the *kehillot* by 'modern' forms of corporations, such as the *Gemeinden* in Germany and the *consistoires* in France. Membership was compulsory for all professing Jews, but in contrast to the *kehillot,* which provided a wide range of services, collected taxes for the government, and supervised the behaviour of members, the functions of the new organisations were mainly limited to the provision of specifically religious services; they only collected taxes to meet the costs of these services, and they had no authority to regulate the social and religious behaviour of their members.

Civil emanicipation, the movement out of the ghettos to areas of residence where non-Jews predominated, the migration from the more rigidly structured rural areas to the more anonymous urban areas, the diffusion into the middle and upper ranges of the occupational structure, and the declining functions and social control of the organised Jewish community, all resulted in an increasing number of Jews entering a marginal situation. The marginal Jews' social relationships and organisational affiliations were no longer confined to the Jewish sub-society but were extended to non-Jewish society or at least a sub-section of it. Most marginal Jews married within the Jewish group, although intermarriage by members of many rich Jewish families, especially among the Sephardim, was not uncommon in western Europe and North America. Primary relationships were still predominantly held within the Jewish group, but their participation in non-Jewish society was sufficiently great to require an orientation to the beliefs and behaviour patterns of the dominant culture. Both religious organisational patterns and religious practice underwent considerable change.

Organisational change

In feudal Europe the structure of Jewish religious organisation did not vary greatly; the *kehilla,* the semi-autonomous Jewish community, was the norm. In the nineteenth century, with the incorporation of the Jewish communities into the nation states, Jewish organisational patterns differed considerably. Where the political authorities laid down the forms of Jewish communal organisation, they were often patterned on municipal or non-Jewish religious organisation; they varied in the extent to which they were subject to state regulation, the existence and level of state financial assistance, and in their degree of centralisation. The most centralised and hierarchical system was instituted by Napoleon in France in 1808. The peak organisation was the *Central Consistoire* in Paris which was 'charged with over-all supervision of the interests of the Jewish religion'; its major constituents were the departmental *consistoires* and below them there were less important units called *communautès.* The *Central Consistoire* was the official link between the departmental *consistoires,* over which it had financial and religious control, and the *Ministre des Cultes;* it submitted the nomination of rabbis to the government for approval and it had the power (which it never used) to dismiss a rabbi or a member of a departmental *consistoire.* The hierarchical arrangement of the rabbinate appears to have been modelled on the Catholic Church: at its head was the *grand*

69

rabbin of France, chosen by the *Central Consistoire* and two delegates from each departmental *consistoire,* followed by the *grand rabbin* of Paris, the departmental *grands rabbins,* the *rabbins communaux,* and, finally, the *ministres officiants* who substituted for rabbis in the very small communities. The *grand rabbin* of France was a member of the *Central Consistoire* and he had ultimate authority over the *Sèminaire Israelite,* the state-sponsored seminary for the training of French rabbis. [12]In 1848 the *consistoire* system was suggested in Italy but the smaller communities objected to its hierarchical aspects. The local Italian communities retained complete autonomy but a loose Union of Italian Jewish Communities was founded in 1863. [13]

In Germany the level of local autonomy varied between the individual states: in the southern states the Jewish communities were united in officially recognised central councils and Judaism was given a status approximating to the Catholic and Protestant Churches, while in Prussia no central authority governed the local financially self-supporting *Gemeinden.* In 1869 a national organisation, the *Deutsch-Israelitischer,* was formed, but neither the communities nor the rabbinate were organised in a hierarchical system. [14]

Unlike the organisational patterns in mainland Europe, the Jewish organisations in Britain and North America were not imposed by non-Jewish authorities, but their changing forms were clearly influenced by the non-Jewish environment. In the United States, Jewish religious organisation displayed the distinctive features of American religious organisation; it was associational, democratic, and congregational. Since Church and state were separated in America, all religious organisations were voluntary associations, and, more than other religious groups in America, the Jews insisted on the rigid separation of Church and state because they believed that emancipation was only guaranteed by a secular political structure. In their commitment to the local religious organisation Jews were more typically American, but while in Europe the decentralised form of religious organisation was taken for granted, in America it became an ideology, especially in the Reform movement which took the liberal Protestant groups as organisational models. When, in 1841, and again in 1849, Isaac Leeser, a member of the conservative-historical school, tried to found a federal union of American synagogues, he met considerable opposition from Reform synagogues. One opposing Reform resolution stated that 'all conventions, founded or created for the establishment of any ecclesiastical authority whatever ... are alien to the spirit and genesis of the age in which we live, and are wholly inconsistent with the spirit of American Liberty'. A rabbinical assembly met in Cleveland in 1855 to discuss the possibility of a synod, but the rabbis were unable to agree and a second meeting was not called. In 1873, a loose federation of thirty-four 'modernised' synagogues called the 'Union of American Hebrew Congregations' was formed, but religious authority remained firmly in the hands of the local congregation. [15]

Taking the Anglican and more centralised Nonconformist British churches as their organisational models, the Anglo-Jewish leaders were less averse than American Jewish leaders to the financial and religious amalgamation of synagogues, and in 1870 a number of synagogues in London joined to become constituents of a centralised organisation called the United Synagogue. The number of congregations affiliated to the United Synagogue grew considerably over the years but the organisation was limited to London and the provincial synagogues remained independent. However, the centralised religious authority of the Chief Rabbinate, which was recognised in the constitution of the United Synagogue, extended not only to the provinces but also to the Jewish congregations throughout the British empire. In contrast to the traditional rabbinate, which was neither centralised nor formally hierarchical, a two-tier ecclesiastical hierarchy evolved in England, consisting of a single chief rabbi, in whose office religious authority was almost exclusively concentrated, and Jewish clergymen who performed non-rabbinical roles such as preacher, pastor, and secretary to the synagogues. A number of factors, including the centralisation of English Jewry in London, contributed to the development of the Chief Rabbinate, but one important factor which contributed to the strength of the office after 1870 was the concern of the lay leaders of the United Synagogue to have a religious head who would have a position of authority somewhat parallel to the Archbishop of Canterbury in the Anglican Church.[16] Thus, where Jewish religious organisation was voluntarily based, the organisational patterns which emerged combined the traditional community-centred emphasis with models taken from the non-Jewish environment.

Levels of acculturation

The traditional Jewish community continued longest where Jews remained separated from non-Jewish society and where the Jewish community continued as a powerful agent of social control. The majority of eastern European Jews continued to adhere to the traditional religious culture up to the last decades of the nineteenth century. After the hassidim and *mitnagdim* were reconciled, a revival of traditional learning occurred in the first half of the century. A *Haskalah* movement emerged in Russia at the beginning of the nineteenth century, but although it espoused a more moderate rationalism than the German *Haskalah,* it attracted only a tiny proportion of Russian Jews. The early Russian *maskelim* (adherents of the *Haskalah*) were not necessarily anti-religious or assimilationist; they stressed the need for secular knowledge but they were normally orthodox in their religious observance. Nevertheless, they were fiercely opposed by the traditionalists, and the co-operation of the formally antagonistic hassidim and *mitnagdim* was, in part, a defence against the exponents of secular knowledge and behaviour. Since almost all acts, roles, and institutions were defined and regulated by religion, any secular innovation was regarded as an attack upon the total religious system. A short jacket or a trimmed beard was regarded as only a short step away from the baptismal font.

Up to the 1850s, the language and cultural orientations of the Russian *maskelim* were German. In the 1850s a new type of *maskil* not only sponsored secular knowledge but also advocated the Russian language and culture in preference to the language, clothes, and habits of the 'ghetto' culture. This small group maintained that they differed from other Russians only in their religion, calling themselves 'Russians of the Mosaic religion', but this distinction between religion on the one hand and culture and nationality on the other was not accepted by the majority, and the few attempts that were made to introduce changes in the synagogue service met with little response. [17]

By 1880 the traditional religio-culture was found only in eastern Europe; the British and North American communities had been secular from their beginnings, and in central and western mainland Europe the traditional religio-culture had given way to a rapid process of secularisation. In contrast to the majority of eastern European Jews, who made no distinction between religion, culture, and nationality, the western Jews came to insist that their Jewishness was limited to the specifically religious sphere and that they did not differ from their gentile neighbours in their 'non-religious' cultural and national identity. They were no longer simply Jews but 'Germans of the Mosaic Faith', 'Englishmen of the Jewish Persuasion', and so on. In the multinational states of the Austrian monarchy there was a problem of which national group to identify with: German or Czech in Bohemia-Moravia; Magyar or German in Hungary; Magyar or Slovak in Slovakia; German, Polish, or Ukranian in Galicia. At first most Jews under the Austrian monarchy identified with the Germans, but with the emergence of nationalist movements throughout the empire they gradually came to identify with the numerically dominant nationality. In Galicia hassidism spread in the first half of the nineteenth century and the majority remained traditionalist, but a German-oriented *Haskalah* was influential in the larger towns in the 1830s and 1840s, and from the 1860s the assimilationist minority moved away from German culture to an identity with Polish culture and nationality. [18] In Hungary the powerful but numerically weak Magyars sought the alliance of minority ethnic groups, and the Jews responded more than any other group: in 1880 59 per cent of the Jews in Budapest identified with the Magyars and 34 per cent identified with the Germans. [19] In Bohemia-Moravia most Jews continued to identify with the Germans who constituted the top social stratum and were predominant in both the culture and the economy. [20] In Vienna, where the population was almost completely German, the problem of which non-Jewish group to identify with did not arise.

Acculturation to non-Jewish society was most evident in those cultural areas which many now defined as 'non-religious' (clothes, language, food, etc), and only a small minority adopted the religion of the national group with whom they identified. [21] But although acculturation did not extend to religious conversion, accommodation to non-Jewish society involved an extensive deviation from the observance of the Jewish religious law. By about 1870 or 1880 most native-born Jews in western and central Europe and North America were either lax or entirely non-observant with respect to the Sabbath, the dietary laws, the use of lustral baths *(mikvaot)*, daily prayers, and many fasts and festivals. In the traditional eastern European communities the majority of men attended synagogue at least once a week and a large proportion attended every day, but most western Jews came to limit their attendance at synagogue to two or three times a year, on the High Holy Days and on special occasions such as weddings and *barmitzvahs*. It became increasingly difficult to obtain a *minyan* for the daily services, and many congregations either abolished daily services or employed '*minyan* men' to continue them. The number of Jewish males who attended synagogue regularly on the Sabbath shrank to a small minority. [22] By 1880 there were almost no native-born Orthodox Jews in western Europe and North America, and in Germany the Orthodox were concentrated in the small-town rural communities in the eastern province of Posen and South Germany where continued separation from the non-Jewish population and the social cohesiveness and control of small communities preserved the religious components of traditionalism. The communities in Posen included many hassidim and were closer to the traditionalism of Russian Jews

74

than the Orthodox communities in Bavaria and other parts of southern Germany which combined meticulous observance with accommodation to the 'non-religious' components of the environmental non-Jewish culture. Many small-town Jews migrated to the cities where they formed their own Orthodox congregations, but Orthodoxy rarely lasted beyond the first generation in the urban environment. [23]

The French Jews were the most secularised of all western Jews since they came to concentrate in areas such as Paris where anti-clericalism and secularism were prominent among the non-Jewish population; [24] but even in those countries such as England and the United States where anti-religious movements were unimportant and where attendance at church was associated with respectability, most native-born Jews found that the costs of Orthodoxy were too great. Most men worked on Saturday and it is an indication of acculturation that many congregations came to depend on women to fill their synagogues. In France, in particular, the ladies were relied upon to form the congregation at ordinary services, and since few were able to get up early enough to attend the morning Sabbath services, special Saturday afternoon services were instituted with a sermon as the major attraction. [25]

In addition to the economic cost of not working on the Sabbath and religious holidays, many aspects of Orthodoxy, such as the laws of *kashrut* and family purity, were found incompatible with 'modern' living and clearly inconsistent with a desire for social acceptance by, and cultural orientation towards, non-Jewish society. Most secularised Jews continued to observe the religious rites of passage (circumcision, *barmitzvah*, a religious marriage, and burial), but in general, where rituals survived, they did so in a highly attenuated form; for example, many broke all the laws of *kashrut* apart from eating pork, and during Passover many Jews served unleavened bread on the same table as ordinary bread. [26] From an Orthodox point of view such compromises held no religious value, but for the secularised Jews they served as a minimal religious indication of their Jewish identity.

Although few Jews attended synagogue regularly, most entered a synagogue at least two or three times a year, and since the public service was also a central focus of Christian religious observance, the religious concerns of many acculturated Jews were concentrated on the synagogue services and the need for their reform. Throughout the nineteenth century an increasing number of native western congregations modified or altered the traditional parts of the service and adopted other practices influenced by or modelled on the services of the Christian religion. Reforms in the synagogue services may usefully be classified as changes in the form or external appearance of worship on the one hand, and changes in the content of the prayerbook on the other. One important change in form was to substitute the vernacular for Hebrew in the reading of some or almost all the prayers. Other changes in form (beginning with the least and ending with the most radical) included: a general emphasis on decorum, the abolition of the sale of *mitzvot* and the *misheberach,* the introduction of regular sermons in the vernacular, a male choir, a mixed choir, an organ, mixed pews, special Sunday services in addition to the Sabbath services, the abolition of head-covering, and the moving of the Sabbath services from Saturday to Sunday. Changes in content varied from the omission of a few traditional prayers to a complete revision of the prayerbook.

Jewish communities are commonly distinguished by the terms 'modern Orthodoxy', 'Conservative', and 'Reform'. The meaning of these terms has varied between different countries, and the point where modern Orthodoxy ends and Conservatism begins or where Conservatism ends and Reform begins is not always clear; but there is sufficient consensus on the use of these terms to allow us to use them in a fairly consistent fashion. The term 'modern Orthodoxy', sometimes 'decorous Orthodoxy', refers to those communities or congregations where, apart perhaps from some minor changes, the services are traditional in content, but differ from 'traditionalistic Orthodoxy' in their form: an emphasis on decorum, regular sermons in the vernacular, a male choir. In general, Conservative services are still largely traditional in content, but there is a more considerable change in form: a mixed choir, an organ, mixed pews, perhaps a more extensive use of the vernacular. Reform services are highly acculturated in form and many or most of the traditional prayers are omitted or replaced by new ones. In the more radical Reform congregations head-covering is prohibited, the Sabbath service is moved to Sunday, and the vernacular is the predominant language of prayer.

Minor changes in content made by the modern Orthodox and Conservative groups included the omission of repetitions, and the removal of cabbalistic prayers and *piyuttim* (synagogue hymns which called for the slaughter of Jewish martyrs to be avenged). These changes reflected a desire for shorter services and indicated the secularisation of thought and the improved social position of the Jews. Major changes in content made by Reform congregations included the removal of prayers referring to Jews as God's chosen people, the supernatural revelation of the Torah, the coming of the Messiah, the return to Zion, the rebuilding of the Temple, the restoration of the sacrificial cult, and the resurrection of the dead. These changes reflected a desire to 'depoliticise' and 'denationalise' the Jewish religion. The particularistic prayers were replaced by universalistic ones which reinterpreted the Messianic doctrine to mean the coming of a period of peace and harmony when mankind would be united in one faith.

The forms and degrees of religious acculturation of the synagogue service varied between the western communities, but one aspect of religious accommodation was common to all the secularised communities: the concern with decorum. Acculturated Jews disliked the outward emotionalism and demonstrativeness of the traditional service – the loud chanting of the prayers, the body movements, the coming and going during the service, and the inappropriate 'secular' business of selling *mitzvot* and making material offerings when called to the reading of the law. As religion became more compartmentalised in the lives of acculturated Jews, they found such activities as the sale of *mitzvot* and offerings incongruous with a 'sacred' service. In eastern Europe, where there was little differentiation between the 'religious' and the 'secular', the question of decorum did not arise, but for the more secularised western Jews, who observed few rituals outside the synagogue, it was important to display special role behaviour within it. Moreover, many acculturated Jews accepted the standards of decorum prevailing in the middle-class churches and they had no wish to be embarrassed when gentiles visited the synagogues. Thus the acculturated congregations abolished the sale of *mitzvot* and offerings and developed a decorous, rigidly patterned service with a passive audience of worshippers listening to the *hazan*, choir and rabbi.

Most western congregations introduced reforms in the direction of greater decorum but far more radical reforms in the synagogue services were made in central Europe and North America than in southern and western Europe. The movement for the Reform of the synagogue services began in the last decade of the eighteenth century in Germany when a few limited reforms, including German hymns, prayers, and a sermon, were introduced in the services of a number of Jewish free schools. [27] The first Reform temple was established in 1810 in Seesen on the initiative of I. Jacobson, a rich businessman and a leader of the Westphalia *consistoire* under the Napoleonic occupation. The first religious ceremony in the Seesen temple began with a procession where, in the words of an observer, 'one could see persons of distinguished rank, scholars, Jewish, Protestant, and Catholic clergymen, officials, businessmen of all kinds'. The procession was followed by music from an organ and a choir of 'sixty to seventy musicians and singers', prayers, an address by Jacobson, the carrying of the scrolls around the temple, several chapters of the Pentateuch, read first in Hebrew and then in German, an address by a church counsellor, and a chorale with full orchestra sung first in Hebrew and then in German. [28]

The reforms introduced by Jacobson in the Westphalia *consistoire* between 1810 and 1813 included the shortening of prayers, the introduction of some prayers in German, the removal of mystical prayers and the removal of prayers which

78

contained derogatory references to gentiles. Jacobson did not take a consistent line with regard to the Messianic prayers; the omitted prayers referred to the coming of the Messiah and the return to Zion, but other Messianic prayers were retained. Unlike another early reformer, David Friedlander, who advocated the removal of all Messianic prayers and all the 'foreign laws' of the Talmud, Jacobson was careful to restrict changes in order to obtain the support of larger numbers. The Seesen temple was closed when the *consistoire* was abolished following the end of the French occupation, but Jacobson moved to Berlin where he started a Reform group. Other private services were instituted by several rich Jews in Berlin, and in 1817 a Reform prayerbook, compiled by two Berliners, was published. The changes introduced were similar to those of the Westphalia *consistoire,* and again the treatment of the Messianic prayers was not consistent; the German translations of some of the prayers blurred the Messianic messages and other Messianic prayers were said only in Hebrew.

The Berlin Reform groups were forced to close in 1817 after the Orthodox rabbis in Berlin had succeeded in obtaining the support of the Prussian government against the introduction of ritual reforms. E. Kley, who was joint author of the Reform prayerbook, moved to Hamburg and founded a Reform society, and in 1818 a Reform hall was opened in the city. The Hamburg reformers abolished the traditional cantillation, introduced German prayers, a German sermon, choral singing and an organ, and they were consistent in the omission of particularistic Messianic prayers. The omission of a personal Messiah and return to Zion, and the reformulation of the Messianic beliefs as a coming period of universal peace and harmony, now became a central feature of the Reform movement. [29]

The Reform movement grew more rapidly after 1820 and temples were opened in Frankfurt, Breslau, Konningesburg, and Offenbach.[30] These first Reform temples were not financially supported by the *Gemeinden* or community organisations but by the voluntary contributions of their members. However, with the election of Reform Jews to the leadership of the *Gemeinden,*

Reform temples became community rather than associational synagogues, reforms were introduced into some previously Orthodox synagogues, and reformist rabbis were appointed as community rabbis. By 1870, in the majority of the large urban German communities, Reform Jews had either gained the dominant position in the communal administration or shared control with the Conservatives. But German Reform Judaism had itself divided between the moderate reformers or Liberals, who held the majority of communal offices, and the smaller radical Reform section. An example of a radical Reform group was the 'Association for Reform in Judaism' which opened a synagogue in Berlin in 1846. The association's services were almost entirely in German, males were permitted to worship with uncovered heads, and eventually services were only held on Sundays.[31]

Reform Judaism was particularly successful in the cities of north Germany. In general the services in central and southern Germany were more conservative, but, like Reform Jews, most Conservatives were secularised Jews who performed little of the traditional ritual outside the synagogue. The small modern Orthodox movement, which began in the rural areas of Bavaria and became centred in Frankfurt, was non-traditionalistic in its emphasis on decorum and qualified acceptance of secular culture, but its members adhered to Jewish law as codified in the *Shulhan Arukh*. Under S. F. Hirsch, the Orthodox in Frankfurt formed a religious organisation independent of the *Gemeinde*, and in 1876, after a law of 1873 which had allowed Christians to secede from the state churches was extended to cover the Jews, eighty-five Orthodox Jews seceded from the Frankfurt community. In spite of the *Gemeinde* leaders' offer to maintain financially the Orthodox organisations, Hirsch argued that secession was necessary because not to secede would have been tantamount to sanctioning the denial of Judaism.[32]

In the Austro-Hungarian empire Reform Judaism was slower to develop, less radical, more localised, and restricted to a smaller segment of the population than in Germany. In those areas such as Galicia and Bukovina where the socio-economic

80

position of the Jews was similar to that in Russia, Reform Judaism made little progress. A moderate Reform temple was established in Vienna in 1826 and its form of service was adopted first by the major synagogue in Prague and eventually by the majority of synagogues in Bohemia, Moravia, and Silesia.[33] In Hungary there arose a deep religious division between a moderate Reform Judaism, or Neologism as it was called there, and an uncompromising Orthodoxy. Neologism was particularly strong among the urban Magyarised middle class, largely of Moravian and Bohemian origin, in central Hungary, while hassidism and Orthodoxy drew their strength from the poorer strata, mainly of Polish and German origin, in the rural northern and eastern provinces. Neologism developed from the 1830s, and when in 1868 a Jewish congress was convened by the Hungarian government to establish new communal regulations, the Hungarian congregations were represented by 126 Neologists and 94 Orthodox. The delegates could not agree on the reorganisation of the communal structure: the Neologs proposed a centralised system but the Orthodox were afraid that they would be outnumbered by the Neologs and they wanted complete independence for each individual community. Finally, Hungarian Jewry split into three sections: the Neologists and Orthodox, each with their own regulations, and the Status Quo, who retained the pre-Congress regulations.[34]

Reform Judaism developed later in North America then in Germany but by 1880 the American Reform congregations were more extreme in their deviation from the traditional synagogue service. The first demands for reforms in the synagogue service were made in 1824, in Charleston, South Carolina, which at that time had the largest Jewish population in the country. Forty-seven members of the Charleston congregation sent a petition to the synagogue leaders asking for an English sermon, the abolition of money offerings, the omission of certain prayers, and the reading of prayers in English. The rejection of the petition was followed by secession and the formation of the 'Reformed Society of Israelites' which

81

abolished head-covering in the synagogue and held a brief English service with some original hymns, based on Christian models, and instrumental music. [35] The society was not, however, successful, and in 1855 only nine of the fifty major North American Jewish congregations were Reform. [36] The movement developed rapidly in the 1860s and 1870s; groups of German-Jewish immigrants formed Reform societies which in time became temples with Reform rabbis imported from Germany; and Reform practices, such as English or German translations of prayers, regular sermons, confirmation, family pews, organ music, mixed choirs, the removal of particularistic prayers and the introduction of universalistic ones, were also introduced into synagogues which had previously been Orthodox. By 1880, perhaps a dozen of the two hundred major congregations had strictly Orthodox services, a larger minority had radical Reform services, and the majority had moderate Reform services. [37]

The progress of Reform Judaism in America was, to some degree, influenced by the immigration of German Reform rabbis who believed that a more democratic and liberal country would be a more congenial environment for Reform Judaism. The Reform rabbis often took the initiative in introducing reform practices into previously Orthodox synagogues, but the rabbis could only, at the very most, anticipate the religious requirements of the laymen. Congregations often 'called' rabbis from Germany, and the rabbis either had to follow the religious trend of the congregation or leave it. A number of prosperous, educated, reformist German laymen also emigrated to America, but the vast majority of the 150,000 migrants from Germany between 1800 and 1870 came from the poor and traditionalist villages and small towns of west and south-west Germany. Some of these immigrants founded congregations with Orthodox services but most quickly deviated from their Orthodox background. [38]

For a time German and American Reform Judaism existed side by side, but the former gradually disappeared and the latter came to predominate. German Reform was the religion of the more prosperous first-generation German-Jewish immigrants who settled in the east of the United States. The German language unified German and German-Jewish immigrants; German Jews participated in many German associations and continued to orientate themselves towards German culture. [39] David Einhorn, a leading Reform rabbi, who emigrated to America in 1855, stated that there was an intimate relationship between Reform Judaism and German culture, and he therefore refused to preach in English. In the western communities a more Americanised Reform Judaism developed. Isaac Meyer Wise was its leading theoretical formulator: he correlated Americanism with Judaism, and he believed that the 'Mosaic' faith was fulfilled in the political order of the United States. He called upon Jews to drop their sectarian practices and to mix with Christians in order to make way for the 'universal' faith. In 1857, Wise published his prayerbook according to the 'Minhag America' (American Ritual), and this came to be used by a large number of Reform synagogues. Wise wished to unite the 'modernised' congregations in America, and he was largely responsible for the formation of the Union of American Congregations in 1873, the Hebrew Union College theological seminary in 1875, and the Central Conference of American Rabbis rabbinical association in 1889. [40]

In Pittsburgh, in 1885, a number of Reform rabbis adopted a radical statement which came to be known as the Pittsburgh Platform. They emphasised the universalistic, humanistic progressivism and rationality in Judaism; they rejected those 'Mosaic' laws which conflicted with 'modern civilisation'; and they claimed that the Jews were a religious community and not a nation. The more conservative congregations had begun to break away from the Reform movement in the 1870s, but the radical stand of the Pittsburgh Platform made the break definite, and a set of organisations, parallel to the Reform organisations, were formed by the 'historical' school which later developed into the Conservative movement. However, in 1880, on the eve of the mass east-European emigration, Reform Judaism dominated American-Jewish religious life.

In contrast to central Europe and America, the changes made in the synagogue services in England, France, and Italy in the nineteenth century were mainly limited to the form, as opposed to the content, of the services. The formation of the West London Reform Synagogue in 1842 was denounced by the British Chief Rabbi, but the changes made in the new synagogue's prayerbook were far less radical than the changes made in the Reform prayerbook in Germany and America. The modifications included a choir, English sermons every Sabbath, the discontinuation of being called to the reading of the law, and some abbreviations and eliminations in the prayerbook, but the prayers for the return to Zion and the coming of the Messiah were retained. [41] Reform made little progress in the English provinces; there was a small Reform group in Hull in the 1850s, but only two provincial Reform synagogues were formed in the nineteenth century, one in Manchester and the other in Bradford.

The English Reform Jews were primarily concerned to introduce greater decorum into the service, and this was also a concern of many members of the English congregations with Orthodox services. In May 1843, the vestry of the Great Synagogue, the largest synagogue in London, received a petition from a number of seat-holders asking for a more decorous recital of the liturgy, regular sermons, the deletion of certain parts of the service, and the substitution of the 'indecorous' means of raising revenue by a regular assessment system based on a tax on seats. A counter-petition demanded that the hours of worship and all the prayers should be kept, but they admitted the need for greater decorum. [42] In his 'Laws and Regulations for all the Synagogues in the British Empire', 1847, Nathan Adler, the Chief Rabbi, stipulated that 'a solemn and reverential service should pervade the Synagogue' and, in order that a solemn atmosphere should prevail, the rules laid down that children under four years were not to be admitted into the synagogue, clerical officers had to wear clerical uniform, the sale of *mitzvot* was prohibited, the number called to the reading of the law was limited, and the number and form of the *misheberach* were prescribed. The congregation was expected 'to preserve quiet during the reading of the prayers intended for the Reader alone', and, in other prayers, they had to accompany either the reader or the choir 'in subdued though audible manner' for that part of the service.

Choirs were formed in the London synagogues from about 1840, and by the end of the 1840s there was already a noticeable decline in the worshippers' audible responses to the prayers.[43] Editorials in the *Jewish Chronicle,* which both expressed and formed the opinions of many native English Jews, criticised the lack of participation, but the paper did not propose a return to the traditional audible responses. It argued instead for 'congregational singing'. In 1872 the *Chronicle* suggested that the synagogues adopt 'easily learnt melodies ... such as [the] beautiful hymns of the Church of England'. [44]

Although there was some acculturation in the form of the services, there was very little change made in the content. In 1880 the chief rabbi sanctioned a number of comparatively minor changes submitted by a lay committee of the London native congregations. These included the omission of most of the *piyuttim,* and of passages in the *Selihot* (penitential prayers) which invoked the intercession of angels. He refused to sanction other proposals, including one to omit selections from the Talmud in the prayerbook despite the lay committee's argument that 'The Jewish man of business to-day ... has no taste for those Talmudic studies ... The time has gone by for the study of Talmudic literature in the synagogue.' [45]

In France, Orthodoxy remained strong among the poorer strata in Alsace, but in Paris, in the late 1830s, a small group of *notables,* including members of the *Central Consistoire,* began to press for moderate changes: to shorten the services, abolish the *piyuttim,* translate some prayers into French, and introduce a regular sermon, choir, and organ. An Orthodox group opposed the suggested changes and attacked the tutelage of the *notables* in the *Consistoire,* but they found little support either from the *grand rabbins* or from the young rabbis, trained at the new 'modern' rabbinical seminary, who adhered to a middle or

Conservative position. The lay leaders of the *Consistoire* were careful to choose *grand rabbins* who were adaptive to change, and in 1856 the *grand rabbin* of France summoned the consistorial rabbis to Paris to discuss the matter of ritual reform. The agreement of the rabbinical synod on the need for moderate reforms, such as the reduction of the *piyuttim* and the introduction of the sermon and organ, was met by opposition among the Orthodox, but it was made clear that there was no desire on the part of the religious and lay leaders to impose reforms on those who rejected them. Within a few years the religious conflict subsided: the number of French Orthodox declined, especially after the loss of Alsace to Germany; both Reform and Orthodox ideas were discredited by their association with Germany; the support for a Conservative position was reinforced, especially among the rabbinate; and many French laymen were attracted by free thought and scientism rather than any radical reform of the religious service. [46]

Changes in the content of the French synagogue service were comparatively minor, but the patriotism of the French Jews is clearly stated in the following 'prayer for France' which from 1857 appeared in a widely used book of prayers: 'Almighty protector of Israel and humanity ... if of all religions ours is the most dear to You, because it is Your own handicraft, France is of all countries the one which you seem to prefer, because it is the most worthy of You.' Although many Messianic prayers remained in the prayerbook, they had little meaning for the majority of French Jews; France was seen as 'a second Promised land' and the Messianic era was interpreted as a period of justice which had begun with the French Revolution. [47] There was, moreover, a significant acculturation in form by 1880. One French rabbi noted that 'the very resemblance to the ceremonies of Christian ritual is generally an excellent recommendation in France for every innovation', and this was clearly the case with respect to the emphasis on the sermon and choir, the introduction of the organ, the rabbis' adoption of the Catholic priests' garb, the ceremony of bringing to the synagogue new-born children to receive the blessing of the rabbi, the confirmation ceremony which resembled the Catholic First Communion, the collection that took place at marriage ceremonies, the summoning of rabbis to the bedside of the dying, 'the covering of coffins with flowers and garlands, the hangings at the entry of the mortuary, and all the luxury of the hearse'.[48] Some of these accommodations to the religious environment, such as mixed or female choirs and the organ, were also introduced into the Italian synagogues. [49] In summary: there was acculturation in the form of the religious services in England, France and Italy, but, in contrast to parts of central Europe and the United States, there was little change made in the content.

Environmental culture and social structure

The traditional or Orthodox religio-culture continued in such areas as Galicia, northern Hungary and the rural districts of southern Germany where the Jews remained a petty trading and artisan class separated, economically and socially, from the non-Jewish population. Secularisation and religious acculturation occurred in the urban centres of central Europe, western Europe and the United States where the barriers between Jews and gentiles were lowered and where many Jews moved into the occupational range of the gentile middle and upper classes. The problem here is to explain why socio-economic mobility was accompanied by extensive and radical changes in both the form and content of the religious services in some communities and only moderate changes in others. This can only be answered by comparing the cultural environments of the more prosperous Jews and their relations with non-Jews in the different societies.

It is important to note that the top Jewish stratum provided the leaders of most Jewish communities. In Europe the electorate of the official Jewish communities was generally restricted to a wealthy minority, but even when an extended or universal suffrage was introduced only men from the top stratum were elected to the communal offices. In France, for example, the *consistoire* electorate was extended from a minute minority to all adult males in 1849, restricted again in 1862, extended to universal suffrage in 1870, restricted in 1872, and restored to universal suffrage finally in 1880, but throughout and after these electoral changes the French community continued to be led by its *notables*. [50] The associational London synagogues were also governed by a wealthy elite. A distinction between privileged members and other seat-holders was retained by most London synagogues up to the end of the 1870s; in addition to their right to vote and eligibility for synagogue offices, privileged members often had religious advantages, such as preference in being 'called to the law' and burial in an exclusive part of the cemetery. Past honorary officers elected the new honorary officers from a list prepared by the wardens, and this permitted the governing body to perpetuate itself by self-recruitment. The right to attend and vote in the synagogue vestries, which decided on general synagogue policies, differed a little between synagogues, but it was generally limited to the honorary officers plus a few of the privileged members. [51] Synagogue government was more democratic in the United States: the congregation elected the synagogue board and there were a number of limitations on the power of the wardens and boards. In many cases the American communities may have elected their richest members to the synagogue offices, but the differences in wealth tended to be less sharp than in the European communities.

This prosperous Jewish stratum became acculturated to the high-status forms of Christianity prevailing in its environment; this fact explains, in part, the success of Reform Judaism in Germany and the United States and its lack of success in Britain, France, and Italy. Religious acculturation tended to take more radical forms where the symbols, practices, and ideology of the high-status environmental Christian religion were closer to those of Judaism. The marginal Jews in Germany took as their non-Jewish religious reference liberal Protestant denominations which, like Judaism, had come to reject any form of supernatural mediation between God and man. Beliefs which were alien to Judaism, such as the divinity of Jesus, the Trinity, and the practices associated with them, were rejected by the liberal Protestants. Acculturated and secularised Jews could therefore co-operate with, and adopt the practices of, liberal Protestants, without experiencing a high degree of religious inconsistency. In Prussia, the importance of liberal Protestantism as a religious reference for the urban middle-class Jews declined in the second half of the nineteenth century; the liberals came to accept the values of the Prussian ruling class and took an increasingly polemical stand against Reform Judaism.[52] Hence the greater number of ritual innovations, and the highest level of intellectual discussion in the German Reform movement, occurred in the decade prior to the 1848 revolution, when religious and political liberalism in Germany was at its height. The number of Reform Jews in Germany continued to increase after 1848, but there was little change in the German Reform religious services after that date.

In America liberal Protestantism also served as a religious reference for marginal Jews and facilitated the development of a radical Reform movement. A doctrinal cleavage, which was particularly prominent after 1830, existed in American Protestantism between 'fundamentalists' and 'liberals'.[53] The predominantly urban, socially mobile Jews were more likely to interact socially with the liberals, who were concentrated among the middle class in urban areas, than with the fundamentalists, who were found more among the lower classes in rural and frontier areas. The rejection of Trinitarianism by the Unitarians and their emphasis on a rational interpretation of the Bible made them an important religio-cultural reference for American Jews; the early Reform movement in Charleston followed an upsurge of Unitarianism in the city; by 1880 frequent interchanges of pulpits were taking place between Jewish and Unitarian ministers, regular joint services of Jews and liberal Christians were held in some communities, and in the latter part of the century Reform rabbis annually met liberal Protestants, ministers and laymen, in an annual Liberal Congress of Religion.[54]

89

In England the semi-Catholic practices and symbols of the high-status Anglican Church were too alien from Judaism to be regarded as an appropriate religious model. The influence of Catholic theology, the revival of the sacraments, and the return to regular Holy Communion and the daily Eucharist, particularly after 1850, narrowly limited the extent of Jewish acculturation to Anglicanism. The Church of England remained traditionally oriented throughout the period, although a few innovations were made in keeping with the spirit of its prayerbook. Likewise, the leaders of the Anglo-Jewish community did not feel it was necessary to make radical changes in the Orthodox prayerbook. English Judaism could, however, parallel the emphasis on form that prevailed in the Church of England. In 1872, a writer in the *Jewish Chronicle* suggested that the Reform secession in England in 1842 only occurred because 'the brilliant ceremonial of the High Church, and of the ritualistic party, with their intoning of prayer and attention to form, was then scarcely known in England; and there seemed a strong tendency to assimilate Jewish ecclesiastical customs to the then severe institutional ritual of the dominant church'.[55] Thus the synagogue services remained traditionally Jewish in content, but the West London Reform Synagogue and the native synagogues with Orthodox services followed the Church of England in its increasing emphasis on orderliness, dignity, solemnity, and decorum.

The absence of an appropriate Christian referent helps also to account for the lack of success of Reform Judaism in France and Italy. Cecil Roth's comment on Italian Judaism is also appropriate to other Catholic countries: 'An elaborate ceremonial, and prayer in a tongue no longer spoken, seemed to be natural and proper in Italy.'[56]

The differences in the environmental forms of Christianity can only partly account for the different levels of Jewish religious acculturation. There was no consistent relationship between the religious environment and the level of acculturation; liberal forms of Judaism were more successful in some predominantly Catholic environments (eg the urban areas of southern Germany and the Austrian monarchy) than in others (eg France, Italy), and in some countries (eg the Netherlands), where an appropriate Protestant reference was available, Reform Judaism was unsuccessful. Moreover, although the non-Jewish religious environment might account for some differences in form, such as the introduction of the vernacular into the services in Germany and America compared with its relative absence in France and Italy, it cannot fully explain such differences as the deletion of particularistic Jewish prayers in some countries and not in others. It is clear that some Jewish communities were far more disposed to become acculturated to their environment than others, and this can only be explained by comparing the position of the communities within the different social structures.

The extent of religious acculturation accompanying urbanisation and economic mobility was related to the social and religio-cultural inconsistencies in the Jews' marginal situation. In Germany there was a high degree of inconsistency in the ranking of middle- and upper-class Jews; the movement out of the ghettos and the high rate of economic mobility were not paralleled by social acceptance into non-Jewish circles or by a rise in social honour. The full legal emancipation of the German Jews was slow and erratic, but even when progress was made in legal equality, there continued a high level of social discrimination. The social mixing of a few aristocrats and Jews in the salons around the turn of the century was short-lived, and the growing but highly status-conscious German middle class were careful not to jeopardise their position by visible equal-status contacts with members of the Jewish minority. In the 1830s some voluntary liberal societies and artistic and intellectual groups were open to Jews, but even within liberal circles there was no unanimity on the subject of the civil emancipation and social acceptance of Jews. [57]

Opposition to the civil emancipation and social acceptance of Jews was justified by reference to their 'alien' religion and values. The Junkers perceived the Jew as a symbol of those forces which they detested: materialism, liberalism,

Westernisation. Many Junkers became involved in business enterprises and money became a central concern for them, but they continued to affect a contemptuous disdain for the bourgois material values which they associated particularly with the Jews.[58] In the first half of the century the small but growing middle classes, who were struggling against the aristocracy for political power, were not particularly anti-Jewish, but after about 1850 they gradually came to accept the political dominance and cultural values of the Prussian politico-military elite. Racial anti-semitism, which drew its support from the insecure but aspiring lower-middle class, began to grow in the 1870s, but nationalistic cultural anti-Judaism was a widespread phenomenon in Prussia before that period.[59]

There was a strongly felt need in Germany for a homogeneous culture and strong national identity which would integrate an otherwise non-unified nation. The educated classes venerated and idealised German *Kultur* and both the advocates and the opponents of Jewish emancipation agreed that the particularistic Jewish religious law and Messianism was an obstacle to Jewish identification with the German nation and culture. The opponents argued that the Jews would not change or that citizenship should only be granted if they repudiated their 'alien' culture, but the advocates argued that the Germanisation of the Jews would accompany or soon follow their emancipation. Thus even the advocates of emancipation were by no means cultural pluralists; in exchange for emancipation, it was expected that the Jews would either adopt Christianity or at least radically revise their Judaism. Unconditional political loyalty was demanded of the Jews and this involved a repudiation of their Messianic doctrines; it was argued that any Jew who longed to return to Palestine had no right to German citizenship.[60]

In Prussia Protestantism was incorporated into the exalted German *Kultur,* and Judaism was attacked as a cultural 'fossil', a religion of superstitions without an ethical or spiritual basis. Many Jews internalised the nationalistic critique and negative evaluation of their religion and believed that the removal of the particularistic elements would enable them to enter non-Jewish social groups. In his address to the worshippers at the opening of the Seesen Temple in 1810, Israel Jacobson stated that he did not seek complete religious unification between Jews and Christians, but he did seek 'some rapproachment' between the Jews and their Christian neighbours. He continued: 'For your true and progressive enlightenment depends this rapproachment ... our ritual is still weighted down with religious customs which might be rightfully offensive to reason as well as to our Christian friends ...' Addressing the Christians present at the ceremony, Jacobson said: 'I trust you will be far from receiving my brothers coldly. I trust you will not reject them ...'[61] In his introduction to the 1817 Reform prayerbook, E. Kley wrote that the new forms of prayer rendered in German would show the Germans that there was nothing in Judaism which prevented Jews from being faithful citizens. In reply to the Reform attacks on the Messianic beliefs the Orthodox claimed that their beliefs did not conflict with their faithfulness to Germany, but reformers argued that only religious reform would finally remove gentile arguments against the complete political and social acceptance of the Jews.[62]

The most radical demands for religious reform were made by Jewish professionals educated in the German gymnasia and universities; their occupations involved considerable interaction with gentiles, but they experienced a high degree of discrimination and social avoidance both in the universities and in the professions. They formed the core of the radical lay reform association in Berlin and Frankfurt and expressed impatience with the Reform rabbis who were not sufficiently radical for them. The Reform association in Frankfurt, 'The Society of the Dawn', held that it would not subscribe 'to Talmudical ceremonialism which separates the Israelites from their fellow-citizens'.[63] Thus, many Jews accepted the argument that it was Jewish particularism and separatism rather than gentile intolerance and exclusiveness which prohibited their acceptance by German society.

The situation in the lands of the Austrian monarchy was

similar in some respects to Germany, especially where, as in Bohemia-Moravia, the Jews identified strongly with the German minority but were excluded or restricted in numbers from gentile social groups. [64] In Hungary, where the Jews came to identify with the Magyars, the rich Jewish businessmen sought admission into the society of the Hungarian gentry, but they were strictly excluded from certain professions and social activity which were restricted to the 'genuine Hungarian gentleman'. [65] As in Germany, social exclusion could be interpreted as a consequence of Jewish cultural particularism, but unlike Prussia, nationalism was not generally identified with a specific form of Christianity. Catholicism was the dominant religion throughout the Austrian empire, and in Hungary the aristocracy was divided between Catholics and Calvinists.

In contrast to the rigid, ascriptive social stratification in central Europe, the American social hierarchy was comparatively amorphous. However, the American values of equality and achievement produced ambiguity and uncertainty of social position and Americans tried to overcome this by socially excluding certain groups and emphasising the importance of appropriate behavioural patterns. [66]

In the first half of the nineteenth century American Jews were able to assimilate into non-Jewish membership groups, including upper-class Christian circles; there appears to have been little anti-Jewish prejudice or discrimination. However, with the increase in the number of Jewish immigrants, disparaging comments against Jews became more evident and the beginnings of discrimination were discernible. Discrimination against Jews did not become an important factor until the 1870s, but social discrimination, in the form of non-admittance to membership of WASP (White Anglo-Saxon Protestant) clubs, began to appear about mid-century. Although Jews still belonged to the best clubs in many cities as late as the 1870s, discrimination by WASP clubs was quite apparent in many places in the 1860s. The private club, together with private schools and certain colleges, was becoming an aristocratic status-ascribing institution from which Jews and other non-WASP groups were excluded. Those wealthy Jews who were excluded from the WASP clubs either joined German clubs, in which the criterion of membership was at first based upon date of arrival in America rather than ethnicity or wealth, or founded their own clubs.[67] Even in those small towns where Jews had the most cordial relationships with their non-Jewish neighbours, there were fairly well-defined limits to assimilation, and Jews often felt self-conscious about their integration into non-Jewish society. Thus, according to the historian of the Jewish community in Rochester, despite the Rochester Jews' early acceptance by Christians and their involvement in civic enterprises, interfaith services and meetings, they remained 'on the fringes of the Gentile social world'.[68]

In comparison with most European Jews, the American Jews were highly assimilated into non-Jewish society, but it was just because they were so assimilated that the comparatively low or subtle social barriers that remained assumed great importance for them. American Jews put an important emphasis on their acceptance by non-Jews, and this involved eliminating many of the cultural and religious differences between them. Thus, socio-economic mobility and some degree of assimilation to Christian groups were paralleled by a high degree of religious acculturation. Some of the later, post-1850 German-Jewish immigrants were already Reform Jews, but the comparatively non-acculturated immigrants faced inconsistencies in the ranking of their cultural affiliations; their Orthodoxy was perceived as inconsistent with their desire to be accepted as Americans. In New York, in 1844, a number of Jews formed an association with the object of introducing reforms in Jewish worship. One reason given for the need for reforms was to permit the Jews 'to occupy a position of greater respect among our fellow-citizens'.[69] In 1871 a New York Reform journal bluntly accounted for the success of Reform Judaism: Jews wanted to mix with gentiles, eat at their tables, and have gentiles visit the synagogues. The journal stated that it 'would not do to exhibit the old medieval locality with its musty unintelligible service'.[70] At the opening of a new building for the Reform temple in Rochester, in 1876, the congregation's rabbi explained that 'the Jewish Temple has a new mission to fulfil. It is to dispel prejudice; non-Jewish brethren can come here and hear us pray and be surprised at how little difference there is between them.' The rabbi's statement reflected the attitude of the majority of Rochester's German-Jewish community who wished to 'strip their own religion of all semblances of uniqueness and singularity'.[71] The Rochester congregation was one of the more radical Reform congregations, but the socio-economic position and attitudes of Rochester Jews were not atypical of American Jews of German descent. By 1880, the majority of middle-class American Jews of German descent had expressed their desire to be recognised as Americans by joining, or at least occasionally attending, a moderate or radical Reform congregation.

There were considerable pressures on immigrants to adopt the dominant American religious values and norms. The majority of colonists in pre-revolutionary America were English and Protestant, and they set the American religious normative standards to which other generations of immigrants oriented. The potential centrifugal forces existing in a 'nation of immigrants' lacking a long-established cultural tradition were counterbalanced by an emphasis on the need for the acculturation of immigrants to the dominant WASP values and behaviour patterns which had become synonymous with Americanism. This identification of Protestantism with the 'new' American character, and the legitimation of the American democratic ideology by reference to Christian ideas, as understood and interpreted by Protestants, profoundly influenced the development of both Catholicism and Judaism in America.[72]

In England, the upper-middle- and upper-class Jews, who provided the leadership of the synagogues, were not subject to the strains of social exclusion or the pressures of religious conformity. Their social acceptance within gentile circles was part of a larger absorption of the English *haute bourgeoisie* by the English upper class. Unlike the aristocracies in other European countries, the English upper class was not a rigidly ascriptive estate, but compared with the emerging American upper class it was secure and established. The English upper class retained much of its power and many of its institutions by absorbing the new rich which included a number of Jewish merchants, traders and professionals. [73]

In England, high social status was not rigidly ascribed but was tied to the concept of the 'gentleman'. T. H. Marshall has pointed out that the two most necessary attributes of the gentleman were birth and 'culture'. Birth in the right family entitled a person to the appropriate 'culture', and it was normally accompanied by the means to attain it, but it was possible to acquire the appropriate life-styles of a gentleman without the benefit of birth. Over two, or at the most three, generations, the status of the gentleman could be achieved. [74] In 1833 the right of Jews to own freehold land was secured, and in the 1840s the children of rich Jews began to be accepted by the public schools. Like the rest of the rising bourgeoisie, the wealthy Jewish families achieved social recognition by acquiring titles and country estates, and by sending their sons to the public schools to learn the life-style of the aristocracy. [75]

The upper-class Jews' acculturation to the life-styles of the gentleman, which was an essential prerequisite to acceptance by the English upper class, did not, however, involve accepting the religious beliefs or adopting the religious practices of the Anglican Church. In the sphere of religion the English upper class were comparatively tolerant and pluralistic: the Church of England had a rather vague theology, its teachings extended over a wide area, and it emphasised practice rather than principle. Since the dominant religion in England was non-ideological and had a broad orientation, there was little pressure on Jews to alter their prayerbook to conform more closely to the services of the Church of England.

The Anglo-Jewish middle class was less assimilated into Christian circles than the upper class, but they accepted both the leadership of the upper class and the religious form of the services. There is very little information on the social life and religio-cultural beliefs of the Jewish middle class in the Victorian era, but there is an interesting book by a middle-class Jew, *Jewish Perseverance*, published in 1851. The author, M. Lissack, claimed and demonstrated in his own life, that socio-economic mobility into, and happiness in, a higher stratum was possible without severing an allegiance with 'Orthodox' Judaism. He wrote: 'It is true there exists in England a religion connected with the state, as well as in the countries on the Continent but, it is fair to say that, in reality, liberty of conscience prevails in England. And I, as a Jew, felt myself much more free in this country than I had been in Prussia ... a mild spirit of toleration pervades many, I may confidently say most of my Christian neighbours.' For Lissack, the notion that Jews could 'secure for themselves the respect and patronage of their Christian neighbours' only by denying their religion or ceasing to practise the Jewish ritual was 'altogether erroneous ... For, do there not, in this country, in the metropolis in particular, exist numerous examples of strictly orthodox Jews who have obtained great riches without infringing upon the statutes of their religion? ... As to the idea that a faithful adherence to the religion of Moses is averse to the obtaining of respect and patronage among Christians, my own experience has sufficiently taught me that there is no foundation in it ...' [76] We do not know how representative Lissack was of the middle-class English Jew, but there is no evidence to contradict the statement that a middle-class English Jew could, without difficulty, mix socially with non-Jews and remain religiously 'Orthodox'.

Although rich Jews were not generally socially excluded from English upper-class circles, they could not enter Parliament until 1856, and for many years they were excluded from certain professions because they refused to take the required Christian oath. In the eighteenth century and the first decades of the nineteenth many Sephardim overcame these disabilities by apostasy, but by the late 1830s a few Jews had attained high public positions without conversion. David Salomons was able to dispense with the Christian oath when he became Sheriff of London in 1835, and he was followed in the office by Moses

Montefiore who proclaimed, at his inauguration dinner, that his fatih had not been a barrier to a position 'to which my forefathers would in vain have aspired'. [77] Upper-class English Jews were socially accepted before they attained full political rights and they made use of their personal influence and contacts with members of the English upper class to obtain those rights. Since English Jews were already socially accepted, political emancipation was not given the high priority by Jews and liberals that it had in other European countries, and while some upper-class Jews felt that the political discrimination was an affront to their position, the vast majority of English Jews were indifferent to the issue. Under the £10 householder franchise most English Jews were not qualified to vote at parliamentary elections.

The opposition to Jewish emancipation included many shades of political opinion, but the main opposition came from the High Church Tories who perceived the rich Jew as a representative of the liberal bourgeoisie and were afraid that emancipatory legislation was but a prelude to the disestablishment of the Church. However, support for emancipation came not only from the middle class and Nonconformists but also from members of the aristocracy and a section of the Evangelical Christians in the Church of England. Jews did not, therefore, conclude that the improvement in their situation required a change in the British politico-social structure or the disestablishment of the Church of England. [78] In common with the opponents of emancipation in Germany, the English opponents argued that the Jews were a separate nation and emphasised the union of state and Church, but, in contrast with the proponents of emancipation in Germany, the English proponents argued that the beliefs of the Jews were totally irrelevant to their claim for equal citizenship, that religious beliefs and membership were a private and voluntary sphere of life, and that Church and state ought to be separated. Thus, although English Jews denied that they were a separate nation and maintained that they were only different in creed from other Englishmen, they did not feel the need to deny their religious aspirations to return to Zion. [79]

As in England, the French lay leadership was also recruited from an upper class who combined their ties to the Jewish community with participation in gentile upper-class circles. The French-Jewish upper class was divided into two sections: the titled aristocracy, such as the Rothschilds, who were fully accepted into the upper class, and the very rich untitled businessmen who 'enjoyed at least nominal acceptance in the Parisian world of high society'. Middle-class French Jews felt some gentile hostility towards them, particularly in the competitive business and professional fields, but prior to the Dreyfus case anti-semitism was a comparatively minor problem in France. [80] Similarly in Italy: after the abolition of civil disabilities following the achievement of a United Italy in 1870, the social acceptance of Jews was common throughout the society. [81] Thus, where the dominant gentile groups were disposed to religious pluralism, and where the socially mobile Jews, and in particular the Jewish leaders from the top stratum, were accepted into the equivalent socio-economic gentile circles, the reforms made in the Jewish services were moderate and the particularistic prayers remained in the prayerbook.

4 Period of Mass Migration

Urbanisation, migration, and mobility

The urbanisation of Russian Jews continued at a faster pace after 1881. The 1897 Russian census found that 49 per cent of the 5 million Jews in the pale of settlement lived in towns, 33 per cent in townlets *(shtetls)*, and 18 per cent in villages; the Jews constituted nearly 40 per cent of the entire urban population in the pale and represented large proportions of the total populations in such cities as Minsk (52 per cent), Kovno (36 per cent), Brest-Litovsk (65 per cent), Dvinsk (44 per cent), and Pinsk (74 per cent). Of the total occupied population in the pale, 73 per cent of those in commerce and 31 per cent of those in crafts and industry were Jews. Since there was little heavy industry within the pale, the majority in crafts and industry were artisans, either self-employed or working in small factories and workshops; out of a total 300,000 Jewish industrial workers, only 50,000 worked in medium and large-scale factories. The vast majority of the Russian Jewish population were very poor artisans, small traders or charity recipients; about half of the 5,600,000 Russian Jews in 1914 were impoverished *petite bourgeoisie* while about a quarter were working class. [1]

Pogroms, further restrictions on residence and occupations, proletarianisation and pauperisation all contributed to the emigration of about 2 million Russian Jews between 1881 and 1914. [2] The majority migrated to the United States, others started new communities in Canada, South America, and South Africa, and over 100,000 migrated to England where they soon outnumbered the native Anglo-Jewish community. The eastern European immigrants remained a minority in relation to the native-born Jews in Germany and France, but they added substantially to the Jewish populations in the capital cities. In

101

1880, out of a total German-Jewish population of nearly 562,000, there were 15,000 foreign Jews (2.7 per cent); in 1910 the total was 615,000 and the number of foreign Jews was 79,000 (12.8 per cent). In Berlin there were 3,000 foreign Jews out of a total of 54,000 in 1880, and 22,000 out of a total of 144,000 in 1910. In areas and cities where the native Jewish population was very small, such as Saxony, Leipzig, and Dresden, foreign Jews were in the majority by 1910. [3] In France the vast majority of immigrants were concentrated in Paris; between 1880 and 1914 about 21,000 eastern European Jews were added to the 40,000 Parisian Jews. [4]

In central Europe, internal migration from rural areas and small towns to the cities, especially the capitals, continued at an accelerated pace. [5] This was especially the case in Prussia where the village communities disappeared, and the small-town communities remained stable or declined. In 1885 32 per cent of Prussian Jewry lived in cities with a population of 100,000 or more; in 1910 the proportion was 54.5 per cent, 71 per cent lived in towns with 20,000 or more, and 21.6 per cent lived in Berlin. [6]

Economic mobility was high in urban areas. In the major cities of the Austro-Hungarian empire the Jews contributed a high proportion of the upper-middle-class merchants and professionals, but the majority remained in the lower-middle and lower classes. German Jewry became more economically homogeneous and evidence of their prosperity is provided by income tax returns; in Berlin, 1905–6, the average Jewish tax contribution was 357.42 marks, the average Lutheran contribution was 132.91 marks and the average Catholic contribution was 111.27 marks. [7]

In most Western cities there was a marked class division between the middle- and upper-class native Jews and the lower-class immigrants; this was particularly obvious in New York and London where the immigrant population was much larger than elsewhere. In New York, where the Jewish population increased from 80,000 in 1870 to 1,400,000 in 1915, the major immigrant or first area of settlement was the Lower

East Side of Manhattan which reached a peak of congestion in 1910 and then declined; by 1916 23 per cent of the city's Jews lived in the district compared with 50 per cent in 1903 and 75 per cent in 1892.[8] The first area of settlement in London, the East End, was by 1910 a densely populated two square miles; the proportion of Jews in many streets was more than 75 per cent and in some streets the proportion rose above 95 per cent.[9] The number of Jews in the area appears to have fallen after 1905, but on the eve of World War I approximately two-thirds of the London Jewish population lived in the East End.

As the immigrant areas grew, the more socially mobile of the earlier immigrants migrated to second areas of settlement. In New York Jews migrated to most areas of the city but the major second areas of settlement developed in Brooklyn and the Bronx while the native-born Jews of German descent lived in the more select areas of uptown Manhattan.[10] In London the major second areas of settlement developed in north and north-east London while the more prosperous native Jews migrated from the City, west-central and north London to the more fashionable parts of west and north-west London.[11]

Russia and the immigrant communities in the west

Very few Russian Jews attempted to adopt Russian culture or assimilate to Russian society after the pogroms of 1881. It became clear that anti-semitism was an official Russian policy; pogroms were increasingly provoked and staged by the government as its fear of revolution grew. Jews who had formerly identified with the Russian people turned to Jewish nationalism in a number of forms. There were a few small, short-lived and extremely marginal Jewish-Christian religious movements, but the religious monopolism of the Russian government, and the segregation of the Jews, meant that any attempt Jews might make to adapt to both the Jewish and non-Jewish religio-cultures had no hope of success.[12]

Although the majority of Russian Jews remained traditionally religious up to the end of the century, a number of secular Zionist and socialist movements grew rapidly in the last two decades. In the villages and *shtetls,* where the Jewish community retained a high level of social control, religious traditionalism remained largely intact; in the towns, the relative absence of community sanctions, the proletarianisation of the masses, and the intensive propaganda of the secularist intelligentsia resulted in an increasing deviation from religion. Many urban Russian communities became divided into religious and secularist groups. Apart from the relatively small *Mizrachi* movement, the political Zionist movements were either indifferent to religion or anti-religious, as in the case of the socialistic Poale Zionists. The largest Jewish socialist movement, the *Bund,* was also opposed to religion, although many workers on the periphery of the movement remained religious. Unlike the Zionists, some of the socialist leaders had long-term assimilationist goals, believing that the persecution of the Jews would end only after the proletarian revolution, but in the meantime they had to accommodate to the social, linguistic and religio-cultural divisions between the Jewish and non-Jewish workers. Jews were prominent in the leadership of the Russian revolutionary movement, but the vast majority continued to confine their social involvement and cultural orientations to the Jewish sub-society. [13]

The growing division in eastern Europe between the traditionalists, who made no distinction between religion, culture, and nationality, and the secularists, who rejected religion and redefined their identify along national-cultural lines, was transplanted to the immigrant communities in the west. Rabbis in eastern Europe opposed emigration to the *treyfa* (religiously unclean) western countries, and at least during the first two decades of the mass emigration the secularists were more disposed to emigrate than the traditionalists. [14] The secularists still represented a small proportion of the total emigration and, although the impact of the western societies was to reduce the number of traditionalists and increase their number, they remained a minority within the immigrant communities.

Prior to World War I, socialism was more important than

Zionism in the immigrant communities, but its importance varied between countries. The Jewish socialists in England, unlike the English socialists, were revolutionaries, but the small scale of the major immigrant trades (garment, and boot and shoe making) was not conducive to the growth of a socialist movement. Some of the socialists and anarchists emigrated from London to New York where the larger and more proletariat community provided a more favourable milieu, but the Jewish-American radical movements also began to decline around the turn of the century. [15]

Similar attacks on religion were made by radical Jews in Paris, London, and New York; they distributed anti-religious tracts, held dances on the eve of Yom Kippur, and on the day of Yom Kippur they provoked fights with religious Jews by their ostentatious eating and smoking in the streets and around, even in, the synagogues.[16] The anti-religious movement began in London; from 1885 the first socialist Yiddish journal, the *Arbayter Fraynd,* included anti-religious articles with many parodies of prayers and religious observance, and in 1888 the London radicals initiated the first Yom Kippur ball. The first Yom Kippur ball in New York was held in 1889 and, despite many attempts to stop them, they continued until 1901. At first the socialists joined the anarchists in their attacks on religion, but the socialist leaders soon came to realise that anti-religious activities lost them the support of most Jewish workers, and, from a theoretical point of view, they argued that direct attacks were unnecessary since religion would disappear once capitalism was overthrown. The accommodation of the socialist leaders to the religious feelings of immigrant workers enabled them to obtain the support of at least the nominally religious working-class Jews in socialist-led strikes and demonstrations. The anarchists, on the other hand, saw religion as an evil whose destruction was an integral part of the overthrow of the social order, and they continued their 'direct action' tactics throughout the 1890s until they petered out in the early 1900s. The anarchists believed that their anti-religious acts would help to revolutionise the Jewish workers, but in fact they served only to

105

alienate them; most immigrants held positive attitudes towards religion which provided them with a sense of continuity with the 'Old World' and a sense of security in the 'New'. It was, of course, just because religion was so important in the immigrant society that Jewish anarchists directed their attacks at it; most Jewish anarchists had been socialised in a religious environment and they attacked religion with the ferocity of converts.

The closeness of both the anarchists and socialists to religion is shown by the religious symbolism in which the radical message was often expressed: the coming of the social revolution was identified with the coming of the Messiah, radical texts included quotes from the prophets, and anti-religious tracts were written in the form of traditional prayers. A socialist brochure in 1885 contained a statement of 'The Thirteen Articles of Socialist Faith' modelled after Maimonides' 'Thirteen Articles of Faith'. The following article was included: 'I believe with perfect faith that whoever profits by the labour of his fellowmen without doing anything for him in return is a wilful plunderer.'[17]

Only a minority of Jewish immigrants were anti-religious secularists, but a far greater number became secularised Jews. A decline in religious observance was clearly observable in the immigrant communities, even among the older members: women no longer wore wigs or attended ritual baths, men shaved their beards, cut their sidelocks, and discarded their ritual garments, phylacteries, and skullcaps. A survey in 1912 found that only 25 per cent of Jewish workmen in New York rested on the Sabbath, and in 1913 60 per cent of the shops in the Lower East Side were found to be open on the Sabbath.[18] In 1917 the Jewish Communal Register of New York City reported a total synagogue membership of nearly 80,000 and a total synagogue seating capacity of 415,000 (in permanent and temporary synagogues) for an estimated potential synagogue population of 900,000. Since the total synagogue membership constituted 5.3 per cent of the total New York Jewish population, it can be estimated that approximately a quarter of the adult Jewish males in New York were synagogue members.

Overall, the affiliation of first generation Jews could not have been high, but the register shows that synagogue membership varied considerably between districts. Synagogue affiliation was higher in the Lower East Side (Delancey, East Broadway) than in both the second areas of settlement (Williamsburg, Brownsville, etc) and the more acculturated areas (Borough Park, West Side, etc). [19]

The level of synagogue affiliation does not necessarily indicate the level of religious observance and synagogue attendance; the small synagogues or *hevrot* were also *landsmanschaften* (societies of immigrants from the same home town or district) which performed non-religious as well as religious functions. In addition to providing a room for religious services, many *landsmanschaften* were also burial and friendly societies and social centres, integrating the immigrants in familiar groups of regional origin and social background. For many immigrants the more broadly cultural and social functions of the *landsmanschaften* may have been more important than their specifically religious functions, but there was a tendency for the specifically religious societies to become differentiated from the friendly and social societies. [20] However, the high ratio of permanent to total synagogue seats (ie permanent seats plus temporary seats for the High Holy Days) in the Lower East Side suggests a larger regular attendance than in the second areas of settlement where secular institutions, such as Jewish community centres, replaced the synagogues as the most important foci of social activity. It was certainly higher than the attendance of native New York Jews; Emanu-El, the major Reform synagogue in New York, was barely able to secure a *minyan* for its Sabbath services. [21]

Similar patterns of synagogue membership and attendance were found in London: between one-third and a half of the adult Jewish males in east London belonged to a *hevra* or synagogue in 1914, but only a small minority attended synagogue regularly. Among the predominantly native-born, middle-class Jews living in west and north-west London, the proportion of adult males affiliated to a synagogue was higher but the proportion who attended synagogue regularly was probably lower; a religious census on a Sabbath morning in 1886 found that between 10 per cent and 15 per cent of the Jews in west and north-west London attended the service. [22] There appears to have been no significant difference between immigrant and native Jews in their attendance on the High Holy Days; in both cases, the great majority of adult Jewish men attended synagogue. An extensive religious census in London in 1903 included an enumeration of attendance 'at every Jewish Synagogue in London' on the first day of Passover, which in that year fell on Easter Sunday. [23] If the total London Jewish population was between 120,000 and 140,000, then about one in five attended synagogue on the day. Even if the one or two thousand Jews who worshipped in small *hevrot,* not recorded by the census, are added to the total, less than one in four Jews attended. This was little more than the proportion of Christians who attended church on an ordinary Sunday in 1903. The survey found that a larger proportion of the Jews in west and north-west London attended the synagogue on that day than the Jews in the East End. This difference is largely accounted for by the higher proportion of native Jewish women who attended; the less acculturated immigrants put less emphasis on synagogue attendance on the part of women, and many native women were able to attend the synagogue by leaving the preparation of the Passover meal to their servants.

Synagogue attendance was, if anything, lower in the predominantly native German and French communities. Arthur Rubbin estimated that, by the beginning of the twentieth century, about 10 per cent to 15 per cent of German Jews were Orthodox, and Marrus has estimated that there were only about 500 Orthodox Jews in the whole of France in 1898. An inquiry carried out in 1904 found that only 487 of the 1,850 synagogues in Germany held daily services, 1,147 held services on the Sabbath, and 216 held services only on High Holy Days. On ordinary Sabbaths the Berlin synagogues presented 'a beggarly array of empty benches'. In France the provincial synagogues found it difficult to obtain a *minyan* on the Sabbath, and in Paris the synagogues provided a seating capacity of 5,000 for a total

Jewish population of about 40,000. Synagogues were only full on the High Holy Days, but even these attendances fell off towards the end of the century: in Berlin there were little more than 20,000 seats available for the High Holy Day services in 1897 for a population of 80,000–90,000, and in Paris the attendances were low when the days coincided with the period when middle-class Parisians left Paris for the summer resorts. In Austria and Bohemia-Moravia the native Jews attended synagogue four times a year: the first two days of Rosh Hashanah, Yom Kippur, and the birthday of Emperor Franz Joseph.[24]

The east European immigrants repeated, in many respects, the experience of the emancipated, native, western Jews; they found that the economic and cultural costs of religious traditionalism were too great. Moreover, since very few distinguished rabbis emigrated from eastern Europe, there was no strong traditional scholarly elite to defend traditionalism in the immigrant communities. The religious functionaries employed by the *hevrot* received very small salaries and they generally had to combine the offices of *shammash* and *hazan* in the synagogue with occupations, such as *melammed,* scribe and matchmaker, outside it. In 1888 a number of Orthodox synagogues in New York brought a distinguished rabbi from Vilna to act as their 'chief rabbi', but other rabbis refused to accept his leadership and he was unable to compel the ritual slaughterers and butchers to abide by his regulations.[25] In 1911, thirty immigrant rabbis held a conference in Leeds in which they proposed a return to traditionalism. The chairman said: 'We have met in England with the object of saving Judaism in this country. We know how weak the power of each individual Rabbi is in his town or congregation ... The most important laws of the Torah and *Shulchan Aruch* ... are trampled under foot and left unobserved.' Another said: 'Things had come to a pitch that Jews hide themselves when putting on their *Tephillin* ... Their greatest misfortune was their apish imitation of their Christian neighbours. Every mother in Israel used to lull her baby with the song: "My son will study the Torah". A Jewish

109

mother now rocked her child to sleep with pantomime songs.' Among the resolutions passed by the conference were the following: to establish proper ritual baths; to issue pamphlets explaining all laws concerning sexual morality; to agitate against the dancing together of men and women; to agitate in favour of the married women's wig.[26] Such complete rejection of accommodation to the 'host' society met with little response from most immigrants.

Divided communities

Religious practices were, for most immigrants, only part of a broad Jewish or Yiddish culture, and they felt little identity with the native Jews who were singularly lacking in *Yiddishkeit*. Language was an important element in this cultural difference; most native Jews considered Yiddish, which few could speak, as a despicable 'jargon', but while most immigrants learnt to speak English, Yiddish remained their first language. In addition to differences in culture and identity, the immigrant and native Jews were divided by class and status: they lived in socially distinct districts (uptown/downtown, East End/West End); most immigrants were lower-class workers, artisans or petty traders; most native Jews were middle- or upper-middle-class merchants and professionals. Even though the immigrants were themselves divided by regional background and beliefs, they felt they had far more in common than with the highly acculturated native Jews.

Both religious and secularist immigrants regarded the decorous and unemotional services of the native synagogues with disdain. In America Reform Judaism was seen as a travesty, but immigrant reactions to the decorous 'Orthodox' services in Paris and London were not very different. In Paris, the immigrants decried the natives' tendency to imitate Catholic ceremonies and the predominance of females in the native synagogues,[27] whilst in London the immigrants saw little difference between the Reform synagogue and the synagogues affiliated to the 'Orthodox' United Synagogue with their sedate services, mixed choirs, and ministers who looked like Christian clergymen.[28]

110

The emotionalism, active participation and indecorum of the traditional services were preserved in the *hevrot* which were found in public houses, shops, huts, backyards, and attics. A native London Jew who visited a 'humble *chevra* room' in 1895 reported that, 'the room was not only a kitchen and a bedroom, it was also a *Shul,* or rather a *Chevra*. It seems that a dozen or so of poor foreigners have clubbed together to form a *Minyan*. They subscribed 2d. a week.' The visitor reported that the ark was impressive in relation to its surroundings, but the reader's desk was rickety and the reader's book rested on an old lemonade box. The visitor asked why they did not go to a nearby synagogue. A member replied: 'Oh, that's only for rich people, and we are only poor. If you go there you have to *shnoder* half-a-crown ... For twopence a week we can have as many *mitzvahs* as we want.' [29]

The *hevrot* aroused intense dislike among the native communities; they saw the small, slum prayer rooms as unsuitable for sacred services, and they were embarrassed by the indecorous fervour of the services. In the countries of immigration, anti-alien campaigns condemned the introduction of a 'foreign' culture, and native Jews, who noted that gentiles did not always distinguish between the 'foreign' immigrant and the acculturated native, were concerned that the strange customs of the immigrants would reflect on their own reputation and status. Native Jews tried to discourage immigration, to persuade the arrivals to return to Russia, and, in Europe, to encourage them to re-emigrate to America. The reaction of native Jews to the immigrants was everywhere a negative one, but once the immigrants had settled the native communities differed in their policies towards them. The most antagonistic were the native German Jews; they tried to exclude the immigrants from their organisations and disfranchise them from the *Gemeinden;* and some Jewish students supported the movement in German universities to expel the Russo-Jewish students. French Jews tried to distance themselves as much as possible from the immigrants, but in Paris the *Consistoire* founded a synagogue with a Polish ritual to attract the

111

immigrants from the *hevrot*. Very few immigrants, however, attended the *Consistoire* temples. In both England and America native Jews tried to acculturate the immigrants by providing English language classes, apprenticeship schemes, schools, institutes for leisure, educational pursuits, and special religious services. [30]

In London the United Synagogue financed 'free services for the poor' which were intended to discourage the immigrants from attending the *hevrot* and to familiarise them with a more decorous form of service. Its leaders also introduced a number of 'East End Schemes' to build a large synagogue in the East End which they hoped would induce the immigrants to abandon the *hevrot* and, as one leader put it, 'inoculate these persons with ideas of reverent and orderly Divine worship'. The proposed synagogue was never built; the level of public support which was required before the United Synagogue would commit a large capital outlay was not forthcoming. There was also considerable opposition from the East End-centred Federation of Synagogues, a loose association of *hevrot* and small synagogues formed in 1887 under the leadership of Samual Montagu, a rich, native but Orthodox Jew, who provided loans to the Federation synagogues and funds for its central organisation. In 1914 most *hevrot* and small synagogues in the East End were members of the Federation; only a few East London Jews joined the United Synagogue, although there were others who wanted to join but were unable to pay the high cost of membership. The services in Federation synagogues were traditionalist, but under Montagu's autocratic leadership the Federation displayed some accommodation to English society: board meetings were held in English; as members grew more prosperous they acquired larger and more 'respectable' buildings; and in a few cases they displayed some degree of religious acculturation, such as the abolition of the auction of *mitzvot* and the provision of special services for children.

In the second areas of settlement some of the migrants from the East End established their own *hevrot* or joined a synagogue affiliated to the Federation, but a greater number joined the

United Synagogue; in 1914 about 6 per cent to 8 per cent of the adult Jewish males in north London were members of the Federation, while about a third were members of the United Synagogue. The leaders of the United Synagogue sought the membership of the socially mobile, more acculturated first generation in the second areas of settlement; they lowered membership fees and they made organisational provisions for small congregations who wanted to join the United Synagogue but could not pay the high contributions of a full constituent synagogue toward the communal services of the central organisation. In addition to the organisational accommodations of the United Synagogue, the tendency of the first generation in the second areas of settlement to join was facilitated by the fact that, with only minor modifications, it adhered to the Orthodox prayerbook. The more socially mobile first generation found that the nondecorous services of the *hevrot* were no longer congruent with their new social position, but that it was possible to remain 'Orthodox' by joining the predominantly native, prestigious United Synagogue.[31]

In contrast to England, few Jews in the second areas of settlement in the United States joined native congregations. American Jews were concerned to keep the east Europeans at a social distance and they did not provide or encourage new Reform synagogues for immigrants. A more important factor, however, was that the east Europeans found the Reform beliefs and practices too alien from the Judaism into which they had been socialised. In 1901 a group of rich Reform Jews, recognising that Reform Judaism had little appeal to the immigrants but concerned that 'ghetto' Orthodoxy should not continue as a threat to the status of Jews in America, reorganised the Jewish Theological Seminary to train Americanised rabbis for immigrant groups. Since most native American Jews joined Reform synagogues, the seminary had been unsuccessful as an institution for training rabbis for native, non-Reform congregations. Its goals were, therefore, reformulated: it was to train rabbis who would instil 'culture, refinement and civilisation' into the immigrants, and rid

Orthodoxy of its 'ghetto' characteristics. The seminary eventually became the rabbinical school of the Conservative movement, but it found only a limited response in the first or second areas of settlement where Orthodoxy remained the most important form of Judaism. There were, however, signs of change; many of the older Orthodox synagogues were reformulating their religious services and programmes in a Conservative direction. [32]

Native Judaism and the socio-cultural environment

Prior to 1918 most native western Jews continued to insist that religion was the only factor which distinguished them from their non-Jewish neighbours, but the content and forms of the religious services which accompanied this position continued to vary. In central Europe the number of Reform congregations continued to grow although there was little further acculturation of the religious services. Reform Judaism tended to be more radical in Germany than in the Austro-Hungarian empire, but, compared with American Reform, it retained many traditional elements.

Reform or Liberal Judaism was dominant in Berlin but the Liberal candidates were defeated in the 1896 *Gemeinde* elections by Conservative candidates; the Liberals' official election programme was limited to demands for more prayers in the vernacular, but there were rumours that they intended to abolish Hebrew entirely and alter the Sabbath services from Saturday to Sunday. The Liberals regained power in 1898, when sixteen of their candidates were elected and only six candidates of a more extreme Reform party, advocating Sunday services, were elected. The Liberals were defeated in 1901, when they advocated special Sunday services, but all the Liberal candidates were elected in 1904, after the Sunday service issue was dropped from the Liberal programme. [33] The failure to introduce radical religious change in the official community synagogues caused a number of private associations to hold their own extreme Reform services.

In France and England the majority of native Jews continued

to be satisfied with the acculturated forms of Orthodoxy which had developed prior to 1880. In London, in 1892, the Chief Rabbi sanctioned some ritual modifications which had been proposed by the richer congregations of the United Synagogue. These included: the reading of the ten commandments on the Sabbath by the minister; a brief service for children on the Day of Atonement; English prayers to be composed by the ministers and to be read by them from the pulpits; a special religious service for the pupils of religious classes who had attended their course of instruction and passed the appropriate examination, but the service was not to 'be termed a confirmation, such rite being foreign to our faith'; and a verbal declaration of consent by the bride and bridegroom to the minister's prepared questions before the beginning of the prescribed marriage ceremony. The Anglo-Jewish ministers wore clerical garb, including 'dog-collars', put very little emphasis on religious scholarship, and adopted the roles of preacher, teacher of the young, pastor, and administrative secretary of the synagogue; they tried to meet lay demands that they approximate to the 'cultured gentlemen' clergy of the Church of England, and act as worthy ambassadors to the non-Jewish world. [34]

Few native London Jews were attracted away from the United Synagogue to the West London Reform Synagogue or to the Liberal movement, [35] the Jewish Religious Union, which was formed in 1902. The inaugural service of the Religious Union, which was held on a Saturday afternoon, was mostly conducted in English, retained very little of the traditional Jewish service and included a number of hymns on universalistic themes. The prayers for the restoration of the sacrificial rite, the rebuilding of the Temple and the return to Zion were not included in the movement's prayerbook. The leaders of the Liberal movement said that their object was to attract those Jews who rarely attended synagogue either because they worked on Saturday morning or because they felt little sympathy with the Orthodox services. The Union was not, however, very successful as a 'missionary force'; by October 1903 there were 300 members but in the following year thirty-one members resigned while only thirty-four joined, and at the annual meeting in 1907 it was announced that there had been only a small increase in membership. The Union's leader, Claude G. Montefiore, admitted, in 1904, that he had been mistaken in believing that a 'modern' service would attract a large number of regular worshippers. The idea that the Liberal movement should provide only 'religious services supplementary to those provided by the existing synagogues' was dropped, and in 1911 the Union opened a Liberal Jewish Synagogue in St John's Wood. The main services, held on Saturday afternoons, included certain parts in Hebrew, but the greater part of the service was in English. The Torah scrolls were taken from the Ark and a few verses were chanted in the traditional style, but nobody was 'called up' to the reading of the law. The service, which was accompanied by an organ and a mixed choir, included a Bible reading and an address from the pulpit built above the Ark. By 1915 all the 446 seats in the synagogue were let, but there were continuing complaints about the low attendance at the services. [36]

In France, most middle-class native Jews preferred the services of the *consistoire* synagogues to the highly acculturated services of *l'Union liberale israelite*, formed in 1907, which was able to recruit only a sufficient number of the rich Parisian Jews to support one small synagogue. The Union's services were held on Sunday morning, prayers were read in French, males and females could sit together, and men were not required to wear headgear. [37]

Only in America did radically reformed services attract the majority of middle-class native Jews. The majority of Reform congregations adopted the Union of American Hebrew Congregations' prayerbook, published in 1894, in which the traditional prayers of suffering and revenge were replaced by prayers expressing security and prosperity. [38] English rather than Hebrew was the major language used in the Reform services, and many Reform congregations held their main service on Sunday rather than Saturday. N. Glazer wrote: 'Around the turn of the century, it would not have been far-fetched for a historian of ideas to predict a merger between Reform Judaism and Liberal Christianity.'[39]

The type of Christianity prevailing in the environment continued to influence the form of Jewish religious acculturation in this period, but the success of radical Reform in America, compared with the failure to introduce radical changes in German Reform, and the limited appeal of the Liberal movements in France and England, can only be explained by comparing other important aspects of the socio-cultural environments. An important factor was the varying importance of anti Jewish prejudice and discrimination and forms they took.

In Germany the attacks on Jewish religion and culture continued, but anti-semitism, in a more virulent and racial form, became also an integral part of the social protest of the German lower-middle class who wished to exclude all Jews, even the most acculturated and assimilated, from the competition for white-collar jobs. Supposed differences in 'blood', rather than differences in religion and culture, became the major legitimation for prejudice and discrimination. After 1900 political anti-semitism subsided, but occupational and social exclusion increased; Jews were discriminated against in the civil service, judiciary, and universities, and excluded from student fraternal organisations, professional associations, and more informal groups.[40] The German conservatives continued to argue that the Jews had no place in Germany since the German state was inseparable from the national Church and derived its authority from God. The German liberals attacked the dogma and sacraments of the established Church, but they nevertheless wished to strengthen the Christian character of the state and infuse German society with the spirit of the Gospels. Liberal Christians and Jews shared the rationalistic, historical and ethical approaches to religion, but this intellectual closeness gave rise to new tensions and a reassertion of their differences. Many German liberals argued that only when the Jews had sacrificed their Judaism for the higher goal of German national unification should they be received as equals into German society. Thus, even the political and religious German liberals did not accept that the Jews could both retain their distinct religious identity

117

and gain social acceptance by German society. [41]

Reform and Orthodox Jews accused each other of provoking anti-semitism; Reform Jews argued that Orthodox religious practices had obstructed social acceptance, while the Orthodox maintained that anti-semitism proved the failure of Reform and was a divine action to stop assimilation and lead Jews back to the Torah. The disillusionment of many Reform Jews did in fact make them revise their response to anti-semitism and their interpretation of Jewish identity; the *Central Verein,* which was formed in 1893 and which claimed to represent some 200,000 German Jews in 1916, defended Jewishness in public and came to argue that, in addition to their religious identity, Jews also had a common origin and history. The defence against anti-semitism was conducted by Reform Jews who had abandoned most visible Jewish practices but who had come to recognise that Germans would not accept Jewish acculturation short of conversion, and that there were others who excluded even the converted Jew from the German nation.

The *Central Verein* proclaimed its neutrality in religious matters, but it repudiated the argument of some Jewish intellectuals that liberal Protestantism and Judaism were identical and that this justified conversion. It did not, however, abandon the desire for acceptance within German society, and in 1913 it repudiated the political Zionists who advocated withdrawal from German society and settlement in Palestine. The major support for political Zionism came from the eastern European immigrants, but a small number of young native Jews from highly acculturated middle-class families reacted to anti-semitism by proclaiming the hopelessness of integration and the necessity for a Jewish national consciousness. The radical Zionist position was strongly repudiated by most native Jews who feared that the Zionists would only serve to legitimise the anti-semitic accusations of Jewish disloyalty to the German state and people. [42]The major conflict among German Jews was changing from one between Orthodox and Reform Jews to one between the 'assimilationists', who claimed that religion was either the only or the major difference between Jew and gentile, and secular Jewish nationalists.

In Austria racial anti-semitism originated in the pan-Germanic movements, and Jews were attacked by both the anti-clerical pan-Germans and the anti-liberal Catholics. In Vienna the anti-semitic Christian Social Party defeated the Liberal Party, and Jews were expelled from many *volkisch* German clubs, societies, and fraternities. Despite these developments, however, most Austrian Jews remained liberals, deprecated the importance of anti-semitism, and retained their belief in progress towards their acceptance in gentile society. Prior to 1918, only a small minority of native Austrian Jews became Zionists and challenged the control of the Jewish community by the liberal 'assimilationists'. [43]

The Jews in Bohemia-Moravia were also subject to social discrimination in German circles, but anti-semitism took more virulent forms among the Czechs, and up to World War I the majority of Jews continued to identify with the Germans. In Hungary the trend towards identification with the Magyars continued: in 1905 90.3 per cent of Hungarian Jews identified with the Magyars and 8.2 per cent identified with the Germans. Anti-semitism remained a comparatively unimportant issue in Hungarian politics, although as a prominent group in industry and commerce, the Jews encountered a lot of hostility, especially from the impoverished lower nobility and German town bourgeoisie. [44] In central Hungary, Bohemia, Moravia, and Austria a moderate Reform or Liberal Judaism grew to become the religion of the vast majority of native, middle-class Jews, but, as in Germany, the acculturated form of religion had become stabilised and further innovations in religious services rare. [45]

In contrast with Germany and Austria, where anti-semitism was considered respectable in wide social and cultural circles, the English made a distinction between anti-alienism, which was respectable, and anti-semitism, which was not. Those who campaigned and argued for restrictions on the immigration of eastern European Jews denied that they were anti-semitic and were unanimous in praising the virtues of the native Anglo-Jewry. There is little evidence of discrimination against

119

native Jews and it was clearly far less significant in England than in other European countries or the United States. Some discrimination in the form of social snobbery may have existed in middle-class circles, but upper-class Jews, who provided the leaders of the Anglo-Jewish community, were accepted into the English aristocracy. Discrimination against Jews in the higher professions declined, Jews were accepted by the major public schools and the old universities, the Court circle of Edward VII included a number of Jews, and, from the late 1860s, many rich Jews left the Liberal party and joined the Conservatives. [46]

The secure position that native Jews occupied in England meant that the majority saw little need to make radical changes in the religious services, such as the omission of particularistic prayers. Many native Jews did, however, regard the foreignness of the immigrants and the nationalist proclamations of the Zionist movement as a threat to their position, and they countered both by proclaiming their 'Englishness'. In 1900, Solomon Schechter, the Jewish scholar who later became President of the Jewish Theological Seminary of America, wrote that: 'the now fashionable cry ... of our being Anglo-Saxons or Englishmen of the Jewish persuasion, is but a sickly platitude. We can only be Jews of the Jewish persuasion.' Simeon Singer, the minister who compiled the authorised British Orthodox Prayerbook, wrote in reply to Schechter: 'I am an Englishman professing the Jewish faith. I refuse to recognise a classification according to which my neighbour ranks as an Englishman and I as a Jew.' Israel Zangwill, the novelist, quoted passages from Singer's prayerbook which appeared inconsistent with Singer's proclamations of his Englishness. For example, the prayer for the royal family included the passage: 'In her days and in ours may Judah be saved and Israel dwell securely and may the Redeemer come unto Zion.' [47] But since there was no organised anti-semitic movement and since native Jews were rarely excluded socially because they were Jews, few concerned themselves with changing the synagogue service to bring it more in line with their statements of English identity. Moreover, the particularistic prayers in the prayerbook were part of an

Orthodox Judaism which was itself identified with English culture and society. The *Jewish Chronicle* claimed that the 'spirit of Torah' had been responsible for all that was good in the English nation: it had saved England from revolution and atheism, it had given substance to the Liberal Party, and it had led to the triumph of free trade. [48] For many, to support Orthodox Judaism was also to support the existing institutions of England.

Anti-Jewish prejudice and discrimination was greater in France than England but not as extensive as in Germany. Organised anti-semitism was weak in France prior to the Dreyfus case, and it appeared to break out very suddenly: anti-semitic writings and demonstrations appeared in Paris in the late 1880s and 1890s, anti-semitic riots in French cities followed a few days after Zola's famous *J'accuse* statement on the Dreyfus *affaire* in 1898, and sporadic incidents continued throughout the *affaire*. As in Germany, the major support for anti-semitism was found in the lower-middle class, the *petite bourgeoisie* of small merchants and minor bureaucrats, who were frustrated in their social and economic aspirations. The movement also found support among the Catholic clergy and frustrated professionals in fields such as journalism and law where Jews had been highly successful. Middle-class business and professional Jews felt some degree of hostility towards them, but they experienced little occupational discrimination, and rich Jews continued to be socially accepted in upper-middle and upper-class circles. [49] It was possible, therefore, for French Jews to minimise French anti-semitism as an anomalous import from Germany, to respond passively to its outburst, and to continue to hold the position that they were 'Frenchmen of the Israelite faith'. Most French Jews refrained from any involvement in the Dreyfus *affaire* and lived through it without changing their religious or political views. In contrast with Germany, no large-scale Jewish organisation was set up or took over the task of combating anti-semitism. Some denied that the *affaire* had anything to do with anti-semitism, and those who became active Dreyfusards legitimised their position by arguing

121

that they were defending the principles of the Republic. Only a small minority of French Jews, mostly from eastern Europe, responded to anti-semitism during the Dreyfus *affaire* by rejecting assimilation and asserting a secular Jewish nationhood. [50]

In the United States the correspondence in time between the mass eastern European immigration and the growth of anti-Jewish expression and discrimination would appear to account for the further religious acculturation of native Jews. Discrimination was more widespread from about 1880: Jews were excluded from an increasing number of hotels, clubs, summer resorts, and college fraternities. Scholars differ in their explanations of this phenomenon. Some point to the compatively amorphous stratification which causes anxiety concerning status and leads to an emphasis on 'exclusiveness'; the emerging middle class could define their status more sharply by discriminating against the exceptionally mobile Jews. [51] Others have argued that the mass immigration of east European Jews, with their alien cultural and religious traditions, was a more important factor than the particular features of the American class system. In this interpretation, anti-semitism was only one aspect of the growing antagonism towards all the new immigrant groups from southern and eastern Europe. [52] Both factors probably played a part, but for us it is important to note that the immigrants were a prominent target for anti-semites, and this led many native Jews to believe that discrimination was often motivated by a dislike for 'foreign' cultures and religions. Moreover, if status-consciousness was high in America, discrimination made native Jews even more self-conscious of their status than other Americans; they were, therefore, highly sensitive to the opinions of other people and made great efforts to conform to American cultural patterns. By adopting a Reform Judaism which minimised the religious differences between themselves and other native Americans, they widened the cultural distance between immigrants and themselves, and demonstrated their concern to accommodate to the non-Jewish religious environment.

122

Comparisons

A comparison of Jewish communities from the beginning of the nineteenth century to World War I shows that the traditionalistic Jewish sub-society lasted longest where the Jews remained separated from non-Jewish society and where the Jewish community retained a high degree of cohesiveness. In Russia the majority continued to conform to the traditional religio-culture up to the last decades of the nineteenth century, and in the *shtetls* traditionalism continued largely intact up to World War I. The Russian Jews remained unemancipated, economically distinctive, and socially segregated, and the attempts by the Russian authorities to convert the Jews only served to reinforce the distinctively Jewish cultural identity. Secularist movements emerged in the rapidly growing and highly class-differentiated urban communities, but whether they were religious or secularist, Jewish movements remained separate and culturally distinctive from the non-Jewish environment. Only a very small minority of Russian Jews, who lived in the cities outside the pale of settlement, adopted the Russian language and culture, and since the major division in Russian Jewry was between the traditionalists and the secularists (Zionists and socialists), there was no significant movement for reforms in the synagogue services. There was a process of secularisation without acculturation. At most one can talk of transculturation; the non-traditionalist Jews were influenced by secularist ideologies from the non-Jewish environment, but these ideologies were then given a specifically Jewish content and expressed in the language and symbols of the Jewish milieu.

In contrast with the segregationist policy of the tsarist governments, many central and western European governments, in the late eighteenth and the nineteenth centuries, removed the legal barriers between Jews and Christians. The removal of residential restrictions, the diminishing economic functions in rural districts, and new economic opportunities in the towns, resulted in a continually growing migration from the villages and small towns, where the socio-economic separation of the Jews was rigidly institutionalised, to the more anonymous and loosely

123

structured cities. Within the cities many Jews moved from the ghettos and Jewish areas to predominantly Christian residential districts. Economic and occupational mobility often accompanied vicinal mobility, and in the urban areas the Jewish occupational structure became more heterogeneous and less distinctive. In those areas, such as Galicia, northern Hungary, Posen, and southern Germany, where the Jews remained rural and socio-economically distinctive, traditionalism, in either its hassidic or its more legalistic Orthodox forms, remained strong. In the cities of central and western Europe, where many of the barriers between Jews and gentiles were removed or lowered, and where the functions of Jewish communal organisation were limited to specifically religious tasks, the majority of the vicinally and economically mobile Jews found themselves in a marginal situation: they wished to become equal members of the larger society, but continued at least a nominal adherence to Judaism. Religion was defined by marginal Jews as the only or major content of their 'Jewishness', but the traditionalistic religion was in many ways incompatible with the more secular culture of the urban gentiles. Marginal Jews reduced the cultural inconsistencies by abandoning many traditional religious roles and behaviour-patterns and adopting secular roles and behaviour patterns, and their religious concerns were concentrated on the religious services and the need for their reform.

In the nineteenth century, the religious services, in the majority of the more wealthy Jewish congregations in Europe and America, became more decorous and less emotional; but there were large variations in the extent of acculturation in the form, but more especially in the content, of the services. These variations were related to the following interrelated social and cultural dimensions: the structure of Jewish religious organisations; the ideology and practices of the Christian religion prevailing in the environment; the dominant groups' dispositions toward religio-cultural monopolism or pluralism; and the position of the marginal Jews, especially, the lay leaders from the top Jewish stratum, in the stratification systems.

124

Most Jewish religious organisations in Europe remained under the auspices of the state. Synagogue and other religious facilities in central Europe were provided by the *Gemeinden*, to which all professing Jews had to belong and pay special taxes. At first this type of organisation had a prohibitive effect on the development of non-traditional forms of Judaism; its leaders opposed innovations and modifications in the religious services, and there was little that reformist Jews could do at that stage except attempt to form a voluntary association outside the official community. Once reformist Jews were elected or appointed to the lay and rabbinical offices of the *Gemeinden*, it was the turn of the Orthodox to feel isolated and threatened, and, after legal provisions were made by the states, many Orthodox Jews seceded from the official community to form independent congregations.

The French *consistoires* and rabbinate were organised in a hierarchical fashion. The lay leaders of the *Central Consistoire* favoured moderate reforms and they appointed religious leaders who were adaptable to change. A rabbinical synod, convened by the *grand rabbin* of France, passed a number of reforms, but it was left to each individual community to decide whether to accept the reforms or not.

The synagogues in Britain and America were dependent upon the voluntary association of members, and the environmental Protestant denominations, which were also based on voluntary association, provided the Jewish lay leaders with organisational models. The Jews in America emphasised the autonomy of the local congregation, and each congregation was able to modify its services without reference to a high authority. The lay leaders in Britain, on the other hand, preferred centralised and hierarchical modes of organisation. Rabbinical authority in Britain was centralised in the Chief Rabbinate, and the individual chief rabbis used their position and influence to oppose extensive reform in religious practices. But even the most centralised rabbinical system could act only as a brake on the demand for religious reform; if the laity demanded change, the rabbinate could not prevent it indefinitely. Rabbis were elected or appointed to their posts by laymen, and they could always be replaced after dismissal, retirement, or death by men who would be more responsive to lay demands. In Germany traditionalistic rabbis were replaced by reform rabbis, but in England and France laymen accepted the conservative changes approved by their respective religious authorities because their demands for change were moderate compared with the demands of the German and American Jews. It is necessary, therefore, to analyse the cultural environments and the position of the Jews in the social structures to explain the variations in religious acculturation.

Marginal Jews in north Germany and the United States took as their non-Jewish religious models the high-status liberal Protestant denominations which, like Judaism, had come to reject any form of supernatural mediation between God and man. In Germany, the importance of liberal Protestantism as a religious reference for marginal Jews declined in the second half of the nineteenth century when the liberals took an increasingly polemical stand against Liberal and Reform Judaism. In the United States, liberal Protestantism continued to be an important religious reference for marginal Jews, and at the end of the century, the services in the American Reform synagogues were closer to Unitarian services than to Jewish Orthodox services. In contrast, the semi-Catholic practices and symbols of the Church of England were too alien to be introduced into the Jewish services. English Jews took the Anglican services as a religious model with regard to decorum and the emphasis on form, but the content of the Anglo-Jewish services remained predominantly traditional. The absence of an appropriate Christian referent helps also to account for the lack of success of Reform Judaism in France, Italy, and other predominantly Catholic areas.

The religious distance of the environmental forms of Christianity from Judaism was an important dimension affecting the level of religious acculturation, but it is clear that some Jewish communities felt greater social pressures than others to change their religious services in an acculturative direction.

126

Where the Jews were separated from non-Jews, as in eastern Europe, demands for Jewish conformity to the dominant culture were ineffectual, but where the barriers between Jews and non-Jews were lowered, and where in consequence the Jews came to identify with the dominant nationality, Jews were responsive and sensitive to demands for religio-cultural conformity. Thus, outside eastern Europe, Jewish religious acculturation was greatest where the dominant groups in the wider society took a monopolistic rather than pluralistic disposition toward religio-cultural differences.

In the medieval and early modern period the official pluralistic disposition towards the Jews was based on the economic interest of the rulers and the teachings of the Church. The diminishing importance of the Jews as a specialised economic group, their legal emancipation, and the decline in the power of the Church removed the bases of this pluralism. In the developing nation states, a high level of conformity to the national culture was demanded, and this was particularly the case where national integration was most problematic, as in Germany, the Austro-Hungarian lands, and the United States. In response to the criticisms of the supposed Jewish lack of cultural and national patriotism, the German Jews strongly emphasised their identity with the German nation and culture and altered their religious services accordingly, Furthermore, since German nationalism and German Protestantism were so interrelated in Prussia, the marginal Prussian Jews took German Protestantism as an important religious model. In the Austro-Hungarian lands, where conflicts between the major ethnic groups were growing, there were also strong pressures on the Jews to identify with the dominant national cultures, especially with the Germans in Austria and Bohemia-Moravia, and with the Magyars in Hungary. In contrast with Prussia, however, the importance of Catholicism meant that national cultures were not identified with a particular church, and this may in part explain the more moderate forms of religious acculturation in the Austro-Hungarian lands and southern Germany. In the United States, pressures on immigrants to adopt the dominant Protestant Anglo-Saxon (WASP) values and behaviour patterns influenced the Jewish immigrants from Germany and their descendants to develop a radical Reform Judaism whose services came to approximate those of liberal American Protestantism.

Nationalism was also an important force in France and England in this period, but national identity was more established and secure than in central Europe and North America, and there was a greater pluralistic disposition toward the specifically religious aspects of Jewish culture. In neither France nor England was there pressure to conform to a national church; in France it was possible to be both nationalistic and secular or anti-clerical, and in England, although the Anglican Church was an established church, there was a comparatively high level of tolerance toward religious differences. Thus, the stronger the dominant groups' emphasis on a national culture and the greater the identification of a particular church or religious tradition with this culture, the greater the level of religious acculturation among marginal Jews.

If we compare those societies where Jews had moved out of their ghetto isolation, it was the most 'closed' and 'open' stratification systems which produced the greatest pressures to acculturate. Marginal Jews were particularly sensitive to the dominant groups' demands for religio-cultural conformity where they were excluded from gentile social groups and where their economic mobility was not accompanied by an equivalent rise in social honour. All important urban European Jewish organisations were led by oligarchies of rich men with high social standing within their communities, but only in France and England were Jewish leaders accepted into upper-middle- and upper-class gentile circles on terms of approximate equal status. In central Europe the circles of the gentile upper stratum were comparatively exclusive, and while there were objections to the admittance of the gentile *nouveaux riches,* the objections to the admittance of rich Jews were even stronger. Individual Jews were sometimes socially accepted as 'exceptions' and there were some marriages between impoverished nobles and Jewish heiresses, but in general Jews in central Europe were more likely to be frustrated in their social ambitions than the wealthy Jews in western Europe. In matters of social behaviour the gentile bourgeoisie followed the example of the upper class, and in central Europe mixing with Jews could threaten their own often precarious social position or social aspirations. As noted, social exclusion of Jews was often legitimised by reference to Jewish religio-cultural particularism, and many Jews strove to overcome what they perceived as the major obstacle to social acceptance and honour. In fact, reformed Jews remained social outsiders, and even conversion did not guarantee social acceptance, at least for the first-generation convert; but most central European Jews remained optimistic that they would in time achieve social integration.

Unlike the ascriptive European stratification systems, which left little doubt where people should be 'placed', the emphasis on achievement and equality of opportunity in the United States gave rise to uncertainty over status position, and this in turn produced 'other-directedness' or conformism. As a highly upwardly mobile group, who were neither Anglo-Saxon nor Protestants, the Jews were particularly sensitive to the opinions of others, and this sensitivity increased from the 1870s when Jews became subject to many forms of discrimination. Short of conversion, most American Jews were intent on reducing the differences between their Judaism and the dominant expressions of American culture.

The English and French stratification systems were neither as closed as the central European systems nor as open as the American system. The rich English and French Jews, who provided the lay leaders of the communities, were accepted within aristocratic circles on a pluralistic basis, at least as far as a specifically religious identity was concerned. Social acceptance was particularly extensive in England where the upper class retained its dominant position by incorporating and absorbing the *haute bourgeoisie,* gentile and Jew, and where middle-class English Jews also mixed socially in middle-class gentile circles. In this situation there was little pressure on the Jews to 'prove' their Englishness by removing the particularistic prayers from the religious service. In France the very few titled Jews were accepted into the upper class, but the situation of the non-titled wealthy and middle-class Jews was more ambiguous; they were accepted more than in Germany but not quite as openly as in England. Religious acculturation was more extensive in France than in England, if only in form, but in addition the French Jews had a respectable secularist option which was not so readily available in England; if comparatively little change was made in the content of the French services, one reason was that most French Jews displayed little interest in religion and very rarely attended the synagogue. In England, on the other hand, it was possible for a rich Jew to mix in gentile circles and retain an adherence to, and involvement in, Orthodox Judaism, at least with respect to the synagogue service. A few upper-class English Jews also practised an Orthodox level of observance outside the synagogue, although this was rare.

The differences in the social position of the native communities also influenced their response to the eastern European immigrants. Everywhere the reaction of native Jews was negative, but they differed in the extent to which they either distanced themselves from the immigrants or attempted to absorb them within the established community. In Germany the native Jews were openly antagonistic toward the immigrants whom they saw as threatening their already precarious position and providing material for anti-semitic propaganda. In France, where immigration was mounting at the time of the Dreyfus *affaire* and anti-semitic outbreaks, the native Jews dissociated themselves from the immigrants. In the United States, where immigration was also increasing when discrimination was becoming a serious problem, the native Jews attempted to Americanise the immigrants, but they made no effort to incorporate the immigrants into their religious associations, and their further religious reforms accentuated the differences between immigrant and native Judaism. In England, the native Jews, as elsewhere, proclaimed their differences, and maintained a high social distance from the immigrants, but they attempted to anglicise the immigrants and to incorporate them into the religious and other institutions of the native community.

5 From World War I to The Present Day: Continental Europe

Migration and dispersion from 1918

The distribution of the world Jewish population has changed dramatically since 1918: European Jewry has greatly diminished as a result of emigration and the Holocaust; the United States has replaced Russia as the country with the largest Jewish population; and the new state of Israel has become the second largest Jewish community in the world. (See Appendix 1, Table C.) The slower but continuing rise of the North American Jewish population was due more to natural increase than to immigration. The immigrant restriction acts of 1921 and 1924 ended the period of mass emigration from eastern Europe to the United States; a total of 160,000 European Jews, including over 97,000 from Germany, emigrated to the United States between 1933 and 1944, and a further 105,000 emigrated in the years after the war. [1] England also restricted immigration after World War I, and in the inter-war years eastern European Jews turned to other western European countries, South America, and Palestine. In the 1930s, many central European Jews migrated to Palestine, and after the war they were joined by the remnants of the Holocaust communities.

The Jewish population of the Soviet Union is to-day the third largest in the world. In recent years many thousands of Soviet Jews have been allowed to emigrate to Israel, and although many others wish to leave, there is little doubt that the great majority wish to remain. The major migration in the post-war period has been from Islamic countries to Israel and France. The

132

immigration of North African Jews to France has increased the country's Jewish population to 550,000, the fourth largest in the world. The only other large Jewish community in non-Communist Europe is the British community with 410,000 Jews; this is now the sixth largest community in the world, following Argentina with approximately 500,000 Jews.

Inter-war continental Europe

Prior to World War I eastern European Jewry had remained culturally distinctive from the non-Jewish environment, but it had become increasingly divided between the religious traditionalists and the secularist Jewish nationalists. In the inter-war period this situation of a cultural sub-society, itself divided along a religious-secularist dimension, continued in newly independent Poland, but in Russia the cultural orientations of the Jewish population were radically changed by the wider societal transformations.

In Poland, where the Jews numbered nearly 3,510,000 in 1939, the major conflict between religious traditionalists (a large proportion were hassidim) and secular Zionists and Socialists was institutionalised in the separate Jewish political parties; in the 1926 elections in twenty-six major Jewish communities, 39 per cent of the elected council members belonged to Agudat Israel, the religious party, and 54 per cent belonged to the Zionist parties. Whether they were traditionalists or secularists, the vast majority of Polish Jews remained socially apart from the gentiles; over three-quarters considered Yiddish their first language and they had their own educational system, communal organisation, youth movements, press, theatre, etc. The treatment of the Jews in post-1918 Poland made the assimilationist position appear unrealistic; Poland had signed minority clauses giving the Jews full civil equality, but these proved worthless, and political anti-semitism, economic boycotts against Jewish shopkeepers, official anti-Jewish economic measures, and pogroms occurred throughout the period. Anti-semitic measures were supported by the growing Christian trading class who found themselves in competition with the large Jewish trading class, the vast majority of whom were very poor *petite bourgeoisie*. Although the percentage of Jews among those engaged in trade and industry fell, it still remained high. In 1931 4.3 per cent of occupied Jews were in agriculture, 42.2 per cent were in manufacture, and 36.6 per cent were in trade; the respective figures for the non-Jewish population were 61.4, 19.4, and 6.1 per cent. The Jews owned 74,000 shops as against 123,000 shops owned by non-Jews, and the number of Jewish merchants was twenty times larger than the number of non-Jewish merchants. Seventy-six per cent of Polish Jews lived in urban districts and they constituted 30.1 per cent of the population of Warsaw, 35.5 per cent in Lodz, and 31.9 per cent in Lwow.[2] Thus, although capitalism and a Christian bourgeoisie were developing in Poland in the inter-war years, the country was still predominantly agricultural, and the Jews continued as a socially distinct, urban, middleman class.

In contrast to Poland, where the continued separation of the Jews meant that the conflict between the traditionalists and secularists remained internal to the Jewish sub-society, in the Soviet Union the traditionalists were attacked by Jewish secularists who were organised and supported by the state. In line with their secularist monopolism, the Russian authorities initiated a campaign against the Jewish religion, and, in an attempt not to encounter the charge of anti-semitism, they entrusted the campaign to the *Evsektsiia,* the Jewish section of the Communist party. In the early 1920s the *Evsektsiia* carried out many anti-religious activities including articles attacking Judaism in the Jewish press, lectures in work places, public debates, elaborate show trials of religious functionaries and observances, demonstrations outside synagogues, and free lunches on Yom Kippur. Religious activities were hindered or made impossible by many new laws; the *kehillot* were dissolved, synagogues were forcibly seized, ritual objects were confiscated, religious schools were closed, books in Hebrew and religious instruction to persons under eighteen years were made illegal, and rabbis were deprived of political rights. For many Jews it became economically necessary to work on the Sabbath and the High Holy Days, and a variety of social and political pressures were brought to bear on Jews who sent their children to *cheder* or attended synagogue themselves. Despite the anti-religious propaganda and measures, religion remained important for most Russian Jews, especially those in the small towns, up to about 1930. In the 1920s *chedarim* and *yeshivot* continued an underground existence, and in the Ukraine the number of synagogues fell very slightly from 1,034 in 1917 to 934 in 1929–30. [3]

It was not the anti-religious campaigns of the *Evsektsiia* but the absorption of the Jews in an industrialising society which secularised Russian Jewry. The nationalisation of trade and industry destroyed the economic livelihood of most Jews and brought to an end their distinctive socio-economic situation. At first there was little alternative employment, and many perished, but. from 1929 rapid industrialisation provided new opportunities for employment. [4] Unemployed youths migrated from the *shtetls* of the former pale to the large cities in central Russia [5] where, as workers in the factories or clerks in administration and industry, they were no longer separated from the non-Jewish population. The *shtetls* disintegrated under the impact of industrialisation and urbanisation, the Jews were dispersed over a wide area, in the cities they were no longer concentrated in ethnic neighbourhoods, and Jewish youth was now socialised in Soviet schools and in the Pioneers and *Komsomol* organisations. This rapid absorption into Soviet society inevitably resulted in a high level of acculturation. Furthermore, the monopolistic disposition of the Communists removed the possibility of accommodating Judaism to the new conditions; in an officially atheistic society the secularisation process was more encompassing. [6] The least acculturated and assimilated Jews, who remained in the former pale, [7] were reinforced by a Jewish population of 2 million in the territories gained by Russia in 1939–40, but soon afterwards the communities in western Russia were destroyed by the German invaders.

As in Poland, in Hungary and the territories which had been transferred from Hungary to Czechoslovakia the Jews continued to represent a large, though declining, proportion of the commercial and industrial classes. Hungarian Jewry differed from the communities in Poland and the territories Hungary had lost to Czechoslovakia and Rumania, however, in its wealth, its important upper-middle commercial and professional class, the assimilation of both its working and middle classes into the gentile population, its secularisation, and its adherence to Liberal, as opposed to Orthodox, forms of religion. [8] In the western provinces of Czechoslavia (Bohemia, Moravia, Silesia), Austria, Germany, and western Europe the Jews were also concentrated in commerce and industry but, in contrast to eastern Europe, they represented only a small proportion of the urban middle classes. Only in certain professions such as medicine, dentistry, and law, in certain cities such as Berlin and Vienna, did the Jews represent a significant proportion of the total. [9]

The high rate of intermarriage in central Europe in the inter-war period [10] indicates that at least certain gentile circles now accepted the Jews socially, but the growth of a virulent racial anti-semitism led to a decline in the number of Jews who espoused the assimilationist position and an increase in the number of Zionists. Religious differences within the Jewish communities declined in importance as the majority group increasingly emphasised the importance of 'national' or 'racial' differences rather than religio-cultural ones. In the Berlin Jewish communal elections in 1920 the Conservative and Liberal religious sections issued a combined list of candidates to oppose the Jewish National Party (Zionists) who wanted to replace a religiously-defined community by a nationally-defined one; a vigorous electoral campaign ended with the election of four Liberals, four Conservatives and four Zionists. [11] In 1925 the voters of the Federation of Prussian Jewish communities elected seventy-one Liberals, thirty-one Zionists, fourteen Orthodox, five Religious Centre Party, and two Polai Zion community officers. [12] By 1930 the 'German Jew of the Mosaic Persuasion' had declined considerably in number; the strongly anti-Zionist Union for Liberal Judaism had a membership of only 10,000 in 1933, and the extreme assimilationist organisation, the Association of National-German Jews, formed in 1921, which called upon Jews to acknowledge the truth of some anti-semitic charges, remained very small. [13]

In France, where anti-semitism was less important than in Germany, the native Jews continued to assert the assimilationist position and remained hostile to Zionism. French Jewry was still very much divided between the predominantly middle-class native Jews, mainly of Alsation descent, and the predominantly lower-class east European immigrants who increased in number by about 80,000 between 1918 and 1939. [14] However, whether the central and western European native Jews remained assimilationists or turned to Jewish nationalism, there was little change in their religious practices. By 1918 religious observance was minimal, and, if anything, declined further in the inter-war years; even the rites of passage, such as circumcision, *barmitzvah,* religious marriage, and burial were ignored by a large minority in some communities. [15] There was also little change in the forms of Judaism; in central Europe the majority of native congregations were Liberal or Reform while in western and southern Europe decorous Orthodoxy remained the predominant form. Attendance at synagogue was so small that few concerned themselves with changes in the content or form of the services.

Post-war continental Europe

The Holocaust and the creation of the state of Israel strengthened Jewish identity, but while in western Europe this identity could now be freely expressed, in the Soviet Union the authorities denied the legitimacy of either a religious or a secularist Jewish culture. The Germans had destroyed the more traditionalist Jewish population in the western areas of Russia, and from 1948 the Soviet authorities concentrated on the suppression of the secular Yiddish culture. In 1948 all remaining Jewish organisations and Yiddish publications were closed down, and, in the following years, persons active in Yiddish culture and literature were either executed or imprisoned. At first the authorities paid less attention to the Jewish religion, which they believed was disappearing anyway, but the campaign against Judaism resumed in the early 1950s and was intensified after 1959. Religious observances, such as circumcision and eating unleavened bread on Passover, which were perceived as symbolic expressions of Jewish nationalism, were attacked and prohibited, and most synagogues were forced to close. In 1966 only sixty-two synagogues remained and half of these were located in the non-European parts of the country where only 10 per cent of Soviet Jews lived. The Soviet authorities concentrated on attacking religion among the western Jews since the 'Oriental' Jews were more defiant in defence of their religious institutions and their religion was perceived as less intimately related with a separate national consciousness. [16]

European Russian Jews are today predominantly found in white-collar occupations, the professions, engineering, science, and retailing, and the majority are highly assimilated within Russian society. [17] It is likely that the majority would have become highly secularised even if the authorities had not applied pressures, but there is little doubt that the sharp decline of religious institutions was primarily the result of official measures. It is also the case, however, that the discrimination against Jews in certain occupational spheres, such as in the party bureaucracy, and the attacks on Jewish religion and culture, produced a more intensive sense of ethnic identity among a large section of Russian Jewry, and that since no Jewish secular institutions are left, the few remaining synagogues have become the focus of this identity. The synagogues are full on the High Holy Days, and the festival of *Simchat Torah* has in the last ten years become an important holiday when Jewish youth go to the synagogues to sing Hebrew and Yiddish songs. The non-observance of other festivals, such as *Chanukah* and *Purim,* suggests that the religious festivals which are observed express an ethnic or national identity rather than a distinctively religious one. [18]

138

Outside the Communist countries, most European Jews are now able to express their Jewish identity without the fear that this will compromise their status or social acceptance within the non-Jewish world. The decline of both cultural and racial anti-semitism in the post-war period has meant that the western Jews no longer have to consider their Jewish and non-Jewish identities in either/or terms; they can comfortably remain Jews and full citizens of their respective countries. Although social discrimination has by no means disappeared in all social circles, all forms of discrimination are much reduced, and it is now rare for social acceptance to be made conditional on religio-cultural conformity. As a result of this more extensive pluralism, the classical Jewish assimilationist position has nearly disappeared, but assimilation as a fact, as opposed to an ideology, has increased. Assimilation is now less a conscious act, or series of acts, to replace an identity and milieu by another; it is rather a consequence of social interaction between secularised Jews and non-Jews who differ little in their beliefs and behaviour. In this situation the smallest communities are likely to be the most assimilated, and if we take the intermarriage rate as the clearest indication of assimilation, this is seen to be the case: in Denmark, which had a Jewish population of 5,499 in 1970, three-quarters of the married Jews have a non-Jewish partner; in Holland, with a Jewish population of 29,675 in 1966, the intermarriage rate was 39 per cent; in Britain, with a Jewish population of 410,000 in 1965, the relationship between marriages and deaths in 1960–5 suggests that the intermarriage rate was between a quarter and a third; in the United States the overall current rate of intermarriage is about 30 per cent but it is much higher in some of the smaller communities. [19]

Although most western Jews, however assimilated, now feel little inhibition or embarrassment in acknowledging their Jewish identity, the communities differ in the extent to which this identity is expressed in religious or secular forms. The French Jewish community, the second largest in Europe, is among the most secular.

The east Europeans in Paris, both first and second generation, appear to have been more secularised than those in London or New York. Although they concentrated in certain streets, there was no area in Paris where the Jews constituted a majority, and since the eastern European Jews had little contact with native French Jews, the major influence upon them was the secularist French urban working-class milieu. [20] Evidence for this was provided by a study carried out in 1956–8 in the working-class district of Belleville, where the 11,000 Jews constituted about 5.5 per cent of the population. The author, Charlotte Roland, found that the majority of the first generation subscribed to a Jewish burial association and many commemorated the anniversary of the death of their parents, but hardly any conformed to strict religious observance and only a small minority observed important festivals such as Passover. There were some differences between those who had immigrated before 1914 and those who had immigrated after 1919. The former, who were more likely to have emigrated from a small town, were more observant in, for example, keeping Yom Kippur, than the latter, who were more likely to have emigrated from an eastern European city. The pre-1914 immigrants had discarded observances as impractical when they found that they had to work on Sabbath and could not afford to buy kosher meat; the post-1919 immigrants had deliberately rejected religious observances as part of a way of life from which they wished to escape. Since the second generation did not have to revolt against imposed religious prescriptions, there were few ideological secularists among them, but hardly any kept even a minimum of religious practices; only a minority attended synagogue on the High Holy Days and only one tenth abstained from working on Yom Kippur. Roland argued that although the second generation retained a pride in their ethnic identity, they rejected the cultural past of their parents, took non-religious gentiles as their models, and had no wish to adopt religious practices which would distinguish them from other Frenchmen. [21]

The new immigration from North Africa has changed the demographic and social profile of French Jewry. The native Jews are now concentrated in Paris and in the middle and upper-middle classes. The North African immigrants are more widely dispersed throughout France, and, although they have also been highly mobile, they are more socially diversified in both the middle and working classes. The French community has not, however, divided between natives and North Africans; the more occidental of the North African Jews chose to emigrate to France rather than Israel, and their high level of acculturation enabled them to assimilate into the native Jewish population. [22] Native Jewish organisations have sought the membership of North African Jews; the *Consistoire,* for example, established nine new synagogues in the suburbs of Paris between 1959 and 1964 for the new immigrants.

No more than a quarter of French Jews are members of a religious organisation. The *Consistoire,* with its acculturated form of Orthodoxy, has remained the primary Jewish religious organisation in France, but although it now expresses a stronger ethnic identity and has extended its functions by adding community centres to its synagogues, its membership has remained very low. In Paris, where about half of French Jewry lives, the number of *Consistoire* members is about 9,000, and, excluding Alsace-Lorraine, the total membership of the provincial *consistoires* is about the same. [23] Outside the context of the *Consistoire* there are small groups of traditionalists and liberals. In 1962 the federation of traditionalist organisations, *le Conseil representatif du Judaisme traditionaliste de France,* included two synagogues in Paris, and there were also a number of independent Sephardi, Polish, and hassidic groups. The Liberal congregation in Paris has moved in a conservative direction, abolishing its Sunday services and reintroducing prayers in Hebrew, but it continues in a small synagogue with about 600 members. [24]

A number of surveys have found that a comparatively large proportion of French Jews regard themselves as free-thinkers or agnostics but that this does not necessarily mean that they disregard all religious observance. [25] An extensive survey by Memmi *et al* of Jews in the Paris region in 1967 found that one-fifth of the sample observed many religious practices,

141

one-fifth observed no practices, and the majority observed certain rituals, religious marriage, circumcision, and Yom Kippur, which signified an identity with the Jewish community. There were strong correlations between level of religious observance and membership of a religious organisation, European or North African origin, and socio-economic status. There was little difference between Europeans and North Africans with respect to the observance of a religious marriage and circumcision, but with respect to ritual which required frequent observance, such as *kashrut* and regular synagogue attendance, the Europeans were much less observant than the North Africans. The most observant of the occupational groups, among both Europeans and North Africans, were the artisans and small and middle merchants, the least observant were the intellectual and professional occupations, and in-between were the manual workers and lower white-collar workers. The authors argued that the extent of social ties and participation in the ethnic group was the thread which linked the various correlations together. The North African community had tighter boundaries than the European, and those in professional occupations were more likely to work and live in a non-Jewish milieu than the artisans and merchants.

Many French investigators have found that religious non-observance does not necessarily imply a weak Jewish identity; most respondents stated a preference for marriage with another Jew, and the majority identified strongly with Israel. Memmi *et al* found, however, that the relationship between religious observance and expression of a Jewish identity was stronger for the North Africans than for the Europeans. Among the Europeans the strength of expression of Jewish identity varied relatively little with their level of observance, but among the North Africans a fall in the level of observance was accompanied by a sharp drop in the sense of Jewish identity. There were also differences between the occupational groups: the European small merchants and artisans were closer to the North Africans' pattern than the other European groups, and, among the North Africans, the correlation between identity and

142

observance was particularly strong for the professionals. The major difference between the North Africans and European patterns was explained by reference to their past socio-cultural environments. In Europe, as Jews passed from the traditionalist society to a more secular one, there was a process of differentiating social and cultural definitions of the group from religious ones, and many Jews redefined their belonging to the group in the non-religious terms. In North Africa the Jews inhabited widely divergent socio-economic environments, and with the decline of the local structures, only religious tradition survived as a point of common anchorage. The immigration to France accelerated the abandonment of tradition among the North Africans, and the ties to the community were relaxed at the same time. Thus, although, in general, the North Africans have a higher observance pattern and a stronger sense of Jewish identity, if we restrict the comparison to those who have a low observance pattern, it is the North Africans who are more likely to have a weak sense of Jewish indentity. [26]

6 From World War I to The Present Day: United States and Britain

Demographic and social background

There are good reasons for giving special attention to a comparison of religious developments in the British and North American communities in this period. Both communities fell outside the area of the Holocaust, and unlike the large communities in Israel, France, and the Argentine, the vast majority of British and North American Jews are now native-born descendants of eastern European Jews who emigrated between 1880 and 1920. As in other communities, Jewish identity in Britain and America was strengthened by the Holocaust, and by the creation of Israel and the wars which followed, but the comparative demographic continuity of the two populations permits a more limited comparison of the relationship between religious developments and socio-cultural factors.

Three interrelated changes in the social profile of English and American Jewry provide an important background for an understanding of religious change: the decline in the first generation, occupational mobility, and the movement from immigrant areas in the central cities to the suburbs. The decline in immigration after World War I changed the generational profile of both countries. Only 9 per cent of British-Jewish marriage partners were born abroad in 1964 compared with 17 per cent in 1934 and 71 per cent in 1904. [1] In the United States, the proportion of foreign-born adults is now in the 20 to 30 per cent range in middle size and larger communities and very low in the smaller communities. [2] Jewish occupational mobility has been high in both countries. The general trend has been away from wage-earning in the traditional Jewish trades, such as tailoring, to white-collar work and the professions. A study of the Jews in Edgware, a suburb of London, in 1963, found that 1.8 per cent of respondents were unskilled or semi-skilled wage-earners, compared with 17 per cent of their parents; 42 per cent of respondents and 21 per cent of their parents were employers or managers; and 15.5 per cent were professionals compared with 3.9 per cent of their parents. [3] A survey of New York Jews in 1935 found that half of the first generation were manual workers, one-third owned their own businesses or were managers, one-tenth were clerks and less than one-twentieth were professionals, but 60 per cent of the second generation were in 'clerical and kindred' work. By the 1950s, the proportion of Jews in manual occupations had declined considerably; two-thirds of the Jews in New York were in non-manual occupations and, in the communities outside New York, the proportion in non-manual occupations was generally much higher. In the 1950s and 1960s, there was a rise in the proportion of professionals and a fall in the proportion of Jews in small trade and lower white-collar occupations. New York still has a sizeable Jewish lower-middle class, but, in general, the American Jewish population today is predominantly middle and upper-middle class. [4]

Jewish migration from the first areas of settlement to the better neighbourhoods of the cities occurred in the inter-war years, but migration to the suburbs was very much a post-World War II phenomenon. In the inter-war years the New York Jews migrated from the Lower East Side to the better parts of Manhattan and the adjoining boroughs of the Bronx, Brooklyn and, to a lesser extent, Queens. In the post-war period the Jewish population of the Bronx and Brooklyn declined while greater numbers migrated to Queens and the outer suburbs, such as Nassau and Westchester counties. The East End of London contained the largest concentration of London Jewry up to World War II, but wartime evacuations from London and the bombing accelerated the already quickening migration from the area, and, by 1949, the Jews in the East End accounted for less than a tenth of the total London Jewish population. In the inter-war years the most popular second area of settlement for East End Jews was north and north-east London, but in the post-war period there was a substantial migration from these areas to the more prosperous area of north-west London and the outer suburbs. This process of migration from the inner city 'ghettos' to the suburbs can also be traced in other large Jewish urban communities such as Leeds and Manchester in England and Boston and Chicago in the United States.

Synagogue affiliation

In both Britain and the United States, the migration to the suburbs and occupational mobility were paralleled by a rise in the proportion of Jews affiliated to a synagogue. The proportion of the London Jewish population affiliated to a synagogue increased from between one-third and two-fifths in 1930 to 61 per cent in 1960–65.[5] There are no accurate statistics for the provinces but the evidence suggests that synagogue affiliation may be higher than in London. In the United States statistics are not complete enough to allow us to make exact comparisons over time, but there is little doubt about the general trend: the proportion of American Jews affiliated to a synagogue remained fairly stable in the inter-war period, increased rapidly in the post-war period until about 1960, and remained fairly stable at a comparatively high level in the 1960s. The proportion rose from between a quarter and a third in 1939 to about 50 per cent in the late 1950s and 1960s, but the proportion varies quite considerably from between a 25 to 55 per cent range in large cities to a 55 to 90 per cent range in smaller cities, towns, and suburbs.[6]

In the United States the rise in affiliation to a religious organisation has not been peculiar to the Jewish population. From statistics given in the Yearbook of American Churches, it has been estimated that the proportion of church members in America rose from 43 per cent in 1920 to 47 per cent in 1930, dropped to 41 per cent in 1940, and then rose again to 57 per

cent in 1950, 60 per cent in 1955, and 66 per cent in 1966. [7]
These figures might appear to provide evidence for Will
Herberg's contention that joining a synagogue has become a
means of self-identification for the American Jew, both as a Jew
and as an American. Herberg stated that the three basic faiths in
America had become integrated as parts of the 'American Way
of Life'. Among other things, this means that, in order to be
considered a 'good' American, it is necessary to be affiliated to,
and identify with, one of the three faiths. Religion is regarded as
'a good thing', no matter which particular faith it is. Thus,
American Christians expect Jews to be affiliated to a synagogue,
just as they expect other Christians to be affiliated to a church. [8]
It is probable that the high church affiliation and interest in
religion among non-Jewish Americans provides a favourable
environment for Jewish synagogue affiliation and involvement,
but it is doubtful whether the non-Jewish religious 'revival' is a
sufficient or even a necessary condition for the rise in synagogue
affiliation. The evidence from England suggests that it is not a
necessary condition. In England, church affiliation and interest
in the churches has been falling among the majority of the
population for a long period, but the rise in synagogue affiliation
has paralleled that of America. Joining a synagogue in England
is not a means of self-identification as an Englishman; it is only
a means of identifying as a Jew.

Similar social and cultural changes in the American and
English Jewish populations have led to a similar result.
Migration from the predominantly Jewish to non-Jewish areas,
mobility from the traditional Jewish trades to occupations where
many work associates and colleagues are gentiles, and adoption
of the language and cultural patterns of the dominant society
have made the question of the continuation of Jewish identity a
more problematic one. In the immigrant areas of the cities,
where the majority of a Jew's neighbours and work associates
were Jewish and where a Yiddish culture, both religious and
secular, was prominent, the question of a continuing attachment
to the Jewish group was less likely to arise. In the suburbs, on
the other hand, the need of most Jews to acknowledge formally

147

their Jewish identity and instil a sense of Jewish identity in their children is expressed by joining a synagogue and sending their children to the congregational religious classes. This explains why synagogue affiliation in the United States is highest in the small communities (eg 87 per cent in Flint, Michigan, where the Jewish population is under 3,000), lower in communities of intermediate size (eg 78 per cent in Providence, Rhode Island), and lowest in the large cities (eg 53 per cent in Boston and 27.2 per cent in Los Angeles). The smaller the community, the greater the threat of assimilation, and the higher the symbolic significance of synagogue membership.[9] Many Jews do not attempt to conceal their 'non-religious' reasons for joining a synagogue. In 'Lakeville', 'parental status and the consequent sense of responsibility for Jewish continuity is readily acknowledged as a reason for affiliation, especially by those who are religiously alienated'.[10] In three New Jersey suburbs, only 22.2 per cent of the synagogue members gave 'religious' reasons for affiliation, 26.7 per cent indicated that the main reason was for the 'sake of the children', and 31.1 per cent gave social reasons.[11]

Community surveys in the United States have shown a high correlation between children reaching school age and parents joining a synagogue. In the past the provision of religious education for the young was not an important function of the synagogue; prior to World War I special religious classes were organised in the schools in immigrant areas, but most parents preferred to send their boys to the traditional *chedarim*. The migration from the immigrant areas to the suburbs resulted in a decline in the *chedarim* and the special religious classes, and the provision of religious education was taken over by the synagogues along similar lines to Sunday schools among Christians. In England and America most synagogues accept only the children of members, or charge non-members special fees.

The rate of affiliation falls only slightly, however, after the children have reached post-school age.[12] It is possible that the adult-centred social and other activities in the synagogue assume a greater importance in the leisure-time activities of those parents whose children have left school. Prais and Schmool suggest that many English Jews join a synagogue for the financially beneficial burial rights which accompany membership;[13] in fact, this may be an important reason for *retaining* membership after the children are past school age rather than an important reason for joining in the first place. Other secondary considerations in accounting for the rise in synagogue membership include the rise in real income, which has enabled Jews to pay the high membership fees, and the guarantee of a seat in a synagogue on the High Holy Days.

Religious practices

It has been suggested that membership of a synagogue today appears to signify more a concern with ethnic identity than a specifically religious commitment. There is certainly no evidence pointing to a rise in synagogue attendance in the post-war period. The pattern of majority attendance on the High Holy Days and very low weekly Sabbath attendance which became common in the nineteenth century has continued up to the present day. Krausz found that, in 1963, 13.6 per cent of the adult Jews in Edgware attended synagogue once a week, 31.4 per cent attended on festivals and some other occasions, 42.5 per cent attended only on the High Holy Days, and 12.5 per cent never attended.[14] A British National Opinion Poll reported in 1971 that 15 per cent of its Jewish sample attended synagogue weekly or more, 87 per cent observed Yom Kippur and 86 per cent observed Rosh Hashanah. These attendance patterns are similar to those found in the United States, (see Appendix 1, Table D) and the proportion who attend weekly is very close to weekly church attendance in England (about 15 per cent). In the United States, however, church attendance is much higher: in 1959 74 per cent of American Catholics and 40 per cent of American Protestants attended church weekly, but only 18 per cent of American Jews attended synagogue weekly.[15]

Public prayer is, of course, only one of a large number of religious observances enjoined upon the Jew. Surveys in

England and America have found that rituals which require regular attention or are inconsistent with 'modern' living are observed by only a small minority. Very few men put on *tefillin* (phylacteries worn during weekday morning prayers) and most Jews do not avoid riding on the Sabbath. Most Jewish families keep at least some of the dietary laws at home, but only a small minority abstain from eating non-kosher food outside the home. Rituals which involve voluntary segregation from the 'host' society are observed only by a minority, but other rituals, which are performed in the home and centre on the family, are observed by the majority or a large proportion. An example of a popular ritual is the lighting of Sabbath candles on Friday night. Apart from the High Holy Days, the most popular festivals are those which involve family and children celebrations, such as Passover, with its *Seder* night meal, and *Chanukah,* with its candle lighting and children's parties. (See Appendix 1, Tables E and F).

The majority of English and American Jews observe the religious rites of passage: most Jewish couples marry in synagogues; most Jews have a religious burial; a large proportion observe some of the observances enjoined on members of a family after a death; most Jewish boys of thirteen years have a *barmitzvah,* and the non-traditional *batmitzvah* ceremony for girls has become popular, especially in America. For the majority, the *barmitzvah* no longer has significance as a ceremony to mark the beginning of the adult male's religious obligations, but as a social occasion and as a ceremonial confirmation of group identity the *barmitzvah* has grown in importance.

The secularisation of the synagogues

The synagogue is used infrequently by most members for worship, but many parents join in order that their children should attend the congregational classes, absorb a sense of Jewish identity, and associate with other Jewish children. In addition to the provision of religious education for children, the synagogues have extended their functions to include facilities for

150

social and recreational activities. In 1944 the Welfare Committee of the London United Synagogue argued that 'the synagogue should be the pivot of all activities: religious, educational, cultural and recreational', and it recommended that all United synagogues should have meeting rooms and club rooms in order to 'provide more fully for enlisting the interests and support of the younger generation'. A youth committee was appointed at every synagogue to assist, co-ordinate and promote the youth groups and their activities, and in a few synagogues special youth ministers were appointed.

The provision of social facilities was not limited to youth. In a memorandum to the United Synagogue in 1945, a rabbi wrote that the destruction of European Jewry made the survival of Anglo-Jewry a 'dire necessity', and one means of survival was to educate the Jewish public 'to regard the Synagogue not solely as a devotional institution to be visited once a year, or even once a week, but as a focal point of all communal activity'. A Synagogue Community Centres Scheme was instituted to provide large social and communal halls, attached to the synagogues, for educational, social, cultural and recreational activities.[16] Lay leaders recognised the community halls as an important aspect of the synagogue's institutional survival and expansion, and many British congregations have built communal halls, but in general English synagogues have not become such important centres of social activity as the synagogues in America.

Most American synagogues have many auxiliaries or clubs organised along lines of sex (brotherhoods, sisterhoods), age and marital status (youth, singles, young couples, and senior citizens clubs), and interests. The auxiliary organisations of the Reform temples have both increased their representation on the temples' boards and committees and taken over much of the planning and provision of synagogue activities from the temple boards and programme committees. The following table[17] gives the programme content of the auxiliaries of 113 Reform temples which responded to a questionnaire from the central Reform organisation.

151

	Percentage of meetings devoted to		
	General culture	Jewish culture	Entertainment and soc
Mens' associations	40	24	36
Sisterhoods	38	38	24
Couples' clubs	31	27	42
Single adults	29	23	48

Apart from the sisterhoods, which devoted over a third of their meetings to Jewish culture, only a quarter of temple club meetings were devoted to Jewish culture. Since non-religious Jewish topics were no doubt included under the heading 'Jewish culture', it appears that only a very few temple club meetings were concerned with specifically religious matters. By all accounts, the Conservative synagogues have a similar scale of activities. A content analysis of 300 Conservative synagogue bulletins found that 75 per cent of their space dealt with synagogue organisational activities, 10 per cent was devoted to advertising, 5 per cent contained a message from the rabbi or a summary of his sermon, and 10 per cent was given to listing the donors of the various synagogue funds. [18] In three New Jersey suburbs, where all three synagogues were Conservative, respondents were asked to list the synagogue activities in which they were most interested: 30.2 per cent chose social activities, 22.7 per cent chose the Hebrew school, 19.1 per cent chose the religious services, 9.2 per cent chose adult education, 12.9 per cent chose congregational meetings, and 5.9 per cent chose adult sports. [19]

The sisterhoods are the most numerous and largest of the temple or synagogue clubs, and they often wield a great deal of power in the congregations. It is not unusual for a sisterhood to be formed before a congregation in a new suburb or for the number of sisterhood members to outnumber the members of the synagogue. Given the high degree of acculturation of suburban Jews, the importance of the sisterhood is hardly surprising; the women remain in the suburbs during the day, and they generally have more leisure time to devote to synagogue activities. The sisterhoods have instrumental goals, such as fund-raising for the synagogue and charities, but their major function is to provide a context for social activity: 'weekly bridge parties, luncheons, dances ... fashion shows, skits, bingo nights and penny auctions ... book reviews, cooking classes, musical programs'. [20]

The emphasis on secular activities in the synagogue has had repercussions on the timetable and content of the religious services. In the majority of both Reform and Conservative synagogues, the non-traditional late Friday evening service has come to replace the Saturday morning services as the major weekly religious service. In 1950, in reply to a questionnaire sent out to a national sample of Conservative synagogue members, 40 per cent wrote that they never attended Sabbath morning services, but only 7 per cent wrote that they never attended Friday evening services, and half of the respondents wrote that they attended the Friday evening service 'often' or 'quite regularly'. The much longer Sabbath morning services were more traditional and geared to the older members of the congregations, while the Friday evening services were more Americanised, pulpit-centred family services, with a predominance of women in attendance. The comparative popularity of the Friday evening service may be attributed, in part, to the social hour which follows the service. The rabbi's sermon, which generally took up about a third of the Friday evening service time, was the main attraction for over a third of the Conservative respondents, nearly half thought it was of 'secondary importance', and 12 per cent believed that it was 'not at all important'. The majority of respondents preferred to hear a sermon on the 'general problems of Jewry' rather than one on 'biblical interpretations' or 'religious observances' which were only a little more popular than 'current political and social affairs'. [21] Attempts to revitalise the Sabbath morning services have included centring the services on barmitzvahs and batmitzvahs, dedicating the services to secular organisations, and organising junior congregations. Thus, not only have secular activities come to predominate over religious activities, but the religious activities have themselves been secularised.

Both the rise in synagogue affiliation and the secularisation of the synagogue were related to the decline in non-religious or secular Jewish ideologies and organisations. The Yiddish-speaking culturalists and socialists disappeared with the acculturation and embourgeoisement of American Jews and, with the establishment of the state of Israel, the Zionist organisations became less ideological and concerned almost exclusively with the welfare of the state of Israel. The local affiliates of the service-oriented Zionist and philanthropic organisations of American Jewry function as centres of sociability, but, since the organisations' overt purposes are obviously instrumental, they cannot entirely fulfil the expressive needs of Jewish identification. The non-synagogue community centres were very successful in the inter-war period, but their association with the immigrant settlement houses, from which they had evolved, and with the Americanisation of unacculturated Jews, made them less appealing to the post-war, acculturated, middle-class Jews. Moreover, the synagogue centre had a further advantage over the community centre in that it legitimised ethnic sociability by placing social activities under its religious canopy.

Generation, class, and religious groups

In both Britain and the United States there are proportionally small minorities of hassidic and non-hassidic ultra-Orthodox groups who continue to live in a society where religious law and tradition determines, in large part, residential patterns, economic activities, family life, and education. [22] The hassidim are generally distinguishable from the non-hassidic Orthodox by their appearance (side-locks, uncut beards, traditional eastern European garb) and they are themselves divided into the dynasties of the *zaddikim,* but all the ultra-Orthodox groups tend to concentrate in certain neighbourhoods, such as Williamsburg in New York and Stamford Hill in London, where they represent a minority within a minority, living among or close to a large secularised Jewish population which provides a more immediate negative reference than the non-Jewish society.

154

The ultra-Orthodox are mostly the immigrants of the 1930s and 1940s and their descendants, who preferred to set up their own organisations rather than join the declining Orthodox organisations of the earlier east European immigrants. Their social cohesiveness is dependent upon voluntary commitment to a distinctive religio-culture, and to concomitant social separation, rather than segregation enforced by a majority, and, unlike the earlier Orthodox immigrants, they have had considerable success in retaining the commitment of the second generation. Since they are sheltered from the 'open' society and socialised entirely by Orthodox agencies, the second generation experience little conflict between their parents' religio-culture and the culture of the wider society. The Jewish day schools provide an important socialising agency, and they are staffed by ex-students of the *yeshivot* which are the pivotal organisations of the ultra-Orthodox community.

The number of ultra-Orthodox Jews is much smaller in Britain than in the United States; in London, where they are concentrated, they are associated in a loose union of synagogues, the Union of Orthodox Hebrew Congregations, with a total congregation of about 6,000. The major British synagogue groups are the 'Central Orthodox', the Reform and the Liberals. The 'Central Orthodox' group, which is by far the largest, refers to those congregations which hold modern or decorous Orthodox services but whose members do not, in the majority, observe an Orthodox level of religious practice outside the synagogue. Unlike the Reform and Liberal synagogues, the 'Central Orthodox' synagogues are not organised in a national federation, but in London most 'Central Orthodox' synagogues belong either to the United Synagogue or to the Federation of Synagogues. In the pre-World War I period the United Synagogue represented native Orthodoxy and the Federation represented immigrant Orthodoxy. Today there is little difference either between the form of the religious service in the Federation and the United Synagogue or between the standards of religious observance of the members of the two organisations, but the United Synagogue has benefited more than the

Federation from the demographic and social trends of London Jewry. The following tables[23] show the distribution of the synagogue branches in London from 1920 to 1970.

Number of synagogues

Synagogue group	Year						
	1920	1930	1940	1950	1960	1965	1970
United Synagogue	24	34	54	68	77	79	81
Federation	59	64	66	63	56	50	56
Reform	1	1	3	5	6	10	10
Liberal	1	3	3	7	10	11	12
Union of Orthodox Hebrew Congregations		7	22	44	46	45	42

Male membership (in thousands)

Synagogue group	1930	1970
'Central Orthodox'		
United Synagogue	9-10	30
Federation of Synagogues	6	10
Independent and Sephardim	not known	6
'Ultra-Orthodox'		
Union of Orthodox Hebrew Congregations	½	1½
'Progressive'		
Reform	¾	7
Liberal	1¼	5¼

The male membership of the United Synagogue increased by 150 per cent in the inter-war period, from 6,300 in 1915 to about 15,000 in 1940, and in the twenty-five year period after 1940 the male membership doubled to 31,533 accounting for half of the adult male London Jews who were affiliated to a synagogue of any kind. In comparison, the Federation members accounted for one-fifth and the combined members of the Reform and Liberal synagogues accounted for one-sixth of those affiliated to a synagogue. It is clear that the majority of the second generation who affiliated to a synagogue joined the United Synagogue. They did so because the religious services of the United Synagogue represented a suitable mediation between the more traditional services they had known in the East End *chevrot* and an acculturated form of worship. The United Synagogue enabled the second generation both to become anglicised and to remain formally and officially Orthodox. Although the services in the Federation synagogues came to approximate to the type of services performed in the United synagogues, few Jews in the second and third areas of settlement wished to join an organisation which had been clearly associated with the religio-culture and low status of the first generation. If the Federation was too 'foreign', the services of the Reform and Liberal synagogues were too anglicised for the majority of the second generation, and, from the point of view of social status, they had no advantage over the United Synagogue whose membership included most of the socially esteemed and older-established native Jews.

In the years immediately following World War I there was some desire for changes in the religious services among the seat-holders in the prosperous synagogues in north-west London, where the older-established native Jews were still predominant. In 1922, special confirmation services for girls were introduced, and in 1923 a group of seat-holders suggested to a special committee of the United Synagogue that the segregation of the sexes during services should be abolished and that a congregation should have the right to introduce ritualistic changes, such as the organ and more English, if they were approved by a local majority and the congregation's minister. The suggestions were either overruled by the Committee or defeated at a meeting of United Synagogue seat-holders in 1925, and from then on there were no further demands for changes in an acculturative direction. In some cases, the newer suburban congregations of east European descent did not adopt all the non-traditional practices of the older-established native congregations. For example, a proposal to introduce a mixed choir at the Golders Green Synagogue in 1937 was overwhelmingly defeated at a seat-holders' meeting despite the minister's contention that there was no religious objection to the practice. After 1945, many synagogues discontinued their 'confirmation' services, and substituted male choirs for mixed

157

choirs. In 1963, only four United Synagogues had a mixed choir, and in 1973 the Hampstead Synagogue was the last remaining United synagogue with a mixed choir. [24]

Deacculturation of the United Synagogue's services was paralleled by a deacculturation of the roles and appearance of its ministers. From about 1930 there was an increasing tendency for the United Synagogue ministers, and Anglo-Jewish ministers in general, to model their roles on those of the traditional rabbinate rather than on those of the Christian clergy. At the Conference of Anglo-Jewish ministers in 1958, one rabbi said that religious knowledge was the most desirable qualification of the minister and that they could no longer be satisfied with 'more or less efficient religious functionaries primed chiefly in the practical duties of their office and pastoral methods of preaching, reading the service, congratulating and consoling'. [25] The number of ministers in the United constituent synagogues who had rabbinical diplomas increased from four (out of seventeen) in 1930 to twelve (out of twenty-one) in 1960. Anglo-Jewish ministers have discarded the clerical garb of the acculturated minister. Prior to World War I nearly all the United Synagogue ministers wore canonicals. A photograph of the Anglo-Jewish Preachers (Ministers) Conference in 1935 shows that forty-three out of the fifty-six ministers present wore canonicals, and the majority wore no headgear or beards. No ministers can be seen wearing canonicals in a photograph of the ministers at their conference in 1956, but their heads were covered and many had short or trimmed beards. [26]

Deacculturation within the United Synagogue was related to three developments: the assimilation of the second generation into the organisation, the secularisation of the 'host' society, and the influx of foreign rabbis. In the inter-war years the second generation Jews who joined the organisation accepted the decorous Orthodoxy of the older-established native families, but in the post-war period, when the second generation themselves attained high class and status positions, the importance of the nominally Orthodox but rarely observant older-established native families declined. The leadership of the men from the old

158

native families who, although rarely rigorous in their religious practice, felt it their duty and right to follow their parents and grandparents in the governing of the United Synagogue, gave way to the leadership of the 'new' millionaires from the second generation. The change in the social composition of the leadership was gradual and the old native élite monopolised the top leadership positions long after the majority of wardens and Council members were recruited from the second generation, but in 1962 the election of Isaac Wolfson, a second-generation self-made multi-millionaire, to the presidency of the organisation, marked the end of the rule of the old élite.

Less than 10 per cent of the United Synagogue seat-holders attended the annual meetings of the synagogues, and there were very few contests for wardenships and United Synagogue Council members.[27] The indifference of the majority to synagogue affairs enabled the active, and generally more religious, of the second generation to abandon the non-traditional practices which had been introduced by the older native families, and to return to a more traditional service. Up to about World War I, the church-going middle and upper classes were important religio-cultural models for the middle- and upper-class native Jews, but with the decline in church-going and the importance of the churches in English society, acculturated Jews no longer referred to non-Jewish religious models. There was a decline in the number of Jews who were both acculturated in the religious sphere and active in synagogue affairs, and there was little opposition to the increasingly Orthodox policies of the rabbinate.

From about 1933 an increasing number of new immigrants from central and eastern Europe were employed in ministerial and rabbinical positions by the United Synagogue. Of particular importance was the replacement of native *dayanim* by more traditionalistic rabbis from abroad. The importance and authority of the London *Beth Din* grew considerably after 1939, and the *dayanim*, conscious of their importance as the most important *Beth Din* in Europe, endeavoured 'to apply the full range of *halacha* to the problems of the community'.[28] The

159

dayanim and chief rabbis have used their influence and authority to remove such practices as the mixed choirs, and they have adopted strict policies towards intermarriage and conversion of non-Jews who wish to marry Jews. [29]

It is possible that the Orthodox trend in the United Synagogue may have alienated a number of the more acculturated Jews, especially among the third generation. In the early 1960s the increase in membership began to slow down, and in recent years there has been a decline in membership. Up to the middle 1960s it appeared that the United Synagogue was losing members or potential members to the Reform and Liberal movements. Neither the Reform nor Liberal synagogues attracted a large proportion of the second generation in the inter-war years, but their membership rose at a fast rate in the post-war years up to about 1966. The total Reform and Liberal family membership in London rose from about 6,000 in 1940 to 22,000 in 1960–5. The success of the 'Progressive' congregations in the provinces was particularly striking; between 1949 and 1970 seventeen new synagogues were opened, and of these twelve were Reform or Liberal. Although the total annual average of synagogue marriages has declined since World War II, the annual average of marriages performed in Reform synagogues rose from 130 in 1941–50 to 191 in 1961–5, and the annual average of marriages performed in Liberal synagogues rose from 86 in 1941–50 to 155 in 1961–5. In comparison, the number of synagogue marriages in the 'Central Orthodox' group of synagogues fell from an annual average of 2,660 in 1941–50 to 1,476 in 1961–5. The ratio of marriages to deaths in the Orthodox group of synagogues was 73 per cent in 1961–5 compared with 123 per cent in the Liberal synagogues and 154 per cent in the Reform synagogues. However, the total Liberal-Reform membership in London has risen only slightly since 1965, and between 1967 and 1971 the distribution of marriages between the synagogue groups in Britain has remained virtually unchanged: 82 per cent Orthodox (81 per cent in 1972), 11 per cent Reform (12 per cent in 1972), and 7 per cent Liberal (7 per cent in 1972). [30]

The Liberal movement has continued to represent the most radical departure from traditional Judaism. The Sunday services, which the Liberals began in 1920, as an 'addition to the regular Sabbath service', were very similar in form to Christian services; Hebrew was practically eliminated, and mixed choirs sang Hebrew psalms in English. Before about 1920 the religious services of the West London Reform Synagogue were closer in content and form to the services in the United synagogues than the services in the Liberal synagogue, but in the inter-war years the Reform members adopted a number of ritualistic alterations which brought their services closer to those of the Liberal synagogues. The members of the West London Synagogue passed a resolution, in 1923, to enable men and women to sit together during the services, and the services were revised in 1928 to meet the 'religious needs of the young'; a number of traditional prayers were omitted, and English prayers and an English hymn were introduced. [31] In more recent years the Liberal movement has moved in a more traditional direction, the differences in the religious ideology and practices of the two movements have narrowed, and they have started to co-operate in a number of organisational spheres. In 1964 they joined in the administration and financing of the Leo Baeck (Seminary) College, and since the future ministers of both movements are now trained in the same seminary the differences between the two movements will probably decline still further.

Up to the 1920s the services of the Reform and Liberal synagogues represented, in part, attempts by acculturated Jews to reduce the religious differences between the Jewish and the environmental Christian groups, but with the continuing decline in the importance of institutional religion in England this aspect became less important. The growth of the Reform and Liberal movements after World War II was not the result of a larger number of Jews directly taking the environmental Christian groups as religious models, but was rather an accommodation to an increasingly secular environment. Many Jews may have simply preferred services in English rather than in Hebrew which they could not understand, or, in some cases, read.

161

The majority of the new Reform and Liberal synagogues in London were formed in the outer suburbs, such as Woodford, Southgate, Pinner, Bromley, and Harrow, where the facilities for religious observance, such as a *kosher* butcher, are not so readily available. In Edgware, where a Reform Synagogue was formed in 1932 when there were only a few Jews in the area, Krausz found that fewer Reform members observed the religious practices than United Synagogue or Federation members. For example, only 65 per cent of Reform members fasted on Yom Kippur compared with 90.8 per cent of United Synagogue members. The NOP survey in 1971 found that, while 82 per cent of the United Synagogue members kept a *kosher* home, only 19 per cent of the Reform and Liberal Jews did so; 35 per cent of the United Synagogue members said that they never ate non-*kosher* food compared with 6 per cent of the Reform and Liberal Jews; 68 per cent of United Synagogue members said they drove on the Sabbath compared with 84 per cent of Liberal and Reform members. Although they kept few religious practices, the Reform and Liberal Jews wished to continue to acknowledge their Jewish identity and preferred their children to marry within the Jewish community. The most common reason given by Reform members in Edgware for their affiliation to a synagogue was 'to bring up their children as Jews'. This was also an important reason for United Synagogue members, but more important reasons they gave were their religious beliefs and their religious duty as Jews.

It would appear that the Reform and Liberal synagogues attract the more secularised Jews, who wish to give their children a sense of 'Jewishness', but who wish to avoid a conflict between the beliefs and practices taught at the Orthodox synagogue classes and their own beliefs and non-observance in the home. The re-emphasis on traditional practices in the United Synagogue in the post-World War I period may have persuaded many of the more acculturated and less practising Jews to join the Reform and Liberal movements, but there is no sign that 'Progressive' Judaism will replace the 'Central Orthodox' position as the major Anglo-Jewish religious branch.

The relationship of generation, class, and the different branches of Judaism in America were fairly obvious at the beginning of the twentieth century; the lower-class, unacculturated, first-generation Jews from eastern Europe were associated with Orthodox Judaism, and the middle- and upper-class, acculturated Jews of German descent were associated with Reform Judaism. In the inter-war period, Orthodoxy declined as its first-generation adherents died or moved out of the ghetto; the Conservative movement began to attract many of the second generation and the more acculturated of the first generation; and Reform Judaism ceased to be the exclusive preserve of the Jews of German descent.

The congregations affiliated to the United Synagogue of America (Conservative) grew from the original 24 in 1913, to 211 in 1926, to 260 in 1945, to 508 in 1956, to about 850 in 1970, which, together with another 100 congregations who identified with Conservative Judaism, represented a total congregation of about $1\frac{1}{2}$ millions. [32] The Conservative synagogues attracted the largest number of the socially mobile second generation because they took a middle course between the unacculturated Orthodoxy of the first generation and the extremely acculturated Reform Judaism of the native Jews of German descent. The Conservative services are similar to the services of the London United Synagogue in so far as they represent a change in form rather than content from the traditionalistic services. However, the Conservative congregations differ from the British 'Central Orthodox' congregations in a number of important respects: in the great majority of Conservative synagogues men and women are seated together; and it is common for the Saturday morning service to be supplanted in importance by a special short Friday night service which requires only a minimum familiarity with the Hebrew language and liturgy, includes a sermon as a central feature, and is followed by a 'social hour'. [33]

The Conservative movement developed to fill the void in America between traditional Orthodoxy and radical Reform, but neither Reform nor Orthodoxy remained unaffected by the changing generational and class composition of American Jewry. The congregations affiliated to the Union of American Hebrew Congregations (Reform) rose from 175 in 1910, to 210 in 1920, to 261 in 1930, to 293 in 1940, to 420 in 1950, to 616 in 1960, to nearly 700 in 1970, representing a total congregation of about 1 million. [34] The most socially mobile of the second generation, and even some of the first generation, were attracted to the Reform synagogues, which were associated with the high-status Jews of German descent. A survey conducted by the Union in 1931 found that 70 per cent of its members in the large cities were born in America, but only about 20 per cent were third or subsequent generations, and half of the members were of east European descent. A quarter of the members were university graduates, and of those in occupations, 57 per cent were self-employed, 23 per cent were professional or semi-professional, and 20 per cent were employees. [35]

The influx of the most mobile of the second generation into the Reform synagogues together with the rise of Jewish ethnic feeling in the 1930s in response to prejudice and discrimination, both in Europe and America, led to a religious reorientation of the Reform movement. The universalistic, rationalistic and anti-Zionist stands were modified and an increasing emphasis was put on ceremonialism and Jewish ethnicity. In 1937, the Reform rabbinical association, the Central Conference of American Rabbis, replaced the 'classical' Reform position of the 1887 'Pittsburgh Platform' with the 'Columbus Program' which stressed both the importance of the Torah and the relationship between the Jewish religion and the Jewish 'people'. In 1942, the Conference revised its stands still further, and its approval of Zionism led to a number of rabbis seceding from the Conference to form the American Council for Judaism which continued to uphold the rationalistic, anti-ceremonial and anti-Zionist stands of 'classical' Reform Judaism. The Council attracted little support, however, and the Reform movement continued in a more traditional direction: the Reform prayerbook was revised to incorporate more Hebrew, Zionist hopes and traditional liturgy, a more elaborate ceremonial was introduced for the

164

Sabbath and festival services, and ceremonies were prepared for observance in the homes.[36] The traditional direction of the Reform movement continued in the post-war period and the new members of east European descent raised the average level of ritual observance of the Reform membership. The following table gives the replies to questions on religious observance which were sent out to samples of Reform members in 1931, 1953, and 1970.[37]

	Percentage who observed ritual		
	1931	*1953*	*1970*
Light Sabbath candles	26	59	50
Friday night *Kiddush*	15	26	-
Light *Chanukah* candles	40	81	90
Passover *Seder*	33	74	93

In addition to the changing membership, the deacculturation of American Reform Judaism may also have been related to the decline in the importance of non-Jewish religious models for Americanised Jews. Since Judaism has risen to a position where it is widely accepted as one of the three major American faiths, it is unlikely that any form of Protestantism will be as important a religious referent for acculturated Jews in the twentieth century as liberal Protestantism was for acculturated Jews in the nineteenth.

The second and third generations who joined the Conservative and Reform synagogue were not attracted to the unacculturated Orthodoxy of the first generation, but an acculturated, 'modern' Orthodoxy grew to sizeable proportions in the post-war period. In the inter-war years, Yeshiva College (later University) in New York and the Hebrew Theological College in Chicago trained 'modern' Orthodox rabbis who founded their own rabbinical association, the Rabbinical Council of America. In the post-war period, the rapid growth of the 'modern' Orthodox movement was reflected in the number of congregations which affiliated to the Union of Orthodox Jewish Congregations. There are today approximately 700 congregations in the Union, and it has been estimated that about three-quarters of a million are either affiliated or identify with Orthodoxy.

The committed members of the 'modern' Orthodox movement accept fundamentalist religious beliefs and adhere to the *halakah,* but, unlike the traditionalists or ultra-orthodox, they are acculturated; they permit social and secular activities in the synagogue; their lives are not so strictly governed by religious law; and they associate with non-Orthodox Jews. The majority of Orthodox synagogue members are uncommitted and lax in observance; their involvement is limited to occasional visits to the synagogue. This group includes the remnants of the pre-1930s east European immigrants who are more likely to be older, poorer, and less educated than the majority of American Jews. However, the 'modern' Orthodox synagogues have attracted an increasing number of more affluent, acculturated, non-observant Jews who may have joined because of a nostalgic preference for Orthodox services or because they prefer smaller, more intimate congregations. With the 'modernisation' of Orthodoxy and the related influx of more prosperous Jews into the Orthodox ranks, fewer Jews associated Orthodox membership with low status.[38]

Despite the changes in the generational and socio-economic characteristics of the members of the three branches of Judaism, the Jewish community studies of the 1950s and 1960s continued to find that the Orthodox contained the highest proportion of the first-generation, lower-income and less-educated categories, and the Reform membership contained the highest proportions of the native-born, higher-income and better-educated categories.[39] Recent studies have also shown, however, that the differences in the socio-economic characteristics of the members of the three branches are becoming narrower: there is a greater heterogeneity of class composition within each branch and a greater homogeneity of class composition between the branches. The 'modern' Orthodox synagogues have spread into more affluent areas and their membership is no longer confined to the lower-class category. The Conservative and Reform movements continued to build synagogues in prosperous neighbourhoods but the class composition of their memberships continues to widen. [40]

Parallel to the growing socio-economic homogeneity of the members of the three branches, there has developed a greater variation in synagogue ritual within each branch and a greater overlap of ritual between the three branches. This has been possible because the central offices of the Jewish religious unions have had neither the power nor the desire to draw up fixed rituals to which affiliated synagogues should conform; each individual congregation has been free to work out its own preferred ritual. In the post-war period, the suburban synagogues have shown a great flexibility in constructing their rituals, and, in consequence, there has developed a considerable diffusion of ritual between the three movements. Within single synagogues, a fusion of Orthodox, Conservative, and Reform rituals is sometimes found. [41] Flexibility of ritual has always been a characteristic of the Conservative movement; [42] but in the post-war period, the wide range in ritual also became a characteristic of Orthodox and Reform synagogues.

The majority of synagogues find it advantageous to be affiliated to national denominational organisations, but this affiliation is not always reflected in their synagogue ritual. In new suburbs the need for a synagogue is felt so strongly by Jewish residents that a synagogue is often formed before a decision has been reached on the form of synagogue ritual or denominational affiliation. The primary motive behind the formation of a synagogue in a new suburb is rarely the desire to pray according to a particular interpretation of Judaism but rather the desire for an organisation which will serve as a means for ethnic group association and identity. The reasons suburban Jews join one synagogue rather than another are often not based on ideological or ritual preferences. The cost of membership, the quality and characteristics of the Hebrew school, the social and cultural activities of the congregation, and the class, status, educational, and 'intellectual' levels of the congregations are often more important factors in both the choice of a synagogue and the degree to which members are satisfied with their synagogues. [43] The lack of commitment to the particular branches of Judaism is demonstrated by the financial support given by Jews to religious institutions other than those to which they are affiliated.

Both the diffusion of ritual and the decline in the class differences of the members of the three branches were related to the acculturation and embourgeoisement of the majority of American Jews. The three major branches are now competing for very much the same 'market' of acculturated, middle-class Jews. In the competitive 'market' of the suburbs, a syncretistic synagogue ritual was instrumental in gaining larger memberships. Sodden found that in Nassau County, New York, the 'marginal' synagogues, which combined both Conservative and Reform rituals, were usually more successful than the synagogues which kept strictly to either Conservative or Reform ritual. [44]

The increasing homogenisation of socio-economic class and the diffusion of ritual of the three Jewish denominations may be compared with somewhat similar developments among the Protestant denominations in America. Both the theological differences of the liberal and moderate Protestant denominations (Episcopalians, Presbyterians, Methodists, Congregationists, etc) and the differences in the class composition of their memberships have narrowed. [45] There are still, of course, considerable theological differences between the liberal and moderate Protestant denominations, on the one hand, and the conservative and fundamentalist groups, such as the Southern Baptists and the small sects, on the other, [46] just as there are considerable differences in ritual practices between the major Jewish denominations and the 'right-wing' Orthodox groups.

Where the theologies of certain denominations and the rituals of synagogues have become standardised, the religious organisations need to differentiate marginally their 'products' to enable the 'consumer' to distinguish between them. The extreme congregationalism of American-Jewish organisation has meant that marginal differentiation is particularly important at the local level when there are a number of synagogues in competition with one another. In 'Lakeville', for example, Sklare and Greenblum studied an acculturated middle- and upper-middle-class Jewish population who were distinguished by their affiliation to five synagogues, one Conservative and four Reform. Only in the case of the one 'classical' Reform synagogue was the form of the religious service an important factor differentiating the synagogues from one another. The emphasis on the sermon, the briefness of the excerpts read from the Torah, the absence of Hebrew, and the lack of lay participation made the 'classical' Reform service recognisably different from the services of the Conservative and the three neo-Reform synagogues. The differences between the services of the other synagogues were very marginal: the Conservative synagogue retained more of a traditional character in its Saturday morning service, and one of the Reform synagogues had a more informal service and unusual features in its liturgy such as 'creative prayers' written by its members.

There were, however, other perhaps more important features differentiating the synagogues. One Reform synagogue was differentiated from the two other Reform synagogues with similar rituals by its emphasis on intellectual rather than purely social pursuits. Again, the membership of one of the Reform synagogues was composed of modest-income, less-educated, young couples who, like one other of the Reform congregations, put an emphasis on social activities, but who were differentiated from the other congregation by their stress on an intimate and sociable climate between members. As this last example suggests, the factors which distinguished the characteristics and programmes of the synagogues were correlated to certain social characteristics of the membership. The members of the five synagogues were differentiated statistically by their frequency of synagogue attendance, level of home ritual observance, the extent to which they wished to associate with non-Jews, their involvement in non-Jewish activities, their levels of income, education and residency in high-status areas, their age and, finally, by their generational composition. With a very few exceptions, concern for integration, greater involvement in non-Jewish activities, higher socio-economic status, higher educational level, and more advanced generation were all correlated with lower levels of synagogue attendance and home observance. [47] Thus, although four out of the five congregations were Reform and, with one exception, their religious services were very similar, they differed in their social composition, cultural programmes, and social activities. These differences appear marginal compared with the differences between congregations in the past, but they were considered important by the synagogue members.

Finally, mention should be made of the Reconstructionist movement which is the only religious branch whose origins are entirely American. [48] In many respects, the Reconstructionist ideology articulates explicitly what Charles Liebman has called the 'folk', as opposed to 'élite', American Judaism: the social nature and function of religion is emphasised; the Jewish religion is seen as serving the Jews rather than the Jews serving the religion; ritual is regarded not as a law to be obeyed but as a means of group survival and personal fulfilment; faith in man's goodness and progress are substituted for supernaturalism and other-worldly salvation; the American Jew's first loyalty is said to be to America and only secondly to Jewish culture and civilisation; and great emphasis is put on the need to adapt Judaism to the American environment.

As a movement, Reconstructionism has attracted very few American Jews. Its institutional history began in 1922 when Mordecai Kaplan, whose books formed the basis of the movement's ideology, founded the SAJ (Society for the Advancement of Judaism) with twenty-two or twenty-three families. By the end of the 1920s the SAJ still had only about 150 members; its core was one New York congregation and a small group of rabbis and teachers around Kaplan. At first Kaplan saw Reconstructionism as an adjunct to the major branches of American Judaism, but when Reconstructionism did emerge as a self-conscious movement with affiliated congregations, its growth remained very limited; in 1969 there were ten member congregations of the Federation of

Reconstructionist Congregations and Fellowships, and of these one was also affiliated with Reform and four with the Conservative federations.

Liebman argues that it is the very explicitness of Reconstructionism in its articulation of the major values and attitudes of American Jews which explains its numerical and institutional insignificance. Supporting his arguments with the results of a survey of lay and rabbinical leaders in all three major American religious branches, Liebman contends that American folk Judaism is oriented to the survival of the ethnic group but that most American Jews would not join a synagogue which made this the cornerstone of its ideology. In America religious separatism is seen as more legitimate than ethnic separatism, and the Jews have accommodated to this situation by stating their differences with non-Jews in religious rather that ethnic terms. American Jews would feel uncomfortable if they had to admit that their religious observances focused around ethnic rather than specifically religious concerns.

7   Judaism and Secularisation: Further Comparisons

The significance of ancient Judaism for the cultural development of the modern Western world was emphasised by Max Weber, and, more recently, by Peter Berger. A major theme in Weber's sociology was the process of rationalisation in the West, and he argued that ancient Judaism was of great significance in the *early* stages of this development. The 'world-historical significance' of Judaism lay in its rejection of magic, its rational religious ethic of social conduct, and its rational quest for salvation. Weber wrote that the uniqueness of Judaism among the ancient Near Eastern religions was not so much its monotheism, which had existed elsewhere, but its elimination of magic, its contribution to the 'disenchantment of the world'. In magical religions the same laws of causality applied to both the natural and the supernatural, and a heterogeneous array of prescriptions and proscriptions were obeyed for fear of the direct and inevitable consequences of breaking a taboo. Judaism was, in contrast, an internally consistent religion which gave meaning to the world, and the Hebrew prophets demanded obedience to the religious law, which God had revealed to them, as an ethical duty. While magical practices were oriented to the achievement of mundane goals by the manipulation of supernatural forces, the Hebrew prophets promised the Israelites a collective salvation if they adhered to the ethical norms. Moreover, in contrast to the salvation religions of the East, Judaism was 'this-worldly'; salvation was not to be achieved by ecstatic means and withdrawal from the world, but by obedience to God's law in the everyday world.

In incorporating the Old Testament as one of its sacred books, the Pauline mission innoculated itself against the gnostic sects and mysteries which were not conducive to an ethic of everyday life. At the same time it was the Pauline mission's break with the Jews' ritualistic prescriptions, the basis of their 'caste-like segregation', which made possible the diffusion of Christianity and laid the foundations for the further rationalisation which occurred centuries later with the Puritans. The extension among the Jews of ritual segregation safeguarded their distinct identity and social continuity, but it also meant that their contribution toward rationalisation was at an end.

Weber noted that Judaism was a 'historical precondition' of rational capitalism, but he disputed Sombart's contention that there was a direct link between the two. Weber wrote that the Jews' commercial and financial activities made a distinctive contribution to the medieval and early modern economy, but that they took no part in the origins of modern rational capitalism, that is, the rational organisation of formally free labour in industrial production. One reason for this was that the precarious situation of the Jews in Europe hardly permitted an involvement in industrial enterprise with fixed capital. More important, however, were those aspects of the Jewish religion which, in contrast with Puritanism, were not compatible with modern rational capitalism: its traditionalism, ritualistic segregation and restrictions, ethical dualism, the conception of suffering as having a quality of religious merit, and the *relative* absence of a systematic inner-worldly asceticism. Weber accepted that the Jews perceived economic success as one indication of God's reward for personal adherence to the religious law, but he argued that, unlike the pious Puritan, the Jew had no conception of demonstrating his religious merit through economic activity; the Jewish ideal was the religious scholar who studies the sacred texts at the expense of his business. Thus, the contribution of Judaism to the process of rationalisation was confined to an early stage, and it was Puritanism, not Judaism, which was conducive to the development of modern rational capitalism, which was itself to have enormous rationalising effects on the world. [1]

Peter Berger's analysis of Judaism owes much to Weber but

he is less interested in showing the relationship of religion to modern capitalism than in showing the extent to which the Western religious tradition contained the seeds of secularisation within itself. Berger defines secularisation as 'the process by which sectors of society and culture are removed from the domination of religious institutions and symbols', and argues that its roots in the West are to be found in the Old Testament. Ancient Israel came to reject the cosmological monism of ancient Egypt and Mesopotamia in which there was no radical break between the world of men and the world of gods; the archaic cosmologies conceived the natural and social orders as reflections or manifestations of the divine order and this was continually reaffirmed in their rituals. Berger describes Judaism's differences from, and denial of, the surrounding cosmologies in terms of its transcendentalism, historisation, and rationalisation of ethics.

In place of the integrated sacred universe of the archaic societies, the Jews differentiated a transcendental God from a basically disenchanted world and thereby greatly extended the distance between man and the divine. The Old Testament God does not permeate but stands outside and confronts the cosmos. He is not a national divinity tied to Israel for all past, present, and future time but is linked to Israel by a historical covenant. Hence, Judaism is a historical religion: the Old Testament contains not cosmological myths but historical accounts of the acts of God and distinct individuals; the major cultic festivals celebrate not an annual renewal of the cosmic forces but particular events; and laws and ethics are not part of a timeless cosmic order but historically-placed commandments of God. Berger follows Weber in emphasising Judaism's ethical rationalisation. Both the priests, in their elimination of magic and orgiastic practices and their development of the religious law, and the prophets, in their insistence on the whole of life as service to God, were 'carriers' of this rationalisation.

The disenchantment of the world was by no means a unilinear process. The form of Christianity that became dominant in Europe, Catholicism, re-enchanted the world of ancient Judaism by introducing supernatural mediations between man and God, such as the incarnation, saints, and the Virgin Mary, and it drew back from the ethical absolutism of the Hebrew prophets, segregating it safely in the monastaries. Nevertheless, after the break with Judaism, it was Christianity which carried the seeds of further secularisation. Catholicism preserved the secularising potential within it, firstly because it remained a historical religion, and secondly because of the institutionalised specialisation of religion in the Church. An important distinction was made between the Church, in which religious activities and symbols were concentrated, and 'the world'. During the period when the Church had a virtual monopoly of defining the world-view the secularising potential of this distinction could be 'contained', but, with the disintegration of Christendom, 'the world', which had been defined outside the sacred realm, was then subject to secularisation. However, it was Protestantism, in its rejection of Catholicism's channels of sacred mediation and its radical re-statement of the polarisation between a transcendental God and immanent world, which opened up society to the penetration of secular forces. In disenchanting the world of medieval Catholicism, Protestantism left an empirical reality which was open to the exploration of science and the manipulation of technology. [2]

Developments in ancient Judaism may have made secularisation possible, but this did not mean that secularisation was inevitable. The religious institutions and symbols of Judaism did not decline but took on different meanings. The demarcation of the supernatural and the natural meant that man was now centrally concerned with salvation, and in Judaism this was to be achieved by conformity to the law of God in man's everyday life. In the traditionalistic Jewish society, which continued up to the eighteenth century in most of Europe, religious beliefs explained the world and gave life meaning, institutions were organised according to the religious law, and ritual pervaded all spheres of behaviour. If there was a more radical differentiation in Judaism between a transcendental God and a non-sacred world, there was very little differentiation in the traditionalistic society between religious and secular institutions, roles, and spheres of behaviour. There was no equivalent in Judaism to the Catholic distinction between the Church and 'the world'; the synagogue was not a special realm of the sacred but one of a number of community religious institutions where men prayed, studied, and discussed community affairs.

Religious institutions and symbols remained dominant in a Jewish community or sub-society which was economically distinctive, often vicinally segregated, socially apart, and judicially semi-autonomous from the dominant gentile society. The Church, in wishing to protect its monopolistic position in defining the world of the majority religiously, had contributed to the segregation of the Jews, and this, in turn, had protected the distinctively Jewish religious culture from the incursion of Christian beliefs and practices. This separation, which lasted in most European countries until the second half of the eighteenth century and in eastern Europe until the twentieth, largely insulated Jewish culture from the revolutionary developments in thought and science in the seventeenth and eighteenth centuries. In the Christian world an intellectual gulf grew in the seventeenth century between the lower strata, who continued to rely on mystical explanation and magical practices, and the educated classes who began to see the universe as subject to immutable natural laws and susceptible to technical control. [3] Intellectual effort in the Jewish community remained devoted to the interpretation of the Talmud and its commentaries, and there was no equivalent drawing apart of the world-views of the intellectual élite and other strata. There was a growing interest in mathematical and scientific knowledge among a few rabbis in the first half of the eighteenth century, but it was only in the second half of the eighteenth century, with the emergence of the Jewish Enlightenment movement, the *Haskalah,* that the intellectual changes in the wider society can be seen to have made a significant impression on Jewish thought. The movement of the Jews out of the separate Jewish sub-society was the crucial factor; as Jews entered gentile society, their religion lost its dominant position in explaining and interpreting the world.

176

The effects on the Jews of the interrelated changes in the economy, political structure, and belief systems of the wider society came at a relatively late stage, but it was just because of this lag that, when the absorption of the Jews into 'the modern world' did occur, it was an extremely rapid process. In a few decades the separation of the Jews in western and central Europe was broken down, transforming their culture and way of life. In the wider society, institutional religion was weakened as large sections of the population moved away from small, tightly-knit rural communities to the fast-growing urban centres. Religious practice was part of belonging to a community and it lost its meaning once the community was abandoned or transformed. It is not surprising, therefore, that the loss, over a comparatively short period of time, of the Jewish community's functions, cohesion, and social control and the extensive migration of Jews from rural to urban centres were accompanied by a reduction and compartmentalisation of religious practice. For the Jews, the secularising effects of urbanisation and the loss of community were accentuated by problems of identity. Most wished to remain Jewish but they also wished to be accepted into the dominant society, and this appeared possible only if Judaism was restricted to the home and the synagogue and took forms which would meet the demands of Occidental culture.

In the traditional communities there was no distinction made between religion, culture, and national identity. In the acculturated communities Jews minimised their religious practices but maintained that it was only their religion and not their more general culture and national identity which distinguished them from non-Jews. The native, middle-class Jews in central and western Europe and the United States were secularised but not secularists. In eastern Europe, where society was devided more by ethnic-cultural groups and where the urbanisation of the Jews was concomitant with their proletarianisation, there arose a division *within* the nationally and culturally distinctive Jewish society between the religious traditionalists and the secularists.

In the industrialising societies of the nineteenth century there was a clear relationship between proletarianisation and secularisation; industrialisation broke down the old communities with their associated paternalistic values legitimised by the churches and created sharper class-conscious interests and ideologies. In some European societies church-going came to be associated with the privileged classes and the churches largely failed in their attempts to incorporate the working class. Among the Jews the only substantial proletarianisation occurred in eastern Europe and in the large immigrant communities of the West, and it was in these communities that the secularist movements achieved some success. The majority of the Jewish working class did not, however, reject religion, and in eastern Europe a large proportion remained traditionalists. Even where the Jews were proletarianised, they were largely artisans, working in small unmechanised plants, rarely in large mechanised factories. Moreover, in the West, Jewish proletarianisation rarely lasted beyond the first generation; as the second generation moved into middle-class occupations both secularism and traditionalism declined.

The predominantly native, middle-class Jewish communities in western Europe and the United States today are neither secularist nor traditional: Judaism is rarely entirely rejected and Jewish identity is commonly expressed through religious institutions and symbols, but the majority practise only a minimal number of religious observances. The traditionalistic society, where life is organised according to the religious law, is found in a few large cities where the hassidim and ultra-Orthodox have voluntarily segregated themselves, residentially and socially, both from the wider society and from the wider Jewish community. Outside the voluntary 'ghetto', which is found in Jerusalem as well as in New York, London, and Antwerp, the dominant pattern of Jewish observance varies little from country to country: the most commonly practised observances are yearly rather than weekly or daily, and include synagogue attendance on the High Holy Days, which have become important as a public acknowledgement of Jewish identity, and those rituals, such as the *Seder* night Passover meal and lighting candles on *Chanukah,* which centre on the family. In western Europe and especially in the United States, *Chanukah* has become a more important festival in the Jewish calendar than in the traditional community. *Chanukah* occurs close to Christmas and for many Jewish families it answers the pressing problem of what to do at Christmas-time: the candles are lit, '*Chanukah* cards' are exchanged, and the children receive presents and have parties. In Israel, where the problem of Christmas does not arise, *Purim,* which commemorates the deliverance of the Jews from Haman of Persia about 500 BCE, is a more important festival. Even the religiously non-observant Israelis celebrate the festival: the children go out into the streets in fancy dress and adults attend fancy dress parties.

Jewish religious observance is most attenuated in Communist eastern Europe where religious practice has been discouraged by official measures and propaganda. Unlike the religious monopolism of the medieval Catholic Church, the secular monopolism of the Communist authorities stood no exception and was comparatively successful in suppressing Judaism. The anti-religious campaign against the Jews in Russia was not immediately successful, but after industrialisation, urbanisation, and the changes associated with the Revolution had weakened Jewish religious commitment and the Jewish communities, the suppression of Judaism was extensive.

If we compare the large national Jewish communities outside the Communist sphere, the Jewish community in Argentina stands out as having an exceptionally low level of observance. Many synagogues in Argentina are only used on the High Holy Days but even then attendance is not high; only 8 per cent of the 350,000 Jews in Buenos Aires attended synagogue on the High Holy Days in 1973. In many of the smaller Argentinian communities organised religion is non-existent. The Jews in Argentina join community councils which provide a forum for communal socialising, and there is a strong ethnic identity which is focused on the Yiddish language and support for Israel. The highly secular institutional context and cultural expression of

179

Argentinian Jewry is related both to the characteristics of the Jewish immigrants and to socio-cultural features of Argentina.

South America attracted few traditionalists and the majority of immigrants, who came from eastern Europe in the inter-war period after the United States had restricted immigration, adhered to Socialist and Zionist variants of secular Yiddish culture. The maintenance of a secular ethnic culture centred on an ethnic language is a common phenomenon in Argentina where there are important social divisions between ethnic groups. Minorities from Europe, including the Italians, Germans, and the British, have retained their language, established ethnically delimited communal associations, and maintained ties to their country of origin. This pattern of ethnic division, together perhaps with the lack of influence of the major institutional forms of religion in the country, reinforced the secular rather than religious expressions of Jewish identity. However, the second generation speak Spanish and they have not accepted the Yiddish language as an appropriate expression of cultural identity; unlike other ethnic languages, Yiddish is not associated with a country of origin with which they can identify. [4]

Outside eastern Europe and Argentina, the large national Jewish communities do not vary greatly in their levels of religious observance; in all cases, there is a minority of strict observers, a minority of complete non-observers, and a majority who practise a few selected rituals. The proportions do vary, however, within this overall picture. France has a higher proportion of non-observers than England and the United States, and the contrast is particularly striking if we exclude the French Sephardim, a large proportion of whom are recent immigrants. About a third of the French Ashkenazim never observe any rituals in the home or attend synagogue. Most community surveys in England and the United States have shown that no more than 15 per cent observe no rituals in the home; the proportion who never attend synagogue services is 10 to 15 per cent in England and ranges in the United States from 6 to 13 per cent in most small and medium-sized communities to 20 to 30 per cent in the large city communities. The comparatively low level of observance of native French Jews is not a new phenomenon and must be seen in the context of the repudiation of institutional religion and strength of secularism, organised and diffused, among large strata in the wider society.

Israel has a comparatively high proportion of both strict observers *and* non-observers. A 1969 survey in Israel reported that, in answer to the question 'do you observe the Jewish religious law?', 12 per cent replied 'to the letter', 14 per cent 'quite a bit', 48 per cent 'only somewhat', and 26 per cent 'not at all'; 5 per cent of respondents attended synagogue every day, 13 per cent every Sabbath, 36 per cent a few times a year, 19 per cent only on Yom Kippur, and 27 per cent never attended. [5]The fact that Israel is a Jewish nation where the Jews are the dominant majority accounts, in part at least, for the comparatively high proportion of strict observers and non-observers. In western Europe and the United States many Jewish immigrants who had been strictly observant in eastern Europe abandoned many practices when they found that the costs of Orthodox observance, economic and cultural, were too great. In Israel the costs are much less: there are no economic pressures to work on the Sabbath, Holy Days, and festivals, since these are national holidays, and there is less pressure to abandon visible religious practices since even the more secular Israelis are not likely to perceive them as 'foreign' or deny their legitimacy as religious expression. But if the strictly observant position is easier to maintain in Israel, so is the complete non-observant position. In many diaspora communities the communal or ethnic identity of the religiously uncommitted or even agnostic Jew is typically expressed by attendance at synagogue once or twice a year and by one or two yearly ceremonies in the home. In Israel the non-religious Jew finds it possible to maintain his identity both as an Israeli *and* as a Jew without religious observance. The need symbolically to confirm group identity is not so great because the question of loss of identity or assimilation into a non-Jewish group does not arise. It may be that the religious Israelis feel a greater sense of identity with the Jews of the diaspora than the non-religious

Israelis, but this does not detract from the fact that a large proportion of Israelis have retained a specifically Jewish (as distinct from Israeli) identity despite their lack of religious observance. Elihu Katz reports that most of the traditionally religious holidays continue to have meaning for non-religious Israelis since the non-religious aspects of the holidays (national, familial, historical, etc) are given primacy. [6]

The differences in the proportions of the national Jewish communities affiliated to a synagogue are greater than the differences in the levels of religious observance. There is a clear contrast between those communities where only the strict observers are affiliated to or associated with a synagogue (France, Israel) and those communities where the majority are affiliated to a synagogue (Britain, United States). As noted in the last chapter, synagogue membership has become a major symbolic expression of Jewish identity in Britain and the United States, but in neither country is it strongly predictive of a high level of religious observance. In some large American communities there is an inverse relationship between synagogue membership and religious observance; synagogue membership, which is generally quite costly, is correlated with income, and there are fewer members among the lower income Orthodox than among the higher income Conservative and Reform Jews who observe fewer practices. [7] In France, where there is a very close correlation between synagogue membership and high religious observance, synagogue affiliation has not taken on such symbolic significance and a greater proportion belong to the secular Jewish, particularly Zionist, organisations. Apart from the more important secularist tradition in France, the notion of voluntary affiliation to a religious organisation is not so established: it is not a feature of Catholicism, and voluntary membership only became an option for French Jews in 1905 with the separation of the Church (and the Jewish *consistoires*) from the state. In Israel, of course, non-religious Jews feel no need to acknowledge their Jewish identity by affiliation with a synagogue. It is the nationhood of Israel and not the synagogue which is seen to guarantee Jewish survival. The occasionally

182

observing Israeli, who does not attend synagogue regularly but who wishes to attend public prayer in a synagogue or hall on the High Holy Days, will buy the use of a seat for those particular days.

If American and English Jewry are similar in so far as the majority are affiliated to a synagogue, the functions of the synagogues differ significantly. In addition to their religious functions, American synagogues are also community centres: they provide a great range and variety of secular activities with which most English synagogues could not begin to compete. This difference is related to the different forms that the process of secularisation has taken in the wider societies. In England, secularisation has taken the form of the abandonment of the churches whereas in America it has taken the form of society's absorption of the churches and the extension of the churches' functions to cover communal sociability. Bryan Wilson has argued that the American churches have come to function as agencies of community feeling in a 'nation of immigrants' who have broken with their past, and where high social and geographical mobility have attenuated 'natural' stable communities.[8]

The secularisation of American synagogues appears to have gone even farther than the secularisation of American churches; Jews attend synagogue services less often that Christians attend church services, but the synagogues are nevertheless hives of activity. Secular activities are a more important function of English synagogues than of English churches, but the English (and French) synagogues cannot compare with American synagogues in this respect. It is a reasonable assumption that secular activities within American synagogues are given greater legitimacy by the general absorption of religion into the 'American Way of Life', and that the American Jews follow, in a more intense fashion, the general practice in their society, whereas in England and France, where the Christian religious institutions have been in general decline, Jewish sociability and secular activities take place more outside the synagogues.

The most radical contrast to be made with the American

synagogue is the Israeli synagogue whose congregants think in terms of praying at a particular synagogue rather than of a formal affiliation. Non-religious social activities are not a feature of the Israeli synagogues, which generally have a small regular congregation of males who participate in the traditional activities of prayer and study.

The national Jewish communities continue to differ with respect to developments in the forms of synagogue ritual: 'modernised' services have been particularly successful in the United States; decorous Orthodoxy has remained the dominant British form but the Liberal and Reform movements have increased more rapidly in the post-World War II period; the Liberal movement has remained small in France; and the non-Orthodox movements have had little success in Israel. In 1973, there were nearly 6,000 synagogues in Israel but only twenty-two were non-Orthodox (Reform and Conservative) with a membership of a few thousand. The official monopoly of the Orthodox rabbinate in the interpretation and administration of the religious law (which includes marriage and divorce) is bound to inhibit the growth of the 'modernised' movements in Israel, but the fact remains that, despite intensive work of Reform rabbis, 'Progressive' Judaism had made very little impression.

The extent of acculturation in the synagogue services in the nineteenth century was analysed in relation to the forms of Christianity prevailing in the environment and the pressures on Jews to acculturate to the dominant gentile culture. These considerations are quite clearly irrelevant to Israel and they are also of much less relevance in explaining the more recent changes in the diaspora communities. Differences in the environmental forms of Christianity are no longer so important; in Europe institutional religion has declined, and in the United States Judaism has risen to a widely acknowledged position as one of three major faiths. Outside the religious sphere the Jewish communities are as acculturated to the dominant national cultures as they were in the nineteenth century, but there is far less incentive among contemporary Jews to emulate non-Jewish religious forms, and in some synagogue groups ('Central

Orthodox' and Liberal groups in England, Reform in the United States, Liberal Judaism in France) there has been a deacculturation of the services.

In the nineteenth century there were pressures on many native communities to minimise differences in religious ritual and demonstrate their national loyalty. Social discrimination was widespread but many believed that the removal of the particularisms of the Jewish services would contribute to the opening up of gentile social circles. From about 1880, with the change from cultural to racial forms of anti-Jewish expression, the 'assimilationist' position became less plausible, and in the inter-war period, when in both central Europe and America overt racial prejudice and discrimination increased to new heights, it was largely rejected.

In the post-World War II Western diaspora there was a sharp decline of overt anti-semitism and all forms of discrimination, and if a large proportion of Jews still confine their primary relationships to other Jews it is perhaps because they choose to do so. This is not to say that social discrimination on the part of gentiles has disappeared. In the United States most gentile city and country clubs practise religious discrimination (as do a number of sports clubs in England) and Jews are more likely to be accepted in 'instrumental' associations, which have specific goals, than in 'expressive' associations, whose major purpose is socialising.[9] Nevertheless, there have been significant changes in public attitudes and behaviour toward the Jews: Jews are now rarely taunted with the accusation of dual loyalty, and Judaism is no longer scorned as an inferior religion or cultural 'fossil'. The greater feeling of security of Western Jews has enabled them to openly show their concern and support for Israel. This is true, not only of those communities, such as the Argentinian and French, where Jewish identity is primarily expressed in secular context, and symbols, but also of those communities, such as the British and American, where synagogue affiliation is an important symbolic expression of identity. In the latter, and particularly in the United States, the symbols of Israel and appeals on its behalf have become an important content of

Jewish expression *within* the synagogues.

The constraints on Western Jews to make a choice between two identities and cultures are not so great as they were in many countries in the nineteenth century; most Jews can now comfortably maintain a position of identity with both their country of birth and their ethnic group, conformity to the dominant culture and to the minority religio-culture. The attitudes and behaviour of the dominant gentile groups in the Western nations do not differ so widely as they did in the nineteenth century and up to World War II; religio-cultural pluralism and the social acceptability of Jews are now the norm rather than the exception. Differences in synagogue rituals can no longer, therefore, be explained in terms of a variation in the extent to which Jews are constrained to acculturate to the dominant religio-culture. More important is the variation in the symbolic significance of synagogues in guaranteeing Jewish survival and as institutional contexts of sociability. In those communities where synagogue membership is coterminous with strict religious observance, the members are likely to remain content with an Orthodox service and ideology. This is the case in France and Israel. In those communities where synagogue membership is not coterminous with strict religious observance, there are likely to be greater demands for a 'modernised' service which is more in tune with the secular orientations of the congregation. Reform and Liberal Judaism, in particular, represent adaptations to the secular society: their ideology of progressive revelation incorporates scientific advance, legitimises the abandonment of many religious observances which would serve to separate the Jews from non-Jews, and enables Jews to compartmentalise their religion and live like non-Jews without a sense of guilt.

The Reform and Liberal movements in Britain have grown sharply in the post-World War II period, but it is in the United States that the 'modernised' services are most successful. In the United States there is a higher level of participation in social activities in the synagogues than in other countries and this has had an effect on the form and content of the religious services.

The short 'modernised' service which precedes the Friday night social hour in the Conservative congregations attracts a greater proportion of members than the more traditional Saturday morning service. In English synagogues there is no social hour and consequently no demand for a special Friday night service.

Differences in patterns of ritual observance, in levels of observance, synagogue affiliation, and in forms of synagogue ritual are all related to the variant forms that secularisation has taken in the wider societies. In the secularist Communist societies, there are very few Jewish religious institutions and even a minimal religious observance is rare, although a significant minority continue to express their Jewish national identity through the medium of certain religious festivals. In France, where an important aspect of the secularisation process has been an ideological rejection of institutional religion, synagogue affiliation is low, there is a high proportion of non-observers, and Liberal Judaism has had little appeal. Ideological secularism has not been important in either Britain or the United States and in both countries synagogue affiliation is high and complete non-observance is rare. However, in England, as in most other European countries, secularisation has seen the decline of institutional religion. In America, on the other hand, secularisation has taken place within institutional religion: the three major faiths have become an integral part of the 'American Way of Life', and the churches and synagogues have grown and prospered by adopting secular functions and becoming surrogate communities. Thus, the introduction of 'modernised' services has been far more successful in the United States than in England.

Israel is a case apart since there is no question of a Jewish response to the secularisation of a wider non-Jewish society. In contrast with the United States, secularisation in Israel has taken place quite outside the institutions for religious worship: the synagogues are not surrogate communities but houses of prayer and study. Again in contrast with the United States, there is no separation of 'Church' and state in Israel: the state maintains a joint Chief Rabbinate (Ashkenazim and

187

Sephardim) and rabbinical courts, there is no civil marriage and divorce, religious schools are part of the state educational structure, Orthodox religious practices, such as *kashrut,* are prescribed in state facilities. There are also religious political parties whose influence is greater than their voting strength (15 per cent of the vote in 1969) since the Israel Labour Party has depended on their support in the Knesset (parliament) to command a majority. But whereas in the United States political leaders repeatedly make reference to the divine to legitimise American institutions and the 'American Way of Life', this is not the case in Israel where, outside the religious parties, the state and society is legitimised by reference to the political rights of the people and the history of the Jews as a nation.

The process of secularisation in Israel has left the traditional functions of the synagogues unchanged but has involved the transposition of beliefs and practices which formally had a divine point of reference to a secular, largely national, reference. The religious festivals are now celebrated by many Israelis as nature and national holidays with little reference to the divine; there is a re-emphasis on their relationship to the changing agricultural seasons and their commemoration of historical events in the past struggles of Israel. A new festival, commemorating Israel's Day of Independence, has its own secular ceremonies, and, although special synagogue services are held as part of the celebrations, the majority have not accepted the day as a religious festival.

In a sense, Judaism in Israel has returned to its source in its renewed intimate relationship with the land and nationhood of Israel, but there is an enormous difference between Judaism in ancient and contemporary Israel. In the past, Judaism sacralised society: nature and nation were given meaning and legitimised by reference to the divine. Today, Judaism is secularised within society: the festivals commemorating changes in the seasons and historical events remain, but, for a large section of the population, their divine content has been drawn out. Judaism contributed to the disenchantment of the world; the world is now disenchanting Judaism.

Notes and References

ABBREVIATIONS

AJY	*American Jewish Yearbook*
JC	*Jewish Chronicle*
JE	*Encyclopaedia Judaica*
JJS	*Jewish Journal of Sociology*
JSS	*Jewish Social Studies*
JYB	*Jewish Year Book* (Britain)
LBYB	*Leo Baeck Institute Year Book*

Introduction

1 An argument for the comparative study of Jewish communities was made by S. M. Lipset in, 'The Study of Jewish Communities in a Comparative Context', *JJS*, 5 (1963), 157-66. The two most important books on the sociology of religious change in American Judaism are: Nathan Glazer, *American Judaism* (Chicago, Ill, 1957); Marshall Sklare, *Conservative Judaism* (Glencoe, Colo, 1955). A few sociologists have analysed Judaism's contribution to the development of the modern west, but have confined their analyses to ancient Judaism, the Judaism of the Old Testament. See, in particular: Max Weber, *Ancient Judaism* (New York, 1952); Peter L. Berger, *The Sacred Canopy* (New York, 1967), pp 110-25; Weber's and Berger's discussions of the relationship of ancient Judaism with the rationalisation and secularisation of the modern west are summarised in my concluding chapter.

2 See, for example: David Philipson, *The Reform Movement in Judaism* (New York, 1907); Joseph L. Blau, *Modern Varieties of Judaism* (New York, 1966).

3 For a discussion of the distinction between acculturation and assimilation and of the assimilation dimensions see, Milton M. Gordon, *Assimilation in American Life* (New York, 1964), ch 3.

CHAPTER 1

1 Donald Daniel Leslie, *The Survival of the Chinese Jews: The Jewish Community of Kaifeng* (Leiden, 1972), pp 4-24, 60.

2 Schifra Strizower, *Exotic Jewish Communities* (London, 1962), ch 3; David G. Mandelbaum, 'The Jewish Way of

Life in Cochin', *JSS*, 1 (1939), 123-60; Schifra Strizower, *The Children of Israel: The Bene Israel of Bombay* (Oxford, 1971). The Bene Israel claim that they are descendants from the ten lost tribes of Israel and that they reached India about 175 BCE. The Cochin Jews claim that their ancestors came to India after the destruction of the Second Temple in CE 70. There is no independent evidence to support these claims. Although it is possible that there were Jewish communities in India as early as the fifth century CE, the only certainty is that Jews had settled in India before the end of the first millennium CE.

3 Andre N. Chouraqui, *Between East and West* (Philadelphia, Pa, 1968), pp 86-97; S. D. Goitein, *Jews and Arabs* (New York, 1955), pp 109-15, 122-3.

4 Salo Wittmayer Baron, *A Social and Religious History of the Jews* (New York, 1952-1973), Vol 2, pp 191-209; Vol 5, pp 3-20; Vol 6, pp 16-27.

5 Ibid, Vol 3, pp 99-114.

6 Most Middle Eastern Jews spoke Aramaic before they adopted Arabic, but only in the mountains of Kurdistan and Armenia did Jews retain the Aramaic dialect, Goitein, op cit, pp 131-40.

7 A number of Middle Eastern Jewish communities developed Judeo-Arabic vernaculars, but they contained far less Hebrew than Yiddish, the language of the Ashkenazi European Jews. Another difference was that Yiddish, a fusion of Medieval German and Hebrew, was transplanted from Germany and preserved in an area, Eastern Europe, entirely foreign to it.

8 Goitein, op cit, pp 188-92; Chouraqui, op cit, pp 67-79.

9 Nahum Slouschz, *Travels in North Africa* (Philadelphia, Pa, 1927).

10 Goitein, op cit, pp 177-87.

11 Strizower, *Exotic Jewish Communities,* op cit, pp 34-9.

12 Dina Feitelson, 'Aspects of the Social Life of Kurdish Jews', *JJS*, 1 (1959), 201-16; L. C. Briggs and N. L. Guele, *No More For Ever: A Saharan Jewish Town* (Cambridge, Mass, 1964).

13 W. C. White, *Chinese Jews : A Compilation of Matters Relating to the Jews of Kaifeng Fu,* 3 vols (Toronto, 1942); Leslie, op cit, chs 7-9.

14 Strizower, *The Children of Israel,* op cit, pp 27-30.

15 H. J. Zimmels, *Ashkenazim and Sephardim* (London, 1958), pp 188-204.

16 For detailed accounts of the traditional Jewish society see, Jacob Katz, *Tradition and Crisis : Jewish Society at the End of the Middle Ages* (New York, 1961) and Mark Zborowski and Elizabeth Herzog, *Life Is with People : The Culture of the Shtetl* (New York, 1962).

17 Joshua Trachtenberg, *Jewish Magic and Superstition* (Philadelphia, Pa, 1961).

18 Zimmels, op cit, pp 188-204, 251-62.

19 Max Weber, *The Religion of China* (New York, 1964), pp 213-14.

20 Etienne Balazs, *Chinese Civilization and Bureaucracy* (New Haven, Conn, 1964), p 22.

21 White, op cit; Leslie, op cit, pp 108-11.

22 Balazs, op cit, pp 41-2, 70-8.

23 Song Nai Rhee, 'Jewish Assimilation : The Case of the Chinese Jew', *Comparative Studies in Society and History,* 15 (1973), 115-26.

24 Max Weber, *The Religion of India* (New York, 1958), pp 9-29.

25 M. N. Srinivas, *Religion and Society among the Coorgs of South India* (Oxford, 1952), pp 31-2.

26 Baron, op cit, Vol 3, pp 120-72; Chouraqui, op cit, pp 42-55.

27 Goitein, op cit, pp 73-8, 99-124.

28 S. D. Goitein, *A Mediterranian Society,* Vol 2, (Los Angeles, Calif, 1971), chs 5, 7; H. Z. Hirschberg, 'The Jewish Quarter in Muslim Cities and Berber Areas', *Judaism,* 17 (1958), 405-21.

29 Feitelson, op cit; Briggs and Guele, op cit.

30 Baron, op cit; vol 4, pp 5-12, 89-149; vol 9, pp 3-54; vol 10, pp 122-91; Leon Poliakov, *The History of Anti-Semitism :*

From the Time of Christ to the Court Jews (London, 1965), chs 2-7.

31 Guido Kisch, *The Jews in Medieval Germany : A Study of their Legal and Social Status* (Chicago, Ill, 1949), pp 306-16, 323-5.

32 Baron, op cit, Vol 9, pp 3-96; Vol 11, pp 77-121.

33 Ibid, Vol 6, pp 150-277; Vol 12, pp 25-197; Kisch, op cit, pp 318-22, 327-9.

34 Baron op cit, Vol 9, pp 135-236; Vol 10, pp 41-117; Vol 11, pp 3-76, 192-283.

35 Zborowski and Herzog, op cit, pp 66-7, 151-8.

36 S. W. Baron, *The Jewish Community,* Vol 2 (Philadelphia, Pa, 1948), ch 11.

37 Baron, *Social and Religious History;* Vol 3, pp 33-46; Vol 4, pp 27-43; Vol 10, pp 118-219; Vol 11, pp 225-49; Vol 13, pp 3-158; Yitzhah Baer, *A History of the Jews in Christian Spain* (Philadelphia, Pa, 1961).

38 Zimmels, op cit, pp 205-32, 237-46, 262-6.

39 Cecil Roth, 'Jewish Society in the Renaissance Environment', *Cahiers D'Histoire Mondiale,* 11 (1968), 239-50; Cecil Roth, *The Jews in the Renaissance* (Philadelphia, Pa, 1959); Baron, *Social and Religious History* op cit, Vol 13, pp 159-205.

40 Cecil Roth, *The History of the Jews of Italy* (Philadelphia, Pa, 1946), pp 289-394; Baron, *Social and Religious History,* op cit, Vol 14, pp 114-46.

41 Ibid, Vol 13, pp 206-96; Vol 14, pp 147-294.

CHAPTER 2

1 Moses A. Shulvass, *From East to West : The Westward Migration of Jews from Eastern Europe During the Seventeenth and Eighteenth Centuries,* (Detroit, Mich, 1971).

2 S. W. Baron, *A Social and Religious History of the Jews* (New York, 1952-1973), Vol 13, pp 3-158.

3 Herbert I. Bloom, *The Economic Activities of the Jews of Amsterdam in the Seventeenth and Eighteenth Centuries,* (Williamsport, Pa, 1937), p 31.

4 Vivian D. Lipman, 'Sephardi and Other Jewish Immigrants in England in the Eighteenth Century', in *Migration and Settlement,* ed A. Newman (London, 1971), pp 37-62.

5 Raphael Mahler, *A History of Modern Jewry, 1780-1815* (London, 1971), pp 1, 15, 18, 78, 104, 130, 229, 280; Arthur Ruppin, *The Jewish Fate and Future* (London, 1940), p 27.

6 Arieh Tartakower, 'Polish Jewry in the Eighteenth Century', *JJS,* 2 (1960), 110-14; Mahler, op cit, pp 279-85.

7 Ibid, pp 129-40.

8 Arthur Hertzberg, *The French Enlightenment and the Jews* (New York, 1970), pp 1, 121; Michel Roblin, *Les Juifs de Paris : Démographie, Economie, Culture,* (Paris, 1952), p 51.

9 Jacob Rader Marcus, *Early American Jewry,* Vol II, (Philadelphia, Pa, 1953), pp 384-9.

10 Mahler, op cit, pp 78,105; Lipman, op cit.

11 Mahler, op cit, pp 430-535; G. Scholem, *Major Trends in Jewish Mysticism,* (New York, 1961), ch 9; S. H. Dresner, *The Zaddik* (London, 1960); S. Ettinger, 'The Hassidic Movement, Reality and Ideals', *Cahiers D'Histoire Mondiale,* 11 (1968), 251-66.

12 Azriel Shohet, *Beginnings of the Haskalah among German Jewry in the First Half of the Eighteenth Century,* in Hebrew (Jerusalem, 1960), chs 2, 3, 5, 7-10.

13 Selma Stern, *The Court Jew* (Philadelphia, Pa, 1950), ch 9.

14 Isaac Eisenstein-Bazilay, 'The Background of the Berlin Haskalah', *Essays on Jewish Life and Thought,* ed J. L. Blau et al (New York, 1959), pp 183-97.

15 W. Gunther Plaut, *The Rise of Reform Judaism,* Vol 1 (New York, 1963), p 7.

16 Jacob Katz, *Out of the Ghetto : The Social Background of Jewish Emancipation 1770-1870* (Cambridge, Mass, 1973), pp 17-19, 132-6.

17 A. Menes, 'The Conversion Movement in Prussia during the first half of the Nineteenth century', *Yivo Annual of Jewish Social Studies,* 6 (1951), pp 187-205.

18 Hertzberg, op cit, pp 160-1; Roblin, op cit, pp 44-6; Herbert I. Bloom, 'Felix Libertate and the Emancipation of Dutch Jewry', in Blau (ed), op cit, p 108; Cecil Roth, *History of the Jews in England* (Oxford, 1964), pp 225-7; James Picciotto, *Sketches of Anglo-Jewish History* (London, 1875), pp 132-96.

19 Hertzberg, op cit, p 164; Katz, *Out of the Ghetto,* p 116; C. Duschinsky, *The Rabbinate of the Great Synagogue* (Oxford, 1921), pp 14-16.

20 Ibid, pp 28-29, 107-8.

21 Marcus, op cit, pp 389-91, 437-41.

22 Hyman B. Grinstein, *The Rise of the Jewish Community of New York, 1654-1860* (Philadelphia, Pa, 1945), pp 10, 14-15, 43-4.

23 Vaclos L. Benes and Norman G. J. Pounds, *Poland* (London, 1970), pp 61-5.

24 Mahler, op cit, pp 280-91.

25 *JE,* Vol 16, pp 1303, 1308; Mahler, op cit, pp 285-98; Mark Wischnitzer, *A History of Jewish Crafts and Guilds* (New York, 1965), pp 241-4, 254-60.

26 Mahler, op cit, pp 299-303, 446-7.

27 Ettinger, op cit.

28 Mahler, op cit, pp 229-58, 370-423; I. Levitats, *The Jewish Community in Russia, 1772-1844* (New York, 1943).

29 Paul Ignotus, *Hungary* (London, 1972), pp 46-7; Mahler, op cit, pp 268-72;. Erno Marton, 'The Family Tree of Hungarian Jewry', *Hungarian Jewish Studies,* ed Randolph L. Braham (New York, 1966), pp 33-42. The 1735-8 Hungarian census found that 45 per cent of the 11,621 Hungarian Jews were in commerce and 34.9 per cent were craftsmen. The vast majority lived in rural areas and nearly two-thirds were immigrants from the Germanies, Moravia, Bohemia, and Poland.

30 Mahler, op cit, pp 241-7; Katz, op cit, pp 162-5.

31 Mahler, op cit, pp 129-51; Shohet, op cit, pp 9, 21-5, 49.
32 Katz, op cit, pp 43-56, 78, 83-102; Hannah Arendt, *The Origins of Totalitarianism,* (London, 1967), pp 57-60; Michael A. Meyer, *The Origins of the Modern Jew* (Detroit, Mich, 1967), p 26.
33 Hans Kohn, *The Mind of Germany* (London, 1961), chs 3, 4.
34 Arendt, op cit, p 61.
35 On Heine and other marginal German Jews, see, S. Liptzin, *Germany's Stepchildren* (Philadelphia, Pa, 1944).
36 Hertzberg, op cit, chs 5, 7, 8, 9; S. Posener, 'The Social Life of the Jewish Communities in France', *JSS,* 7 (1945), 195-232.
37 Mahler, op cit, pp 78-85; Bloom, *Economic Activities,* intro; Wischnitzer, op cit, p 198; Bloom, 'Felix Libertate', 111.
38 H. S. Q. Henriques, *Jews and the English Law* (Oxford, 1908), esp pp 170-246.
39 A. P. Arnold, 'A List of Jews and Their Households in London', *Miscellanies of the Jewish Historical Society of England,* 6 (1962), 73-111; Vivian D. Lipman, 'The Rise of Jewish Suburbia', *Transactions of the Jewish Historical Society of England,* 24 (1968), 78-102; Cecil Roth, *The Rise of Provincial Jewry* (London, 1950).
40 J. Rumyaneck, *Social and Economic Development of the Jews in England,* unpublished PhD thesis (University of London, 1933); Wischnitzer, op cit, p 201.
41 Marcus, op cit, pp 423-8.
42 Cecil Roth, *Essays and Portraits in Anglo-Jewish History* (Philadelphia, Pa, 1962), pp 10-21; Rumyaneck, op cit. In 1753 the Naturalisation or so-called 'Jew' Bill, which would have given Parliament the power to naturalise individual Jewish immigrants, was repealed after passing the Houses of Parliament. Parry has argued that the religious and political clamour against the bill was more the result of an artificial fanning of prejudice for political ends, in preparation for the general election, than any entrenched anti-semitism in Britain. The violent language used at the time simply

reflected the normal level of eighteenth-century partisan debate, and the artificial nature of the opposition's anti-semitism is substantiated by the absence of any physical violence against Jews and their property. T. W. Perry, *Public Opinion, Propaganda and Politics in the Eighteenth Century : A Study of the Jew Bill of 1763*, (Harvard, Mass, 1962).

43 Marcus, op cit, pp 494-513.

44 Cecil Roth, *History of the Great Synagogue* (London, 1950), pp 67-8.

45 Grinstein, op cit, pp 5-6, 75.

CHAPTER 3

1 Of the 'gainfully employed' Jews in Congress Poland in 1843, 28 per cent were petty entrepreneurs, artisans and wage earners, 24.8 per cent were day-wage labourers, 13.3 per cent were servants and domestics, 11.3 per cent were shopkeepers and petty traders, 6.1 per cent were taverners and innkeepers, 4.7 per cent were agriculturists, 1.2 per cent were in liberal professions, and 0.8 per cent were capitalists, bankers, entrepreneurs and landowners. Aaron Antonovsky and Elias Tcherikower, *The Early Jewish Labour Movement in the United States* (New York, 1961), p 350.

2 Ibid, pp 12-15; *JE* Vol 14, pp 435-43; I. M. Dijur, 'Jews in the Russian Economy', in *Russian Jewry 1860-1917,* J. Frumkin *et al* (London, 1966), pp 120-43.

3 I. Levitats, *The Jewish Community in Russia, 1772-1844* (New York, 1943).

4 *JE* Vol 13, p 1292; Vol 4, pp 345, 644; Ismar Schorsch, *Jewish Reactions to German Anti-Semitism, 1870-1914* (New York, 1972), p 13; P. G. J. Pulzer, *The Rise of Anti-Semitism in Germany and Austria* (New York, 1964), p 10; cf Kurt Wilhelm, 'The Jewish Community in the Post-Emancipation Period', *LBYB,* 2 (1957), pp 47-75; Reinhard Rurup, 'Jewish Emancipation and Bourgeois Society', *LBYB,* 14 (1969), pp 67-91.

5 Schorsch, op cit, p 14.

6 *JE,* Vol 12, p 981.

7 Cecil Roth, *History of the Jews in Italy,* (Philadelphia, Pa, 1946), pp 485-7.

8 Bernard Blumenkranz (ed), *Histoire des Juifs en France* (Toulouse, 1972), pp 308-13; Michael R. Marrus, *The Politics of Assimilation* (Oxford, 1971), pp 30-46; M. Roblin, *Les Juifs de Paris: Démographie, Economie, Culture* (Paris, 1952), pp 52-4, 60-1.

9 Istvan Veghazi, 'The Role of Jewry in the Economic Life of Hungary', *Hungarian Jewish Studies,* Vol II, ed Randolph L. Braham (New York, 1969), pp 35-84; Ruth Kestenberg-Gladstein, 'The Jews between Czechs and Germans in the Historic Lands', *The Jews of Czechoslovakia,* Vol I, (Philadelphia, Pa, 1968), pp 27-8, 39-41; Paul Ignotus, *Hungary* (London, 1972), pp 91-3, 97-8.

10 Vivian D. Lipman, 'Trends in Anglo-Jewish Occupation', *JJS,* 2 (1960), 202-18; Lipman, 'The Rise of Jewish Suburbia', *Transactions of the Jewish Historical Society of England,* 24 (1968), pp 78-102.

11 Marshall Sklare, *America's Jews* (New York, 1971), p 7.

12 S. Debre, 'The Jews of France', *The Jewish Quarterly Review,* 3 (1891), pp 368-85; Marrus, op cit, pp 68-73.

13 Roth, op cit, pp 494-5.

14 Schorsch, op cit, pp 17-32.

15 Moshe Davis, *The Emergence of Conservative Judaism: The Historical School in 19th Century America* (Philadelphia, Pa, 1963), pp 116-19, 125-34, 156-8; David Philipson, *The Reform Movement in Judaism* (New York, 1907), pp 377-81.

16 Stephen Sharot, 'Religious Change in Native Orthodoxy in London 1870-1914: Rabbinate and Clergy', *JJS,* 15 (1973), pp 167-87.

17 Louis Greenberg, *The Jews in Russia,* Vol I, (New Haven, Conn, 1965), ch 9.

18 *JE* Vol 16, pp 1325-9.

19 Nathaniel Katzburg, 'Hungarian Jewry in Modern Times' in Braham (ed), Vol 1 (1966), pp 152-3.

20 Kestenberg-Gladstein, op cit, p 43.

21 The high rate of conversion among the rich Jews in the Prussian cities in the first decade of the century was short-lived; between 1812 and 1846 an average of 108 Jews were converted annually in Prussia. Schorsch, op cit, p 6. De la Roi, a Christian missionary, estimated that 205,000 European Jews adopted Christianity in the nineteenth century: 85,000 in eastern Europe, 45,000 in Austria-Hungary, 29,000 in Great Britain, 23,000 in Germany, 13,000 in North America, 1,800 in Holland, 2,400 in France, and 300 in Italy. 'Judentaufen im 19 Jahrhundert', *Nataniel,* 3 and 4 (Berlin, 1899). In some countries (eg Russia, Germany), these figures are based on official statistics; in others (England, USA) the figures are informed guesses.

22 The 1851 religious census in England recorded that just under 3,000 Jewish worshippers, or 9 per cent of the total Anglo-Jewish population, attended synagogue on the Saturday morning of the census. For details see Stephen Sharot, 'Secularization, Judaism and Anglo-Jewry', *A Sociological Yearbook of Religion in Britain,* ed M. Hill, (1971) p 133.

23 Wilhelm, op cit, pp 56-8; Yeshayahu Wolfsberg, 'Popular Orthodoxy' *LBYB,* 1 (1956), pp 237-54. The term 'Orthodox' is used here to refer to an Orthodox level of observance, that is, conformity to the *Shulhan Arukh.* Some Jewish communities (eg the British) continued a largely Orthodox prayer service in the synagogue, but the majority of members did not practise an Orthodox level of observance. The distinction between Orthodox prayer service and an Orthodox level of observance should be kept in mind since the term will be used in the text in both senses.

24 Marrus, op cit, pp 51-9; Debre, op cit, pp 390-2.

25 Ibid, p 411.

26 Ibid, pp 391-2; Stephen Sharot 'Religious Change in Native

Orthodoxy in London, 1870-1914: The Synagogue Service', *JJS,* 15 (1973), esp pp 72-4.

27 Philipson, op cit, pp 11-18.

28 W. Gunther Plaut, *The Rise of Reform Judaism,* Vol 1 (New York, 1963), p 28.

29 Baruh Mevorah, 'Messianism as a Factor in the First Reform Controversies', in Hebrew, *Zion,* 34 (1969), 189-218.

30 Philipson, op cit, pp 21-38. The use of the term 'temple' was significant: the new type of house of worship was distinguished from the more traditional 'synagogue', and the term indicated that the Reform Jews did not expect a new temple to be built in a reborn Israel, that the place of the Jews was in their country of birth.

31 Ibid, chs 3, 8.

32 H. Schwab, *The History of Orthodox Jewry in Germany* (London, 1951).

33 Max Grunwald, *Vienna* (Philadelphia, Pa, 1936), pp 216-18; Hugo Stransky, 'The Religious Life in the Historic Lands', *The Jews of Czechoslovakia,* op cit, pp 331-4.

34 Katzburg, op cit, pp 149-52; Nathaniel Katsburg, 'The Jewish Congress of Hungary, 1868-1869', in Braham (ed) Vol II, op cit, pp 1-33.

35 Philipson, op cit, p 330; Allan Tarshish, 'The Charleston Organ Case', *American Jewish Historical Quarterly,* 54 (1965), 411-49.

36 Davis, op cit, p 141. Davis estimates that there was a total number of 110 synagogues in 1855 (p 130).

37 Nathan Glazer, *American Judaism* (Chicago, Ill, 1957), pp 31-3, 38.

38 Bernard D. Weinryb, 'The German Jewish Immigrants to America', *Jews from Germany in the United States,* ed Eric E. Hirshler (New York, 1955), pp 103-26.

39 R. Glanz, *Jews in Relation to the Cultural Milieu of the Germans in America up to the 1880s* (New York, 1947).

40 Glazer, op cit, pp 38-9; B. H. Levy, *Reform Judaism in America : A Study of Religious Adaptation,* (New York,

1933), pp 44-52; Will Herberg, *Protestant, Catholic, Jew* (New York, 1955), p 176.

41 A. M. Hyamson, *The Sephardim in England* (London, 1951), ch 15; Cecil Roth, *History of the Great Synagogue,* (London, 1950), ch 16.

42 *Voice of Jacob* (26 May, 4 Aug 1843).

43 *Voice of Jacob* (3 September 1842); *JC* (3 November 1848).

44 *JC* (15 November 1872).

45 *JC* (5 March 1880); Sharot, 'Synagogue Service', pp 63-5.

46 Blumenkranz, op cit, pp 318-26.

47 Marrus, op cit, pp 100-19.

48 Debre, op cit, pp 386-90, 411-25.

49 *JE,* Vol 9, p 1142; Cecil Roth, *History of the Jews of Italy,* p 493.

50 Blumenkranz, op cit, pp 312, 322-3; cf Walter Breslauer, 'Notes on Organisational Problems of German Jewry', *LBYB,* 14 (1969), pp 259-65.

51 *JC* (31 March 1848); Vivian D. Lipman, 'Synagogal Organization in Anglo-Jewry', *JJS,* 1 (1959), 80-93.

52 Uriel Tal, 'Liberal Protestantism and the Jews in the Second Reich', *JSS,* 26 (1964), 23-41.

53 Winthrop S. Hudson, *American Protestantism,* (Chicago, Ill, 1961), pp 99-109.

54 Tarshish, op cit; Glazer, op cit, p 53.

55 *JC* (12 April 1872); For an illustration of the appeal of Anglican services to upper-class Jews see the extracts from the diaries of Lady Louise Rothschild and her daughter, Constance. Lucy Cohen, *Lady Rothschild and her Daughters, 1821-1931* (London, 1935), pp 68, 110.

56 Roth, *History of the Jews of Italy,* p 493.

57 Jacob Katz, *Out of the Ghetto : The Social Background of Jewish Emancipation 1770-1870* (Cambridge, Mass, 1973), pp 193-4, 201-3.

58 Fritz Stern, *The Failure of Illiberalism* (London, 1972), pp 30-47.

59 E. K. Bramsted, *Aristocracy and Middle Classes in Germany* (Chicago, Ill, 1964), chs 4, 5; George L. Mosse,

Germans and Jews (London, 1971), chs 1-4.

60 Katz, op cit, pp 91-102, 199-200; H. D. Schmidt, 'The Terms of Emancipation', *LBYB,* 1 (1956), pp 28-47.

61 Plaut, op cit.

62 Mevorah, op cit; Michael A. Meyer, 'Religious Reform and Wissenschaft des Judenthums', *LBYB,* 16 (1971), pp 19-41.

63 Philipson, op cit, p 115.

64 Kestenberg-Gladstein, op cit, pp 53-4.

65 Ignotus, op cit, pp 97-8.

66 Seymour Martin Lipset, *The First New Nation* (New York, 1967), pp 125-35.

67 Rudolf Glanz, 'The Rise of the Jewish Club in America', *JSS,* 31 (1969), 82-99; E. Digby-Baltzell, *The Protestant Establishment* (London, 1965), ch 5; John Higham, 'Social Discrimination Against Jews in America: 1830-1930', *Publications of the American Jewish Historical Society,* 47 (1957), 1-33.

68 Stuart E. Rosenberg, *The Jewish Community in Rochester, 1843-1925,* (New York, 1954), p 119.

69 Quoted by Hyman B. Grinstein, *The Rise of the Jewish Community of New York, 1654-1860* (Philadelphia, Pa, 1945) p 354.

70 Hyman B. Grinstein, 'Flight from the Slums', *Essays on Jewish Life and Thought,* ed J. L. Blau *et al,* (New York, 1959), p 295.

71 Rosenberg, op cit, p 91. See also Stuart E. Rosenberg, 'Some Attitudes of Nineteenth Century Reform Laymen', in Blau *et al,* pp 411-21.

72 Hudson, op cit, pp 4, 7, 109.

73 This is clearly illustrated by the following letter from Lord Granville to Queen Victoria: '[Rothschild] represents a class which is great by their wealth, their intelligence, their literary connections and their numerous seats in the House of Commons. It may be wise to attach them to the aristocracy rather than to drive them to the democratic camp. The Carlton Club sent a Jew to be their candidate at Sandwich, Lord Shaftesbury wrote to Mr. Gladstone to press for Sir M.

Montefiore's claim to a peerage.' Quoted by Rumney in *JC*, 7 August 1936.

74 T. H. Marshall, *Class, Citizenship and Social Development* (London, 1965), pp 201-5.
75 For a popular account of the Anglo-Jewish aristocracy see Chaim Bermant, *The Cousinhood* (London, 1971).
76 M. Lissack, *Jewish Perseverance* (Bedford, 1851), pp 88, 235.
77 Lucien Wolf, *Essays in Jewish History* (London, 1934), p 315.
78 Israel Finestein, 'Anglo-Jewish Opinion During the Struggle for Emancipation, 1828-1858', *Transactions of the Jewish Historical Society of England,* 20 (1964), 113-43; Polly Pinsker, 'English Opinion and Jewish Emancipation', *JSS,* 14 (1952), 51-94. See *JC* 3 December 1847 for statements of Anglican clergymen supporting Jewish emancipation.
79 Finestein, op cit; U. R. Q. Henriques, 'The Jewish Emancipation Controversy in Nineteenth Century Britain', *Past and Present,* 40 (1968), 126-46.
80 Marrus, op cit, pp 36-45, 124-5; Blumenkranz, op cit, pp 339-42; Robert F. Byrnes, *Antisemitism in Modern France* (New Brunswick, NJ, 1950).
81 Roth, *History of the Jews of Italy,* p 175.

CHAPTER 4

1 *JE,* Vol 14, p 450-1; Ezra Mendelsohn, *Class Struggle in the Pale* (Cambridge, 1970), pp 4-5; Zvi Y. Gitelman, *Jewish Nationality and Soviet Politics,* (Princeton, NJ, 1972), pp 17-18, 20-7,71.
2 Mark Wischnitzer, *To Dwell in Safety : The Story of Jewish Migration Since 1800* (Philadelphia, Pa, 1948), pp 28-140. Economic conditions in Galicia were no better than in Russia, and of the 280,000 Jews who emigrated from the Austrian Empire between 1881 and 1910, the majority were from Galicia. Arieh Tartakower, 'Jewish Migratory Movements in Austria in Recent Generations', *The Jews of*

Austria, ed Josef Frankel (London, 1967), p 287.

3 S. Adler-Rudel, *Ostjuden in Deutschland, 1880-1940* (Tübingen, 1959), p 164.

4 M. Roblin, *Les Juifs de Paris : Démographie, Economie, Culture* (Paris, 1952), p 73.

5 Within the Austro-Hungarian empire there was both a substantial migration from Galicia to the cities of Hungary, Bohemia-Moravia, and Lower Austria, and a migration within the countries from the rural to urban districts. In 1910, when the total Hungarian Jewish population was 932,187, the Jews of Budapest numbered 203,687, representing 19.7 per cent of the total city population. (Erno Laszlo, 'Hungarian Jewry : Settlement and Demography', *Hungarian Jewish Studies* Vol 1, ed Randolph L. Braham (New York, 1966), pp 68, 89.) In 1880 about half of Bohemian Jews lived in towns with over 5,000 inhabitants; in 1921 69 per cent lived in towns with over 10,000 inhabitants. The Jews of Prague remained a small proportion of the city's population, but as a proportion of Bohemian Jews they increased from 21.7 per cent in 1880 to 46.4 per cent in 1930. (*JE,* Vol 13, p 970; Vol 4, p 1179.) In 1918, of the 300,000 Jews in the Austrian Republic, about two-thirds lived in Vienna. (*JE,* Vol 3, p 895.)

6 Ismar Schorsch, *Jewish Reactions to German Anti-Semitism, 1870-1914* (New York, 1972), p 14. In 1910 only 26,512 Jews remained in the eastern province of Posen. (*JE,* Vol 13, p 1292.)

7 The more rural Jews in southern Germany were less wealthy than the northern Jews, but, on average, they were richer than their non-Jewish neighbours. In 1901 the average Jewish income in Baden was 1,229 marks compared with 244 marks for Protestants and 117 marks for Catholics. Schorsch, op cit, pp 14-16.

8 Moses Rischin, *The Promised City* (New York, 1962), pp 83, 94.

9 Lloyd P. Gartner, *The Jewish Immigrant in England, 1870-1914* (London, 1960), pp 144-8; Vivian D. Lipman,

Social History of the Jews in England : 1850-1950 (London, 1954), p 104.

10 Rischin, op cit, pp 92-4.

11 Vivian D. Lipman, 'The Development of London Jewry', *A Century of Anglo-Jewish Life, 1870-1970,* Salmond S. Levin (ed), (London, 1973), pp 43-56.

12 G. Aronson, 'Ideological Trends Among Russian Jews', *Russian Jewry 1860-1917,* Frumkin *et al* (London, 1966), pp 144-71; S. M. Dublow, *History of the Jews in Russia and Poland* (Philadelphia, Pa, 1916-20), ch 25.

13 Gitelman, op cit, pp 71-3; Mendelsohn, op cit, pp vii-ix, 47-61, 117-20.

14 Charles S. Liebman, *The Ambivalent American Jew* (Philadelphia, Pa, 1973), pp 52-3.

15 Gartner, op cit, ch 4; Rischin, op cit, p 159.

16 Ibid, pp 154-5; M. E. Ravage, *An American in the Making* (New York, 1947), p 156; *JC* (23 September 1904); Pierre Aubery, *Milieux Juifs de la France Contemporaine a travers leurs ecrivains* (Paris, 1957), p 60.

17 Aaron Antonovsky and Elias Tcherikower, *The Early Jewish Labour Movement in the United States* (New York, 1961), chs 11, 13.

18 Rischin, op cit, pp 116-17; cf Aubery, op cit, p 75; Gartner, op cit, pp 192-7, 268.

19 *The Jewish Communal Register of New York City* (Kehillah of New York City, 1918), pp 177-286.

20 *JC* (2 March 1906); Rischin, op cit, pp 104-5; Roblin, op cit, pp 59, 158-9.

21 Hyman B. Grinstein, *The Rise of the Jewish Community of New York, 1654-1860* (Philadelphia, Pa, 1945), p 370. In Milwaukee, in 1881, only 125 of the 500 native Jewish families were members of the temples, and synagogue attendance was very low. Louis J. Swichkow and Lloyd P. Gartner, *The History of the Jews of Milwaukee,* (Philadelphia, Pa, 1963), pp 175, 190-1.

22 *British Weekly* (5, 12, 26 November 1886).

23 Richard Mudie-Smith, *The Religious Life of London* (London, 1904).

24 Arthur Ruppin, *The Jews of To-Day* (London, 1913), pp 152-3; Michael R. Marrus, *The Politics of Assimilation* (Oxford, 1971), pp 54-5, 59; *JC* 25 March 1898; Ruth Kestenberg-Gladstein, 'The Jews between Czechs and Germans in the Historic Lands, *The Jews of Czechoslovakia*, Vol I (Pennsylvania, Pa, 1968), p 51.

25 Hyman B. Grinstein, 'The Efforts of East European Jewry to Organise Its Own Community in the United States', *Publications of the American Jewish Historical Society*, 49 (1959), pp 73-89.

26 *JC* (10 March, 17 March 1911).

27 Aubery, op cit, pp 74-5.

28 See, for example, C. Lewis, *A Soho Address* (London, 1955), p 57.

29 *JC* (23 August 1895).

30 *JC* (9 August 1912, 14 February 1913); Adler-Rudel, op cit, pp 25-29; Marrus, op cit, pp 160-2; Roblin, op cit, pp 140, 162-3; Rischen, op cit, pp 101-2; Gartner, op cit, pp 149, 174-5, 221-5, 231-40.

31 Stephen Sharot, 'The Synagogue Service', *JJS*, 15 (1973), pp 59-63; Stephen Sharot, 'Native Jewry and the Religious Anglicization of Immigrants in London, 1870-1905', *JJS*, 16 (1974).

32 Marshall Sklare, *Conservative Judaism* (Glencoe, Colo, 1955), pp 24, 161-5; Rosenburg, *The Jewish Community in Rochester*, ch 15.

33 *JC* (3 January 1896, 16 December 1898, 6 December 1901, 2 December 1904). Never more than half of the Jews on the electoral roll in Berlin voted in the Jewish community elections, and sometimes the proportion fell to less than a third.

34 Sharot, 'The Synagogue Service', op cit, 66-71; Sharot, 'Rabbinate and Clergy', *JJS*, 15 (1973) 176-83.

35 In Germany the term 'Liberal' denoted a less radical position than 'Reform'; in England the term 'Liberal' denoted a more radical position than 'Reform'.

36 *JC* (24 October 1902, 30 October 1903, 17 May 1907, 10

June 1904, 10 February 1911, 31 May 1912); *Jewish Religious Union Bulletin,* 10 March 1915.

37 Roblin, op cit, p 140; Rabi, *Anatomie du Judaise Francais,* (Paris, 1962), p 158.

38 B. H. Levy, *Reform Judaism in America: A Study of Religious Adaptation,* (New York, 1933) pp 38-43.

39 Nathan Glazer, *American Judaism* (Chicago, Ill, 1957) p 53.

40 P. W. Massing, *Rehearsal for Destruction: A Study of Political Antisemitism in Imperial Germany* (New York, 1949); Schorsch, op cit pp 90-1, 137; P.G.J. Pulzer, *The Rise of Anti-Semitism in Germany and Austria* (New York, 1964), p 219.

41 Uriel Tal, 'Liberal Protestantism and the Jews in the Second Reich', *JSS,* 26 (1964), 23-41; Uriel Tal, *Christians and Jews in the Second Reich, 1870-1914,* in Hebrew (Jerusalem, 1970), pp 11-19, 121-72.

42 Schorsch, op cit, pp 108-9, 119, 121, 140, 147-8, 181-207.

43 Walter B. Simon, 'The Jewish Vote in Austria' *LBYB,* 16 (1971), pp 97-121; Pulzer, op cit, pp 25-7, 272, 280-5.

44 Kestenberg-Gladstein, op cit, pp 43-5, 53-4; Pulzer, op cit, pp 139-41; Laszlo, op cit, pp 144-8.

45 Hugo Stransky, 'The Religious Life in Historic Lands', *The Jews of Czechoslovakia,* Vol 1 (Pennsylvania, Pa, 1968), pp 332,338; Nathaniel Katzburg 'The Jewish Congress of Hungary, 1868-1869' in Braham (ed) Vol II, p 21.

46 Sharot, 'Native Jewry', op cit.

47 *JC* (12, 19, 26 October 1900).

48 *JC* (10 October 1890).

49 Robert F. Byrnes, *Antisemitism in Modern France* (New Brunswick, NJ, 1950), esp pp 120-11, 262-300; Marrus, op cit pp 36-45, 163, 208-9; Rabi, op cit, pp 43-61.

50 Marrus, op cit pp 180-285.

51 Seymour Martin Lipset, *The First New Nation* (New York, 1967), pp 127-34; Carey McWilliams, *A Mask for Privilege: Antisemitism in America* (Boston, Mass, 1949).

52 E. Digby-Baltzell, *Philadelphia Gentlemen: The Making of a National Upper-Class* (Glencoe, Colo, 1958), p 286; John

Higham, *Strangers in the Land: Patterns of American Nativism, 1860-1924* (Rutgers, 1965), pp 92-4.

CHAPTER 5

1 Herbert A. Stauss, 'The Immigration and Acculturation of the German Jews in the United States of America', *LBYB*, 16 (1971), p 70.

2 Harry M. Rabinowicz, *The Legacy of Polish Jewry: A History of Polish Jews in the Inter-War Period, 1919-39* (New York, 1965). On the Polish rejection of the Jewish assimilationists, and the psychological strains of the assimilationist position in Poland, see Celia S. Heller, 'Assimilation: A Deviant Pattern among the Jews of Inter-War Poland', *JJS*, 15 (1973), 221-37.

3 Zvi Y. Gitelman, *Jewish Nationality and Soviet Policies* (Princeton, NJ, 1972), pp 292-315.

4 A. Ruppin, *Jewish Fate and Future* (London, 1939), pp 129-30, 168, 250.

5 The number of Jews who migrated east from the pale was over 60,000, 1923-6, and 324,000, 1927-39. Alec Nove and J. A. Newth, 'The Jewish Population: Demographic Trends and Occupational Patterns', *The Jews in Soviet Russia since 1917*, Lionel Kochan (ed) (London, 1972).

6 Gitelman, op cit, pp 269, 500-2.

7 'In 1924-6 the percentage of Jews in Central Russia who had contracted mixed marriages had risen to 16.77, while in the same period the figure for White Russia was only 2.81 and for the Ukraine 4.55.' Ruppin, op cit, p 109. In 1926 48.4 per cent in Central Russia, 76.1 per cent in the Ukraine and 90.1 per cent in White Russia spoke Yiddish (p 250).

8 In 1929 16.5 per cent of the Jews who married in Budapest contracted mixed marriages; the percentage of the working class was 27.7 per cent for men and 29.2 per cent for women. Ruppin, op cit, p 109. In 1930 the Hungarian Orthodox numbered 134,972 compared with 309,599 Liberals (Neologists and Status Quo). *JE*, Vol 15, p 347. In

Budapest, where half of Hungarian Jewry lived, 199,000 Jews belonged to the Liberal and 35,000 belonged to the Orthodox congregations. A. Ruppin, *The Jews in the Modern World* (London, 1934), p 347. In contrast, in Slovakia in 1921, there were 165 Orthodox and 52 Liberal congregations, *JE*, Vol 14, p 1681.

9 Ruppin, *Fate and Future*, pp 164-6.

10 Of every 100 Jews marrying, mixed marriages were contracted by 28.03 in Germany, 29.37 in Berlin and 28.10 in Bohemia in 1933, 14.15 in Vienna in 1932, 56.10 in Trieste in 1927, ibid, p 108.

11 *JC* (2 July 1920). The Liberal/Conservative coalition obtained 8,666 votes and the Jewish National Party obtained 4,516 votes.

12 Walter Breslauer, 'Notes on Organizational Problems of German Jewry' *LBYB*, 14 (1969) p 263; The Zionists were strongly supported by the eastern European Jews who increased in number by 90,000 during and after World War I. Donald L. Niewyk, 'The Economic and Cultural Role of the Jews in the Weimar Republic', *LBYB*, 16 (1971), p 166.

13 *JC*, (27 June 1930); *JE*, Vol 16, pp 105, 110.

14 M. Roblin, *Les Juifs de Paris : Démographie, Economie, Culture* (Paris, 1952), pp 73, 142-77.

15 For example, in Berlin in 1925, only 137 of the total 853 Jewish weddings were religious weddings. A. Ruppin, *Soziologie der Juden,* Vol II (Berlin, 1931), pp 176-7; cf, Hugo Stransky 'The Religious Life in Historic Lands', *The Jews of Czechoslovakia,* Vol I (Pennsylvania, Pa, 1968), pp 331-4.

16 Joshua Rothenberg, 'Jewish Religion in the Soviet Union', in Kochan (ed), op cit, pp 159-87.

17 Nove and Newth, op cit, p 153; the proportion of mixed marriages of Russian Jews rose to over 31 per cent in the period 1966-72. *Jerusalem Post* (23 September 1973).

18 Rothenberg, op cit.

19 *JC* (6 April 1973; 6 March 1970); S. J. Prais and Marlena Schmool, 'The Size and Structure of the Anglo-Jewish

Population, 1960-5', *JJS*, 10 (1968), 5-34; Marshall Sklare, *America's Jews* (New York, 1971), ch 6.

20 Roblin, op cit, pp 83, 86.

21 Charlotte Roland, *Du Ghetto a L'Occident : Deux Generations Yiddiches en France* (Paris, 1962), esp pp 219-37, 262-85.

22 Doris Bensimon-Donath, *L'integration des Juifs nord-africains en France* (Paris, 1971).

23 George Levitte, 'Vers Une Etude des Mutations de la Population Juive En France et du Judaism Francais', *Archives de Sociologie des Religions*, 22 (1966), 89-102; Memmi *et al* found that 25 per cent of their sample belonged to a religious organisation. A. Memmi, W. Ackermann, N. and S. Zoberman, 'Pratique Religieuse et identite juive', *Revue Francaise de Sociologie*, 14 (1973), 242-70. Korcaz found that 66 per cent of her sample belonged to a Jewish organisation, but only 10 per cent belonged to a religious organisation while 22 per cent belonged to a Zionist organisation. Sylvia Korcaz, *Les Juifs de France et l'Etat d'Israel* (Paris, 1969), pp 195-6.

24 Rabi, *Anatomie du Judaise Francais,* (Paris, 1962), pp 156-9.

25 Korcaz, op cit, p 186; Bensimon, op cit, pp 197-9; Doris Bensimon, 'Aspects de l'abandon de la practique religieuse en milieu juif francais', *Social Compass*, 18 (1971), 413-25; Georges Benguigui, 'First Year Jewish Students at the University of Paris', in *Aspects of French Jewry*, Benguigui *et al* (London, 1969). A 1965 survey of Italian Jews found a somewhat higher level of observance than in France: Sergion Della Pergola, 'Identificazione E Observanza Ebraica in Italia', *Annuario di Studi Ebraici* (1971), 73-96.

26 Memmi *et al,* op cit.

CHAPTER 6

1 S. J. Prais and Marlena Schmool, 'The Size and Structure of the Anglo-Jewish Population, 1960-5', *JJS,* 10 (1968), 5-34.

2 Marshall Sklare, *America's Jews* (New York, 1971) p 47.

3 Ernest Krausz, *A Sociological Field Study of Jewish Suburban Life in Edgware, 1962-3, With Special Reference to Minority Identification,* unpublished PhD thesis (University of London, 1965).

4 Nathan Glazer, 'Social Characteristics of American Jews, 1654-1954', *AJY* (1955), 3-41; N. Glazer and D. P. Moynihan, *Beyond the Melting Pot* (Cambridge, Mass, 1963), pp 143-55; Sidney Goldstein, 'American Jewry, 1970 : A Demographic Profile', *AJY* (1971), 68-85.

5 Prais and Schmool, op cit.

6 For detailed references see Stephen Sharot, 'The Three-Generations thesis and the American Jews', *British Journal of Sociology,* 24 (1973), 151-64.

7 *Yearbook of American Churches.* The statistics probably give an inflated picture of the actual post-war growth.

8 Will Herberg, *Protestant, Catholic, Jew* (New York, 1955) ch 5.

9 Sklare, *America's Jews,* pp 123-5.

10 Marshall Sklare and Joseph Greenblum, *Jewish Identity on the Suburban Frontier* (New York, 1967), p 197.

11 Morris R. Werb, *Jewish Suburbia – An Historical and Comparative Study in three New Jersey Suburbs,* unpublished PhD thesis (New York University, 1959).

12 In 'Lakeville', for example, the rate of affiliation rose from 19 per cent of those families with pre-school children (under 6 years) to 56 per cent of those families with early school children (6-9 years), 87 per cent of those families with peak-school children (10-14 years), 91 per cent of those families with late school children (15-17 years), and then dropped to 72 per cent of those families with post-school children (18+ years). Sklare and Greenblum, op cit, ch 3. For a summary of further evidence and a general review of Herberg's three-generation thesis see Sharot, op cit.

13 Prais and Schmool, op cit. Although only 10 per cent of synagogue members in Edgware, in 1963, said that they joined a synagogue for burial rights (Krausz, op cit), it may

211

be a more important reason that people would admit to an investigator.

14 Krausz, op cit. From 3,365 replies to a questionnaire sent out to about 40,000 Jews in London and the provinces, R. L. Henriques reported, in 1949, that 3 per cent attended synagogue daily, 20 per cent regularly on the Sabbath, 21 per cent 'frequently', and 31 per cent on High Holy Days only. R. L. Henriques, *Survey of Jewish Interests* (London, 1949).

15 *Yearbook of American Churches* (1959).

16 *Minute Books of the United Synagogue* (12 June 1944, 12 November 1945).

17 Max Feder, 'The Temple Program and the Temple Auxiliaries', Union of American Hebrew Congregations, *Synagogue Research Survey* (March 1964).

18 D. W. Silverman, 'The Jewish Press', *The Religious Press in America* (New York, 1963), pp 150-1.

19 Werb, op cit.

20 E. M. Rossman, 'The Community and I', *Commentary,* 18 (1954), 393-405.

21 *United Synagogue of America National Survey* (1950).

22 Solomon Poll, *The Hasidic Community of Williamsburg* (Glencoe, Colo, 1962); George Kranzler, *Williamsburg* (New York, 1964).

23 Abstracted from *Jewish Year Books, Jewish Chronicles,* other sources, and, S. J. Prais, 'Synagogue Statistics and the Jewish Population of Great Britain, 1900-70', *JJS,* 14 (1972), 215-28.

24 *JC* (19 May 1922, 2 February 1923, 9 November 1924); *Minute Books of the United Synagogue* (13 November, 18 December 1923, 1 October 1925); *JC* (26 November 1937, 8 March 1963).

25 *JC* (2 May 1958).

26 Photographs in *JC* (7 June 1935, 4 May 1956).

27 See, for example, *JC* (9 May 1924, 8 May 1958). Krausz found in Edgware that 89.9 per cent of the respondents were 'not at all' active in synagogue affairs. Only 2.8 per cent said

they were 'very active', and the remainder were active 'to some extent' or 'very little'.

28 Norman Cohen, 'Trends in Anglo-Jewish Religious Life', *Jewish Life in Modern Britain,* J. Gould and S. Esh (eds) (London, 1964), p 44.

29 *JC* (20 May 1948, 27 June 1958, 6 April 1945, 4 November 1966).

30 Prais and Schmool, op cit; *JC* (27 July 1973).

31 *JC* (29 October 1920, 20 May 1921, 30 March 1923, 24 February, 9 March, 20 April, 4 May 1928).

32 *AJY,* several years.

33 Marshall Sklare, *Conservative Judaism* (Glencoe, Colo, 1959), pp 83-128.

34 *AJY,* several years; *Handbook of the Union of American Hebrew Congregations* (1961).

35 *Reform Judaism in the Large Cities,* Union of American Hebrew Congregations (1931).

36 Laurence Siegel, 'Reflections on Neo-Reform in the Central Conference of American Rabbis', *American Jewish Archives,* 20 (1968), 63-84.

37 *Union of American Hebrew Congregations surveys* (1931, 1953, 1970).

38 Charles S. Liebman, 'Orthodoxy in American Jewish Life', *AJY* (1965) 3-81; Charles S. Liebman, 'A Sociological Analysis of Contemporary Orthodoxy', *Judaism,* 13 (1964), 285-304.

39 See, for example, Sidney Goldstein and Calvin Goldscheider, *Jewish Americans* (Englewood Cliffs, NJ, 1968), pp 177-86; Jack Porter, 'Differentiating Features of Orthodox, Conservative and Reform Jewish Groups in Metropolitan Philadelphia', *JSS,* 30 (1963), 180-94.

40 Charles S. Liebman, 'Changing Social Characteristics of Orthodox, Conservative and Reform Jews', *Sociological Enquiry,* 27 (1966), pp 210-22.

41 Jacob Sodden, *The Impact of Suburbanization on the Synagogue,* unpublished PhD thesis (New York University, 1962).

42 A survey on ritual in synagogues affiliated to the American United Synagogue, in 1933, found that nine different prayer-books, including a Reform prayerbook, were in use, and that the prayers and combinations of Hebrew and English varied greatly. *Rabbinical Assembly of American Proceedings,* 4 (1933), 322-43.

43 Sklare and Greenblum, op cit, pp 198-213.

44 Sodden, op cit.

45 Bryan R. Wilson, *Religion in Secular Society,* (London, 1966), pp 118-19.

46 Charles Y. Glock and Rodney Stark, *Religion and Society in Tension* (Chicago, 1965) ch 5.

47 Sklare and Greenblum, op cit, pp 171-8, 198-213. There were a few exceptions to the correlations. For example, the 'classical' Reform members, who practised fewer rituals than other Lakeville Jews, had the lowest educational level although they had the highest income and lived in the most high-status areas.

48 The following section on Reconstructionism is based on Charles Liebman, 'Reconstructionism in American Jewish Life', *AJY* (1970), 3-99.

CHAPTER 7

1 Max Weber, *Ancient Judaism,* pp 3-5, 417, 423-4; *Economy and Society* (New York, 1968), pp 492-8, 611-22, 1201-4; *General Economic History* (London, 1950), pp 267-70, 358-62. Weber's use of the term 'pariah religion' for Judaism was unfortunate and his delineation of its features has been heavily criticised. See for example, Efraim Shmueli, 'The "Pariah-People" and its "Charismatic Leadership"; A Revaluation of Max Weber's "Ancient Judaism"', *Proceedings of the American Academy for Jewish Research,* 36 (1968), 167-247.

2 Peter L. Berger, *The Sacred Canopy* (New York, 1967), pp 110-25.

3 Keith Thomas, *Religion and the Decline of Magic* (London, 1971), ch 22.

4 *JC* (8 December 1972); Jacob Beller, *Jews in Latin America* (New York, 1969), pp 166-74; Barnet Litvinoff, *A Peculiar People* (London, 1969), pp 204-6.

5 Alan Arian, *The Choosing People* (Cleveland, Ohio, 1973), pp 64-73.

6 Elihu Katz, 'Culture and Communication in Israel : The Transformation of Tradition', *JJS*, 15 (1973), pp 5-21; Simon N. Herman, *Israelis and Jews* (New York, 1970), esp pp 115-25.

7 Stephen Sharot, 'The Three-Generations thesis and the American Jews', *British Journal of Sociology*, 24 (1973), pp 160-2.

8 Bryan R. Wilson, *Religion in Secular Society* (London, 1966), pp 111-18.

9 Benjamin B. Ringer, *The Edge of Friendliness* (New York, 1967), pp 200-21.

Appendices

TABLE A *Jewish population (in thousands)*

	1820-5	1880	1910-11
Russia	1,600	4,500	6,946 (1913)
Austria-Hungary	568	1,625*	2,258
Germany	223	560	615
France	50	60 (excluding Alsace-Lorraine)	100
Italy	25	40	44
Netherlands	45	80	106
Britain	25	65	240
United States	8	250	2,044

*Lower Austria: 95, Bohemia: 200, Moravia: 44, Hungary: 700, Galicia: 686

TABLE B *Increase in Jewish urban population*

	Year	Pop	Year	Pop	Year	Pop	Year	Pop
Russia								
Minsk	1802	2,716	1847	12,976	1897	47,562		
Kovno	1779	1,508	1847	2,013	1897	25,448		
Brest-Litovsk	1766	3,157	1847	8,136	1897	30,608		
Dvinsk	1805	749	1847	2,918	1897	32,400		
Germany								
Hamburg	1816	7,000	1850	10,000	1871	13,796	1910	19,472
Berlin	1816	3,373	1850	9,595	1871	36,015	1910	44,007
Frankfurt	1816	4,309	1850	5,200	1871	10,009	1910	26,228
Breslau	1816	4,409	1850	7,384	1871	13,916	1910	20,212
Vienna	1830	1,600	1848	14,000	1880	72,590	1910	175,318
Budapest			1869	44,890			1910	203,687
Paris	1800	1,000	1850	11,000	1880	40,000	1914	61,000
London	1800	18,000	1850	20,000	1880	45,000	1914	180,000
New York	1800	350	1859	40,000	1870	80,000	1915	1,400,000

TABLE C *Jewish population (in thousands)*

	1918-19	1950	1970
Russia	4,000	2,000	2,151
Poland	4,100	65	9
Rumania	1,000	335	100
Czechoslovakia	349 (1910)	17	14
Hungary	450	160	80
Austria	200	21	8
Germany	500	40	30
France	150	235	550
Italy	43	35	35
Netherlands	106 (1910)	27	30
Britain	275	450	410
United States	3,300	5,000	5,870
Argentine	110	360	500
Israel	85 (1916)	1,115	2,560

TABLE D *Synagogue membership and attendance in the United States*

	Synagogue membership	Attend once a week or more	More than once a month
Washington (1955)	47		
Boston (1965)	53		17
San Francisco (1958)	37		6
Providence (1967)	78	11	38
Milwaukee (1964)	64	17	12
Rochester (1961)	71	14	7
Columbus (1968)	79	13	23
Flint (1967)	87	19	25
New York (1963)	Not known		
native-born Jews		5.8	5.8
foreign-born Jews		23.0	10.8

	Once a month	Occasionally	High Holy Days only	Never or very rarely
Washington (1955)	21	56		19
Boston (1965)	21		39	23
San Francisco (1958)	6	18	31	32
Providence (1967)	7		24	12
Milwaukee (1964)		31	27	13
Rochester (1961)	48		19	11
Columbus (1968)		32	26	6
Flint (1967)		28	18	10
New York (1963)				
native-born Jews			47.9	40.4
foreign-born Jews			44.1	22.1

(Figures in tables D-F given in percentages)

TABLE E *Religious observance in England*

	London and provinces (1949)	Edgware (1963)	London NOP (1971)	'English provincial city' (1972)
Light Sabbath candles	67	85		54
Kiddush	44			26
Mezuzzah on door(s)	74	92		
Not ride on Sabbath	14	11	9	
Observe some of dietary laws	81		67	33
Not eat non-*kosher* food outside home	30	31	28	19
Passover *Seder*	86	94	79	
Chanukah – light candles	59	72		
Fast on Yom Kippur		80	86	62
Barmitzvah (males)		91		
Circumcision (males)		100		

TABLE F *Religious observance in the United States*

	Washington (1955)	New Jersey Suburbs (1958)	San Francisco (1958)	'Lakeville' (1959)	Rochester (1961)
Light Sabbath candles	50	62	32	32	48
Kiddush		24		16	
Mezuzzah on door(s)	46				71
Observe some dietary laws		33	16	9	44
Passover *Seder*	79	87	72	60	86
Chanukah – light candles	68	89	48	68	81
Fast on Yom Kippur			33	34	

	Milwaukee (1964)	Boston (1965)	Camden, New Jersey (1966)	Providence, Rhode Island (1967)	Flint, Michigan (1967)	Columbus (1968)
Light Sabbath candles	66	62	59	42	79	69
Kiddush						
Mezuzzah on door(s)						
Observe some dietary laws	47	27	24		47	44
Passover *Seder*	90	87	93	79	93	92
Chanukah – light candles	81		87	74	87	86
Fast on Yom Kippur						

Appendix 2

Glossary of Hebrew and Yiddish words

barmitzvah
Son of the Commandment. At the age of thirteen a boy reaches religious maturity and it is customary for him to be called up in the synagogue to read a portion of the Law.

Beth Din
Jewish Ecclesiastical Court. House of Law.

Chanukah
Festival of Lights celebrated in commemoration of the re-dedication of the Second Temple.

cheder (pl *chedarim*)
Traditional religious school. Literally, 'room'.

dayan (pl *dayanim*)
A rabbi who is a member of a *Beth Din;* an ecclesiastical judge.

halakah or *halacha*
The section of the Talmud which deals with all legal matters.

hazan or *chazan*
Cantor or reader.

hevra or *chevra* (pl *hevrot*)
A group. Used when referring to the religious societies or rooms of worship of immigrants.

High Holy Days
Rosh Hashanah and Yom Kippur.

kaddish
The mourner's prayer after the death of a close relative; usually after the death of a parent.

kashrut
System of dietary laws.

kehilla (pl *kehillot*)
Community organisation.

kiddush
Blessing over a cup of wine consecrating the Sabbath or religious holiday.

kosher
Food acceptable according to Jewish religious law.
maggid
Preacher.
marranos
Spanish Jews who converted to Christianity but who practised Judaism in secret.
matza
Special unleavened bread for Passover.
melammed
Teacher.
mezuzzah
A small case attached to doorposts, containing a parchment on which biblical verses are inscribed.
mikveh
Ritual bath.
minyan
Quorum of ten males for public religious service.
mitzvah (pl *mitzvot*)
Literally 'commandment'. Also, a good deed.
Misheberach
May He who Blessed. The opening words of short benedictions or prayers recited in the synagogue on occasions when it is customary to promise a donation to a charitable institution.
parnas (pl *parnassim*)
A 'steward'; community leader; the president or senior warden of a synagogue.
piyuttim
Poetical compositions or hymns. Often deal with Jewish history, doctrine, and ritual.
Purim
Festival commemorating the deliverance of the Jews from the hands of Haman, the Prime Minister of Persia about 500 BCE.
Rosh Hashanah
New Year. Day of Judgement, Day of Memorial.
Seder
'Order'. The service at home on the first two nights of Passover.

shammash
Beadle of a synagogue.
shiva
Seven days' intensive mourning on the death of a close relative.
shnoder
Promise to donate in return for religious honour, such as being 'called up to the law'.
shochet (pl *shochetim*)
One who slaughters animals or fowls according to Jewish ritual.
shool or *shul*
Synagogue.
shtetl
Small town in eastern Europe.
shtadlan
Solicitor; interceder. One who uses his influence with the gentile authorities for the welfare of the community.
Shulhan Arukh or *Shulchan Aruch*
Literally, 'prepared table'. The most popular codification of the laws of the Talmud, prepared by Joseph Karo (1488-1575) with added glosses by Moses Isserles (1520-72).
Simchat Torah
Rejoicing of the law. The last day of Sukkot when the regular cycle of weekly readings of the Torah is over and begun again.
Sukkot
The Feast of Tabernacles commemorating the travels of the Israelites in the wilderness where they dwelt in temporary huts or booths (sukkah=booth.) Also marks end of the harvest.
Talmud
Literally, 'study'. Rabbinical compendium.
Talmud Torah
The study of the Torah. Jewish school.
yeshivah (pl *yeshivot*)
Academy of higher learning specialising in the Talmud.
Yiddishkeit
Jewishness.
Yom Kippur
Day of Atonement. A day of fasting, repenting and confessing.

Index